Broadway and
the Blacklist

Broadway and the Blacklist

K. Kevyne Baar

McFarland & Company, Inc., Publishers
Jefferson, North Carolina

LIBRARY OF CONGRESS CATALOGUING-IN-PUBLICATION DATA

Names: Baar, K. Kevyne, 1946– author.
Title: Broadway and the blacklist / K. Kevyne Baar.
Description: Jefferson, North Carolina : McFarland & Company, Inc., Publishers, 2019. | Includes bibliographical references and index.
Identifiers: LCCN 2018056987 | ISBN 9781476672595 (softcover : acid free paper) ∞
Subjects: LCSH: Blacklisting of entertainers—United States—History—20th century. | Blacklisting of authors—United States—History—20th century. | Theater—Political aspects—United States—History—20th century. | United States. Congress. House. Committee on Un-American Activities.
Classification: LCC PN1590.B5 B325 2019 | DDC 792.0973/0904—dc23
LC record available at https://lccn.loc.gov/2018056987

BRITISH LIBRARY CATALOGUING DATA ARE AVAILABLE

ISBN (print) 978-1-4766-7259-5
ISBN (ebook) 978-1-4766-3616-0

© 2019 K. Kevyne Baar. All rights reserved

No part of this book may be reproduced or transmitted in any form or by any means, electronic or mechanical, including photocopying or recording, or by any information storage and retrieval system, without permission in writing from the publisher.

Front cover photograph © 2019 Shutterstock

Printed in the United States of America

McFarland & Company, Inc., Publishers
  Box 611, Jefferson, North Carolina 28640
    www.mcfarlandpub.com

To Howard da Silva
and the People's Theatre of Cleveland
without which my parents might never have met.

Table of Contents

Acknowledgments ix
A Few Words on Spelling and Usage xii
Prologue 1
ONE. Theatre in America Enters the 20th Century 5
TWO. Un-American Theatre: The Short Life and Death of the Federal Theatre Project 17
THREE. Finding Subversives in Hollywood 42
FOUR. Making Work While Blacklisted 58
FIVE. What Has My Union Done for Me? SAG, AFTRA and Blacklisting 70
SIX. Actors' Equity Association: The Chronicle of an Anti-Blacklisting Resolution 83
SEVEN. Investigating Broadway: The 1955 HUAC Hearings 95
EIGHT. After the 1955 HUAC Hearings: A Life in the Theatre Goes On 111
NINE. The Name on the Marquee: Working on Broadway in the Shadow of the Blacklist 120
TEN. Investigating Broadway ... Again: The 1958 HUAC Hearings 137
Epilogue 153

Appendix A: McCarthyism: Why No Joe? 157

*Appendix B: Serving Subpoenas: The Memos
  of Dolores Faconti Scotti* 159

*Appendix C: Who's Who in the Cast of Witnesses
  in 1955 and 1958* 169

Appendix D: An Apology from the Unions 181

Chapter Notes 185

Bibliography 192

Index 197

Acknowledgments

Probably best to begin at the beginning. My parents, Tim and Ella Baar, gave me the gift of theatre even as I was raised in Hollywood. They also educated me politically. They also sent my brother Carl and me to Viola Spolin's Young Actors Company so we would be comfortable in front of people. By the time I was five I knew what was happening: my nursery school was "cooperative" and my teacher was called before the California Un–American Activities Committee. I also learned that, for all intents and purposes, there had been no blacklist in theatre.

Many years later I began my PhD program at Saybrook Graduate School and Research Center (now Saybrook University). One of the things that had attracted me to Saybrook was the ethics requirement. I chose the class "Ethics and Social Responsibility" to fulfill the requirement. Dr. Dennis Jaffe was the professor, and one of the assignments was to find an organization deserving of an "ethics" award he had made up. I asked if I could do it historically: an award to Actors' Equity Association for standing up to the blacklist that was decimating the entertainment industry in the early 1950s. Dr. Jaffe agreed and sent me on my way. He later served as a member of my dissertation committee along with my chair, Dr. Steven Pritzker, who told me to tell a good story, and Dr. JoAnn McAllister, who helped give it a Human Science spin. I set out first to find the material to back up my thesis. A writer acquaintance, Alexis Greene, pointed me in the direction of Gail Malmgreen and the Actors' Equity papers at the Tamiment Library and Robert F. Wagner Labor Archives at New York University (NYU). Gail not only helped me with the collection, three months later she hired me to be its archivist. Thanks to Gail, two years after that the New York Labor History Association asked me to coordinate, along with Actors' Equity, a panel I dubbed "Broadway and the Blacklist," amazed to find that that exact term had never been used. Madeline Lee Gilford who figures prominently in this work, and Peter Friedman who came to the archive to work on the blacklisted actor Philip Loeb, helped pack the room. I spent the next ten years at the archives working on Equity, other labor collections, and finally the archives of the New York office of the American Federation of Television and Radio artists.

One year later I received my PhD with the aid of so many people: Caren Byrd and the late James Borland kept a roof over my head. The late Michael Nash, the director of Tamiment and the Center for the Study of Cold War America, allowed me to further present my work. Thanks to the late Professor Marilyn Young of the NYU History Department and a then doctoral student at CUNY, Andrea Siegel, who helped me develop my syllabi, I became an adjunct professor at NYU. Thanks also for the opportunities and encouragement granted to me by members of the History Department, Dr. Lori Benton, and Dr. Maria Montoya, and by the College of Arts and Sciences' Dr. G. Gabrielle Starr and Dr. Karen Krahulik. One day I was asked by Dr. Edward Ziter of the Tisch School of the Arts if I could do a "theatre version" of the classes I was teaching, and so was born the course that led to this book aided in no small part by my amazing students, one of whom has been my reader throughout my experience of writing this book. Thank you Ellie d'Eustachio. A friend who writes romance novels, Christine Ashworth, a wonderful cheerleader, told me I could do this. There is no real category for my playwright/director friend Michael Van Duzer as he is in a class of his own, and always available to help keep me going.

I didn't just work in an archive; I frequented them as well. Archivists are the best. My first archive home was the Southern California Library for Social Science and Research in South Central Los Angeles. Thank you Ned Comstock at University of Southern California for sharing your expertise. I dove headfirst into the Special Collections at UCLA, the New York Public Library for the Performing Arts, and the Library of Congress. The collections at the Wisconsin Historical Society are amazing, and Mary Huelsbeck and her staff helped make it possible for me to use so many of them. Derek at Photofest left no corner unchecked for me. But nothing can equal my adventures in the collections of the National Archives and Records Administration in Washington, D.C. I walked in their doors at the very beginning in 2002 and was gifted with Katherine Mollan, an archivist who willingly joined me in my journey. She has been there through all my years of coming to NARA. As committee materials are only available 50 years after hearings have been concluded, Kate vetted all of the files I needed first from 1955 and then 1958. When I needed to look to a new area she was always there.

Thanks and appreciation goes to the many who lived through this dark period with grace and good humor and shared these experiences with me. I was introduced to John Randolph and Sarah Cunningham by their extraordinary daughter Martha years before I began this project. They shared stories and materials and introduced me to Madeline Lee Gilford who was invaluable to the work. I met and interviewed blacklisted writers Jean Rouverol, Janet

Stevenson, Joan LaCour, Norma Barzman, and Walter Bernstein. At the age of five I met Pete Seeger for the first time; later I got to interview him for my dissertation. Seeger's colleague in the Weavers, Ronnie Gilbert, like Seeger, never stopped being an activist. Composer Irma Jurist played for me, and Sylvia Jarrico knew everyone. I visited Norma Sullivan, widow of Elliot Sullivan, in her home in London. I promised her a footnote when I finally wrote my book, and I kept my promise in Chapter Eight. I gave Sondra Gorney, wife of songwriter Jay Gorney, a copy of the transcript of our interview and she wrote her own memoir of her husband, *Brother Can You Spare a Dime?* My former boss, George Ives, had been at the 1955 hearings and willingly shared. Bernard Gersten, a witness in 1958, had seen every area of theatre during this period. Our conversations were incredibly valuable.

Others who wrote about this period gave me time and encouragement including Victor Navasky, author of *Naming Names*; Ellen Schrecker, who wrote *Many Are the Crimes*; and Alice Kessler-Harris, who penned my favorite book on Lillian Hellman, *A Difficult Woman*. Newly added to this list is Madeline Lee and Jack Gilford's son Joe, author of the play *Finks*, based on the 1955 hearings. I'm going to put Howard da Silva's son Daniel in this category as he is currently writing a book on his dad. Always good to have someone around who's been where you've been.

In 2015, I moved away from the big city and settled in Davis, California, where I am now writing this. I made the move to be close to family. My brother, the aforementioned Carl, visits often and, as he is older than I am, remembers more and loves to share. I am here because his younger son Keith the scientist and Keith's wife, the amazing legal mind that is Barbara Miltner, decided to move here with their young daughter. I will never be forgiven if I don't add to this list by thanking the love of my life, my great-niece Rowan who at almost 11 is taller than me. She asked me to read her parts of this book and showered me with questions. Serious props to the generations to come. Happy now, kiddo?

During the course of the work that follows, and for theatre in general, great credit is given to the audience. My audience has been those in a dark theater, the many students in my classes, the curious who have attended my presentations and panel discussions, the folks at McFarland, and of course, the person who just picked up this book.

Thank you.

A Few Words on Spelling and Usage

Is it theater or theatre?

When I was growing up I thought that theat*er* was the American spelling and theat*re* was from England. Now that I am, admittedly, a theatre snob, I spell it theatre.

For this book both spellings are used.

1. As I said, if I'm the one speaking, I will use theatre.

2. If the organization uses one or the other as in Federal Theatre Project, I will maintain that spelling.

3. Most of the time committee transcripts use theater, in which case that spelling will be used.

The moral of this story is: it isn't a typo.

Why is the term Negro used?

My reader, a former student who is naturally much younger than I am, was concerned when she first saw me use the word. Her fear was that it might be a slight, or construed as a slight by a younger audience. Please be assured that in the time frame of our story, early 1900s to about 1960, Negro was the preferred reference as in the Negro theatre companies in the Federal Theatre Project.

Prologue

The assignment seemed simple enough: write an essay on "Where do you feel most at home, and what is your responsibility to that place?" Being that it was a class in Ecology and Ethics taught in Seattle, Washington, I figured they wanted me to say, "on a high mountain," and "don't litter."

When I finally allowed myself to approach that door in my mind—the one labeled home—I found myself, as I should have guessed, in a theatre filled with tradition and ghosts. In the still darkness of the house, I walk slowly towards the single unshaded light that sits onstage, and I know exactly where I am. I can stand on that stage with no one around and hear voices, laughter and applause. What country I am in, what city, none of that matters. My commitment to the place has always been simple: do the best I can with whatever I have; treat the space with respect and attention to its traditions while being kind to its occupants and visitors.

Theatre has been my life even when I wasn't working in theatre. It was a place to invest my time, energy, emotions and enthusiasm. It has been my refuge and teacher, my joy and terror, my excitement, and my frustration. I go to the theatre to escape the real world or to live more fully in it. In theatre I found lessons in human behavior, ancient history, and social responsibility while experiencing an involvement in the creative process that left me elated and exhausted. I became a problem solver, mediator, manager, psychologist, and historian.

The British anthropologist Gregory Bateson looks at living things and finds "the pattern which connects." I look at theatre, a most definitely living thing, and find that same pattern. I look at the theatre community and I find family. Although this book is not a memoir, many of the people and organizations that pass through its pages are people I have known and organizations I have been part of. It is one of the reasons why I came back to this story with an urgency to share it.

My parents met at the People's Theatre in Cleveland, Ohio. Howard da Silva was the artistic director and the man responsible for bringing them together. He will be an active participant in any number of chapters to follow. Before they met, my mother attended the American Academy of Dramatic Arts in New York City while my father was in the drama department at Carnegie Tech in Pittsburgh. My father also did Federal Theatre, but we don't get there until Chapter Two. In 1936 they decided to move to California and get married. They were married on January 30, 1937. They chose that date because it was President Roosevelt's birthday, making it less likely to be forgotten in subsequent years.

I was born on the tip of the baby-boom in Los Angeles, where my father had the great good fortune to be working full-time as a union prop maker in motion pictures. And yet, I was always aware that I was born into theatre. The only logical explanation is that while I was in school, he was at the studio. Nights and weekends we did theatre. When I was five I was a member of Viola Spolin's Young Actors Company. I was taking dance classes with Anne and Paul Barlin who were friends of Pete Seeger's. At the time, the blacklist was in full force, and the rule at home was, "if the FBI comes to the door, call your mother." As much as we have discussed it, my brother and I understand that we will never know how or why our father made it through and kept on working, but he did. Not long after, my father built a theatre so my mother could do plays. It all seemed quite normal.

Theatre and this idea of theatre families, the glue holding together this tale of Broadway and blacklisting, grew in my life. I met and worked around, and then with, a wide variety of creative theatre artists. Even now there will be the occasional reunion with someone I worked with 40 years ago, as we pick up the conversation from where it left off. One theme that becomes evident as you continue this journey is that theatre, and making theatre, is different from film and television. This understanding starts to reveal itself almost from the beginning of this story: members of the Group Theatre leave New York for Hollywood's fame and fortune only to join forces to form the Actors' Laboratory Theatre. When the blacklist takes hold they then return to the New York area where work awaits them. Their stories are also affected quite deeply by the unions they belong to as professionals in the performing arts. The strength of this theatre community comes even more strongly into focus first in Chapter Seven during the 1955 hearings into the New York theatre community by the House Committee on Un-American Activities (HUAC), and finally in Chapter Eight which looks at the aftermath of those four days in August.

I am sure it is already quite obvious; I love theatre I love that it can be done virtually anywhere; the Federal Theatre Project made that abundantly clear as they took theatre to every corner of this country. I love the people who make theatre and I love the people who truly make theatre possible, the audience. As Tallulah Bankhead so wisely put it, "If you want to help the

American theater, don't be an actress, be an audience."[1] The value of the audience to our story cannot be overstated. In Chapters Four and Eight, the audience is given its own credit for adding their voice to allow the otherwise unemployable to continue working. A study conducted in London in 2017 went so far as to conclude:

> [We] have now proven what theatre folks have felt for years. The heart beats of audience members actually synchronize and beat together in unison when watching a live performance of a play or musical.[2]

Or as senior editor of *American Theatre*, Diep Tran so cogently put it:

> Theatre is a living, breathing, collaborative art form. To me, that means that every production is different depending on who's working on it. An emphasis on a syllable here, an arched eyebrow there, can drastically change the interpretation of a line. And it changes depending on the audience in the room.[3]

Over the years, this love of mine has grown in so many ways. From this growth came a desire to take my knowledge and skill in a different direction. After a brief return to acting and stage-managing in 2000, I decided to return to school. As one of my nephews remarked, "you are the only person born with the name Baar over the age of two who doesn't have a PhD." It sounded like a great adventure. It has been that and so much more. My original work was centered on the women in entertainment and the blacklist. That work started when I was doing a production of Eric Bentley's *Are You Now or Have You Ever Been...?* One woman, Lillian Hellman, made an appearance in that play. I knew from personal experience there were more. Many had been a part of some of those theatre families I had grown up with. Twenty-five years later I took over 300 of these women to school with me. I started my studies on September 10, 2001.

Thus the world I was living in when I retuned to school in 2001 was not a happy one, but at least I finally found the one ray of positivity in the grim landscape of the blacklist era. For a class in "Ethics and Social Responsibility" we were challenged to find a socially responsible company who we felt deserved a fictional ethics award. Going back into history, I chose Actors' Equity Association (Equity) in 1952, when they became the first and only union to stand up to the blacklist. At the same time they were also standing up for the integration of theatre audiences in the South. My research took me to the Tamiment Library and Robert F. Wagner Labor Archives at New York University, the home of the Equity archives. The archivist told me that no one had ever used the collection to research this subject. I was personally shocked, but academically thrilled that this subject was virtually untouched. A review of the literature for my dissertation proposal proved this all too well. The final product was called *Investigating Broadway: The House Committee on Un-American Activities Meets Members of the New York Theatre*

Community at the Foley Square Courthouse, August 15–18, 1955. It addressed the period of the 1950s, how unions dealt with their members and the blacklist, Equity's anti-blacklisting stance, and the 1955 hearings themselves.

If I thought the world I was living in then was difficult, the morning after school started in 2001, a professor came up to tell me that my work was now taking on a greater relevance. I can only wonder what she would tell me today. In 1935, and for almost four years, the United States government funded theatre across this country. I pray that there is still a National Endowment for the Arts by the time this book is published. But come what may, there will be theatre and it will tell our stories. The work will be important and the work will be frivolous, but it will keep our hearts beating.

On November 21, 2017, the playwright Rajiv Joseph wrote an editorial for the *New York Times*. Joseph was in Houston, Texas, to stage his third production with his "family" at the Alley Theatre. Hurricane Harvey struck five days into rehearsal. The theatre was flooded. He writes about volunteering for the Red Cross where he was put to work, much to his surprise, for his skill as a playwright. Ultimately the play they had started rehearsing opened at a theatre on the University of Houston campus. After closing in Houston, the play had its New York debut at the Off Broadway Atlantic Theater Company. Of his experience in Houston, Joseph writes,

> I have two prevailing and unrelated fears that dovetailed during this time. One is that the vocation I've dedicated my life to is meaningless. The second is that the world might any day experience a cataclysm that alters civilization entirely. This fear is a rather new one, but it grows daily. Who can say why?
>
> In any case, I left Houston with my fears allayed. Sure, all human activity is meaningless, seeing as the world will probably end one day. But with both theater and human existence, as long as there's a show to be put on, the show must go on.[4]

Ladies and gentlemen, audience and readers, the house is open. Please take your seats and make yourselves comfortable. As the house lights dim, know that the artists are in place and ready to tell their stories. Welcome to the theatre.

ONE

Theatre in America Enters the 20th Century

Theatre in the United States at the turn of the 20th century consisted primarily of melodramas, pot-boilers, and drawing room comedies save for the occasional Shakespearean play brought across the ocean by an English company looking for new lands to conquer, which inevitably meant Broadway. The time was opportune for new artists and organizations to be born. These artists and their organizations would be raised in 20th century America and as a result, found more than their share of connections, family and danger through the art of making theatre.

The Theatre Guild

In 1914, as war was breaking out in Europe, an intrepid group of theatre aficionados founded the Washington Square Players. They presented their first production, a program of one acts, at the Bandbox Theatre in New York City in February of 1915.[1]

"The idea behind the Washington Square Players," as Theresa Helburn wrote in her memoir, *A Wayward Quest,* "was somewhat different…. They wanted to present plays which could not, at that time, obtain a hearing on Broadway; better written, more intelligent plays than the public could find in the commercial theater, but plays which they believed the public would be eager to see."[2]

Future Theatre Guild producer Lawrence Langer, along with Edward Goodman and Philip Moeller, prepared a manifesto that read in part, "[the Washington Square Players is] an organization which takes its name from the district where it originated—is composed of individuals who believe in the future of the theatre in America, and includes playwrights, actors and producers, working with a common end in view…. We have only one policy

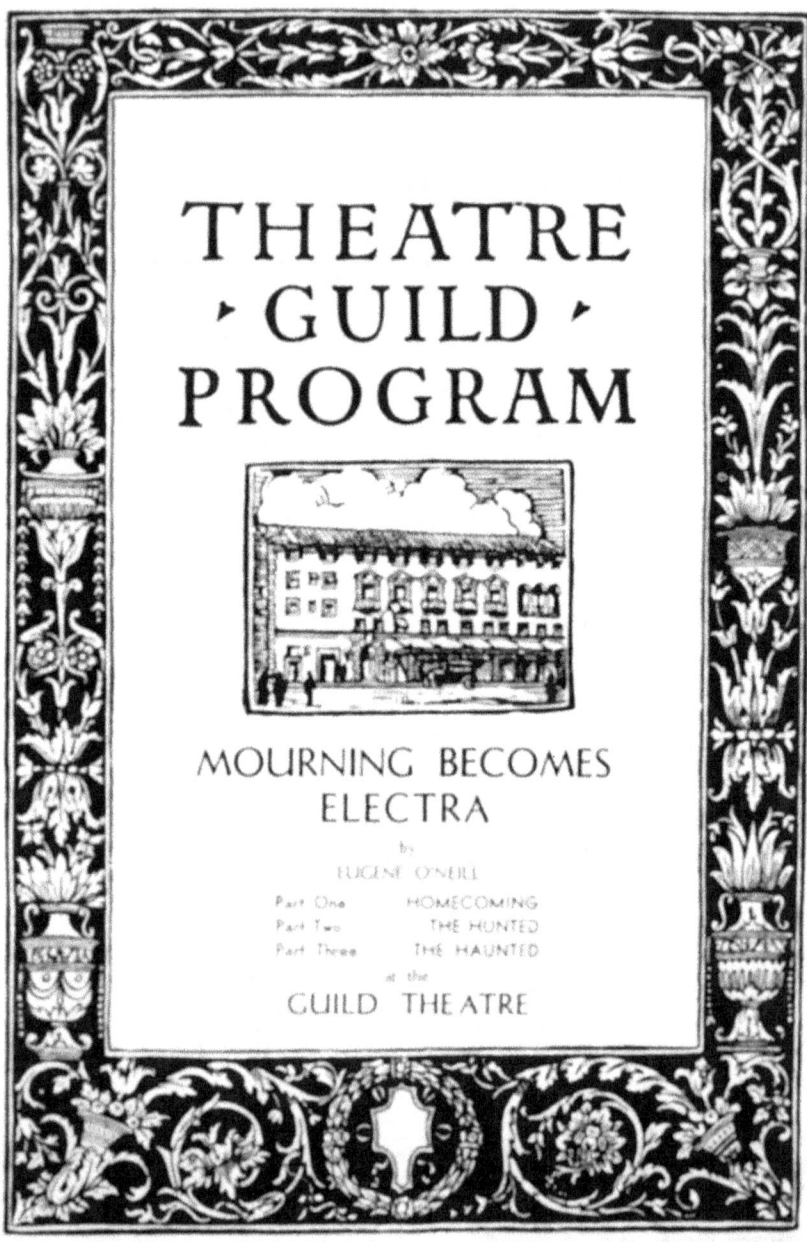

Program from the original Theatre Guild production of Eugene O'Neill's *Mourning Becomes Electra* in 1931. The production starred the legendary Russian actress Alla Nazimova who immigrated to the United States in 1905 (author's collection).

in regard to the plays which we will produce—they must have merit."³ In closing they wrote, "Our ultimate success depends upon our ability to accomplish our purpose AND your interest."⁴ Before they disbanded in 1918, they produced plays that brought the works of George Bernard Shaw across the ocean, helped American audiences embrace the works of Anton Chekov and Henrik Ibsen, gave the American playwright Elmer Rice an early platform, and in Eugene O'Neill, a founding member of the Provincetown Players that began working in the same area in 1915,⁵ helped form the future of the American theatre.

One month after the end of World War I, and one month shy of the beginning of Prohibition, members of the former Washington Square family, a group that was formed "to carry out the idea of an expert theatre,"⁶ met to take the first steps in forming the organization that would become the Theatre Guild. In outlining plans for this new theatre, Langer wrote, "It must be a little theatre grown up.... It should be a professional theatre, employ professional actors and produce only long plays 'which should be great plays.'"⁷

They opened their first production, *The Bonds of Interest*, on April 19, 1919. It was not a critical success, but they persevered. Fortunately, the second production, St. John Ervine's *John Ferguson*, "wrung the emotions of the drama critics so hard that the next day their pens dripped ecstasy."⁸ The Theatre Guild received an additional benefit for their production when

> after *John Ferguson* had been running a few months and calculating a slender fortune for the Guild, the members of Actors Equity Association (the actors' union) and the theatrical managers started calling one another names. The name calling boiled over into a dispute which led to the memorable Actors' Strike. Since [the Guild's] sympathies were with the actors, [the Guild chose] to recognize Equity. They, in turn, decided not to call out [their] actors, with the result that for several months the only play in New York was *John Ferguson*. If you wanted to go to the theatre, you just *had* to see *John Ferguson*.⁹

It wasn't long after that Theresa Helburn, who had been the Guild's play representative, was named executive director.¹⁰

Helburn turned out to be the perfect choice. Her mother took her to her first Broadway shows when Helburn was a child of nine. As she recalled, "From the moment the curtain rose on the first play, I entered a world that was unlike anything I had ever imagined, but that I recognized at once as my own. The theater was not a dream, or a goal—it was home."¹¹ Initially hired on an interim basis, she held the position for over 30 years.

Relationships came to mean everything in the theatre, and Langer's skills in this department drove the young company forward. The Washington Square Players had presented a short play by George Bernard Shaw, then an unknown playwright to Americans; while the first season playwright Ervine was also a friend. Langer convinced Shaw to make the Theatre Guild his home. Between 1920 and 1932, the Guild presented 14 of Shaw's plays starting with *Heartbreak House*. In total they produced 18. It was during this time, 1925, that the Guild opened a Broadway theatre of their own on 51st Street.

Similarly, the earlier company had also produced a short play by Eugene O'Neill. If anything cemented the Guild's reputation for pushing the American theatre forward, it was O'Neill. They produced seven of his plays including the Pulitzer Prize winning *Strange Interlude* in 1928, *Mourning Becomes Electra* in 1931, and *Ah, Wilderness!* in 1933. In 1946, they produced his *The Iceman Cometh*. The Guild also produced musical theatre including the groundbreaking Richard Rodgers and Oscar Hammerstein productions of *Oklahoma* and *Carousel*. The last show produced by the Theatre Guild was also a musical: *State Fair* in 1996.[12]

The Theatre Guild story would not be complete without noting the amazing artists they attracted or introduced to theatre audiences. Katherine Cornell made her theatre debut with the Washington Square Players, while Alfred Lunt and Lynn Fontanne appeared, mostly together but occasionally

The Theatre Guild, looking for a way to support changing ideas of what theatre could be, gave "three young people associated with the Guild" a play to try out, *Red Rust*. The three became the leaders of the newly forming Group Theatre. Left to right are Cheryl Crawford, Lee Strasberg and Harold Clurman (Photofest).

separately, in 25 different productions, many of which they toured making it possible for a young theatre goer in Los Angeles to experience Broadway.[13] The Guild tours brought theatre to most major cities in the United States, whetting an appetite for even more theatre. In 1935, the Federal Theatre Project began feeding that appetite when they brought theatre to those same major cities as well as to areas that had never seen a live production on stage.

Shortly before her death, Theresa Helburn wrote, "In the long run, what made the Theatre Guild the most powerful art theater in the world, what raised the artistic standards of the Broadway theater and Hollywood motion pictures and later of radio and television, was the fact that for every one of us the theater was bigger than any one of us. From the beginning, all of us set aside our desire for personal self-expression for the sake of the basic idea: the play was the thing, and the play came first."

A production still from the first production of *Red Rust*. On the left is Herbert Biberman who also directed. On the right is Gale Sondergaard. They married the year after this production. In 1947 Biberman became one of the Hollywood Ten, and Sondergaard was blacklisted in 1951 (Wisconsin Center for Film and Theater Research).

The Guild continued to produce, started a short-lived theatre school, suffered through and overcame financial and artistic challenges, while finding a way to support changing ideas of what theatre could be. And so it came to pass that "three young people associated with the Guild in different capacities—Harold Clurman as play reader, Cheryl Crawford as casting director, and Lee Strasberg who had a few small parts in Guild plays—felt that we [The Guild] were getting behind the times and that they could inject new blood into the theater."[14]

The Guild had been sent a copy of *Red Rust*, the first Soviet play to reach America. Taking an option on it, Helburn "called Harold Clurman in to my office and told him that we'd like to do it as a special Sunday night performance and suggested that the three youngsters [Clurman, Crawford, and Strasberg] see what they could do with it. They put it on with a fair degree of success."[15] With the further support of the Guild, *Red Rust* opened at Broadway's Martin Beck Theatre on December 17, 1929, less than two months after the stock market crash that signaled the start of the Great Depression. It was directed by and featured Herbert Biberman, and starred Gale Sondergaard who within the year became Biberman's wife. Biberman and Sondergaard play major roles as our story continues.

Of the play, Clurman later wrote:

> *Red Rust* had an engaging quality of youthfulness. The production given it, under Herbert Biberman's direction, was lusty and fresh.... There was no organic connection between the production and the later Group Theatre. The choice of a Soviet play had novelty—it was the first play from the Soviet Union to reach these shores—and it had a strong note of self-criticism in it, though the audience, like myself tended to enjoy the play for its exuberance, which was partly in the script and more markedly in the cast.[16]

Their success with *Red Rust* furthered the desire of Clurman, Crawford and Strasberg to put together an acting company. Letting his "children" go, Langer wrote in his autobiography:

> The best that parents of a child can do when that child wants independence is to help it on its way; and this the Guild Board did even though it was apparent later on that our offspring regarded us as old-fashioned fogies running around the theatre in circles. When they formulated their plans to start the Group Theatre, Terry Helburn was particularly active in helping them to get on their feet. In addition to providing half the funds for their first two plays, we turned over to them a play by Paul Green, *The House of Connelly*, with something of a pang, as well as another play, *1931*, by the Siftons, with a feeling of relief by at least one member of the Board. The umbilical cord thus cut, the Group Theatre began to function, and during much of the time when the Theatre Guild was in the doldrums, artistically speaking, the Group Theatre with its playwrights, Clifford Odets and Irwin Shaw wrote a brilliant page in the annals of the theatre of the thirties, and its individual directors have continued to influence the theatre long after the Group Theatre ceased existing as an entity.[17]

The Group Theatre

"One Friday night in November 1930 Harold Clurman, a twenty-nine-year-old playreader with the Theatre Guild in New York City, began a series of weekly talks for an audience of young actors he hoped to interest in the theatre he wanted to establish with his friends, an actor-director named Lee Strasberg and the Guild's casting director, Cheryl Crawford."[18] These conversations lasted into May of 1931, when at last the people present came to understand

One. Theatre in America Enters the 20th Century 11

Group Theatre Company, 1936. Back row, from left: Art Smith, Walter Fried, Sanford Meisner, Ruth Nelson, Lee J. Cobb, Lief Erickson, Roman Bohnen, Morris Carnovsky, Lee Strassberg, Kermit Bloomgarden; middle row, from left: Luther Adler, Phoebe Brand, Eleanor Lynn, Harold Clurman (behind Lynn), Frances Farmer, Robert Lewis, Elia Kazan; sitting front left: Irwin Shaw (Photofest).

what Clurman's vision for this company was: "an ensemble of artists who would create, out of common beliefs and technique, dramatic productions that spoke to an equally committed audience about the essential social and moral issues of their times." In June the three left the city with 27 actors as their ten-year adventure began,[19] creating relationships that would last a lifetime. Members of this "group" appear over and over again in the chapters that follow.

The entire membership of what was becoming the Group Theatre spent the summer of 1931 in Brookfield Center in Connecticut, before returning to the city to open a show. At this time, the Group Theatre consisted of Stella Adler, Margaret Barker, Phoebe Brand, J. Edward Bromberg, Morris Carnovsky, William Challee, Harold Clurman, Walter Coy, Cheryl Crawford, [Mary] Virginia Farmer, Sylvia Feningston, Friendly Ford, Gerrit [Tony] Kraber, Lewis Leverett, Robert Lewis, Mab Maynard, Sanford Meisner, Paula Miller, Mary Morris, Ruth Nelson, Clifford Odets, Dorothy Patten, Herbert Ratner, Philip

The Group Theatre's first summer away in Connecticut in 1931. The photographs are of the various members listening to one of their leaders, Harold Clurman, seated at far left with a stick in his hand (author's collection).

Robinson, Art Smith, Eunice Stoddard, Lee Strasberg, Franchot Tone, Alixe Walker, and Clement Wilenchick. Of the original group many would take the plunge of going to Hollywood; even more would be blacklisted with several making appearances before the House Committee on Un-American Activities (HUAC), and when this happened, many returned to the all-familiar and still welcoming theatre in New York and surrounding communities. But that was the future; right now they had their summers, which culminated each year in taking a show they were working on to Broadway. In 1931 that work was yet another play the Guild had passed on to them, *The House of Connelly* by Paul Green, "with which the Group Theatre began its notable though brief career."[20] The show was a critical if not financial success as this new family was welcomed into the New York theatre community.

The company grew with each succeeding summer and productions. The future Oscar winning film director Elia Kazan joined them as an apprentice for the second summer and appeared as an actor on several occasions. Following *The House of Connelly*, the 1931–32 season included two additional productions: *1931* by Paul and Claire Sifton, and Maxwell Anderson's *Night over Taos*. They opened their 1932–33 season, after their second summer away, with *Success Story* by John Howard Lawson followed by Dawn Powell's *Big Night*. But it was the final show of that season that marked a major step forward for the Group when the scions of Broadway, the Shuberts, gave them *Men in White* by Sidney Kingsley. It was an atmospheric play set in a hospital. It took full advantage of all the skills they had been working to develop, and thus became the Group's most critically and financially successful project to date, and their only play to win the Pulitzer Prize.

Despite this major success, by the end of 1934, things looked bleak as the leaders of this group struggled to come up with their next production. It was at this turning point that the company members prevailed upon these leaders to look at a play by one of the acting company, Clifford Odets. *Awake and Sing!* opened on Broadway on February 19, 1935. In his review the next day, Brooks Atkinson of the *New York Times* complimented the acting, saying of the nine actors that they "play it with strong power" while calling Harold Clurman's direction "overly wrought and shrill." He also said that the play, " in spite of its frenzy is inexplicably deficient in plain, theatre emotion."[21] The play was revived by the Group four years later, which allowed Atkinson to revise his opinion just a bit as he wrote, "*Awake and Sing!* remains one of the most stirring plays of this generation in the theatre."[22]

Awake and Sing! was one of four of Odets' plays produced and performed by the company in 1935, the others being *Waiting for Lefty, Till the Day I Die,* and *Paradise Lost*. Today one would be hard pressed to not think of the Group Theatre and Clifford Odets in the same breath. Before folding its tent at the beginning of 1941, the company would produce three more new plays by Odets: *Golden Boy, Rocket to the Moon,* and *Night Music,* as well as the aforementioned revival of *Awake and Sing!* As of this writing, *Awake and Sing!* has been given two Broadway revivals, as has *Golden Boy*, which was also made into a musical in 1964.

An early member of the Group, Franchot Tone, was the first to be found by Hollywood. Any number of other members of the company followed him to the west coast, and employment in film as their final production, Irwin Shaw's *Retreat to Pleasure,* opened and ran for a mere two weeks, closing on December 4, 1941, signaling the demise of the Group Theatre as an entity. However, it is its legacy that keeps its name alive for students and fans of theatre. It is found in a way of working that was promulgated by the numerous acting teachers it spawned including Sandy Meisner, Lee Strasberg, Bobby Lewis, Stella Adler, and Phoebe Brand, and by being the ultimate example of the theatre as family ... warts and all.

Above and opposite: In 1934, unable to find a show for their next production, the Group turned to one of their own, Clifford Odets. *Awake and Sing* opened at the Belasco Theatre in February of 1935. Once the reviews were in, this is the flyer they produced. It is interesting to note that none of the blurbs from the critics single out any actor even though the cast included such Group Theatre stalwarts as Morris Carnovsky, Luther Adler, Phoebe Brand, Stella Adler and Jules [John] Garfield (author's collection).

THE GROUP THEATRE
presents

"AWAKE and SING!"

by CLIFFORD ODETS

* "Awake and Sing! kept first-nighters in their chairs until about twenty curtains had lifted and fallen to the tune of bravos, cheers and applause. The reception for this new and powerful play was merited indeed. The youthful newcomer author has arrived. The man can write!"

* "Cheers and bravos at the Belasco. The Group Theatre once more calls for hat-tossing and congratulations. Combining much that was moving in 'Spring Song' with much that was mirthful in 'Another Language,' Awake and Sing! is worthier than either."

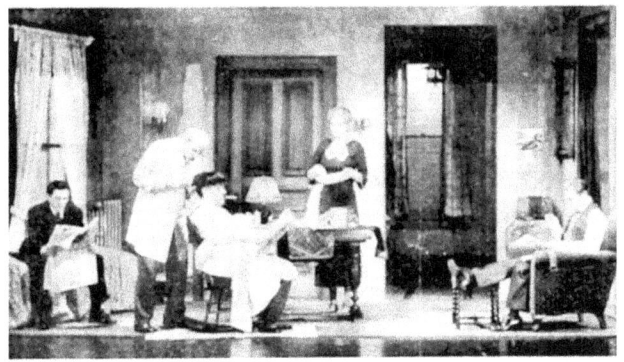

* "The pleasant news is that The Group Theatre has found a genuine writer among its own members and shows how to get his play to rattling on the boards. Clifford Odets has written a drama that is full of substance and vitality; he is not afraid to tackle a big job."

* "There lives a young man in our town who, if he and Hollywood don't look out, is in danger of becoming a foremost dramatist. His name is Clifford Odets. Last night The Group Theatre trusted us in the Belasco to his play, 'Awake and Sing!' A stirring play."

"Laughs Galore!"

BELASCO
THEATRE   W. 44th St.
Mats. Thursday & Saturday

In her exhaustive study, *Real Life Drama: The Group Theatre and America, 1931–1940,* Wendy Smith opines in her preface:

> The story of the Group Theatre told me something I should have known but didn't. Art is part of the real world, the Group said over and over again. It has content, meaning, and implications. There are all kinds of activism, and when art reveals to us our society and ourselves, it is a force for change at least as powerful as any political party.[23]

Sadly, in the real world, an actual political party earning great disfavor in the United States would affect the future of many of this family's members.

Two

Un-American Theatre
The Short Life and Death of the Federal Theatre Project

From the beginning of time, theatre was live. It brought together an often disparate group of people, the audience, with an offer of a hopefully grand communal experience if only for a couple of hours. Over time it has shown that it has the power to amuse, to educate, and on occasion to provoke that same audience. It is this power that in the minds of some makes it dangerous, and for that reason alone, it must be silenced. Such was the fate of the Federal Theatre Project.

With national unemployment at 25 percent by 1933, the Group Theatre had the rare good fortune during the depths of the Depression to be able to supply its members with full-time employment, albeit primarily in New York City. At the same time, the administration of President Franklin Delano Roosevelt and his Works Progress Administration (WPA) was hacking away at that unemployment number with projects across the country that created work for laborers, architects, and tradesmen gifting the country with roads, airports, and even Camp David. But what was to become of the artists not as fortunate as the Group members? Was it possible that the government of the United States could find value in a theatrical performance—a value great enough to employ thousands of actors, musicians, painters, and writers and provide them with a place to work and an audience to work in front of?

The answer came in the form of a tall, dapper career politician and the administrator of the Works Progress Administration, Harry Hopkins. Born in Iowa, a graduate of Grinnell College, he moved to New York City where he became a social worker. When the Depression hit, Hopkins became a leader in emergency relief, catching Roosevelt's attention and becoming one of his closest advisors after Roosevelt was elected president. It was Hopkins who understood that artists also needed a road out of the Depression, and that the country would benefit from their talent.

At the National Theatre Conference at Iowa University in the summer of 1935, Hopkins spoke "'of the new kind of theatre we hoped to create in America.' He concluded with a fearless statement of policy: 'I am asked whether a theatre subsidized by the government can be kept free from censorship, and I say, yes, it is going to be kept free from censorship. What we want is a free, adult, uncensored theatre.'"[1] He introduced the audience to the woman he had chosen to run this new theatrical endeavor: Hallie Flanagan, a diminutive red-haired academic theatre artist and fellow Grinnell graduate, who left her position at Vassar College to become the director of the Federal Theatre Project (FTP). She later wrote, "I took [his] declaration seriously, as did my associates, and that is the kind of theatre we spent the next four years trying to build."[2]

In the brief prepared for her appearance before the U.S. Congress Committee on Patents in February of 1938, Flanagan and her staff wrote about the origins of the project.

> Government support of the theatre brings the United States into the best historic theatre tradition and into the best contemporary theatre practice. Four centuries before Christ, Athens believed that plays were worth paying for out of public money; today France, Germany, Norway, Sweden, Denmark, Russia, Italy and practically all other civilized countries appropriate money for the theatre.
>
> However, it was not because of historic theatre traditions, nor because of contemporary theatre practice that the Federal Theatre came into being. It came into being because in the Summer of 1935, the relief rolls of American cities showed that thousands of unemployed theatre professionals, affected not only by the economic depressions but by the rapid development of the cinema and the radio, were destitute. The Federal Theatre came into being because Mr. Harry Hopkins, Administrator of the Works Progress Administration, believed not only that unemployed theatrical people could get just as hungry as unemployed accountants and engineers, but— and this was much more revolutionary—that their skills were as worthy of conservation. He believed that the talents of the professional theatre workers, together with the skills of painters, musicians and

Harry Hopkins, Administrator of the Works Progress Administration. He is the man who hired Hallie Flanagan to be the Director of the Federal Theatre Project (Photofest).

writers, made up a part of the national wealth which America could not afford to lose.

Therefore, on August 29, 1935, the Federal Theatre Project was set up.

The primary jobs of those of us employed on the project were as follows: to set up boards to review the people sent to us from relief offices; to get them on our payroll; to organized them into companies, having the proper proportion of actors, designers, technicians, etc. It was also necessary to solve many administrative problems, since the Government at that time could not charge admissions, could not pay royalties, could not lease theaters. So complicated were these problems that press and public alike were frankly skeptical as to whether a curtain would ever rise on so vast and uncharted an enterprise. However, by October 1935, projects were set in operation and curtains began to go up all over the United States.

At a time when theatres were dark across America, plays began to be given from the Atlantic to the Pacific, not only in city theatres, but in parks and hospitals, in Catholic convents and Baptist churches, in public schools and armories, in circus tents and universities, in prisons and reformatories, and in those distant and unfrequented [Civilian Conservation Corps] camps where 350,000 of American's youth are learning all they know about life and art.[3]

Hallie Flanagan, the Director of the Federal Theatre Project (Library of Congress).

Finding a quick way to employ its many actors, the FTP turned to the concept of the Living Newspaper. As defined by the *Encyclopædia Britannica*, the

Living Newspaper [is a] theatrical production consisting of dramatizations of current events, social problems, and controversial issues, with appropriate suggestions for improvement. The technique was used for propaganda in the U.S.S.R. from the time of the Revolution in 1917. It became part of the Epic theatre tradition initiated by Erwin Piscator and Bertolt Brecht in Germany in the 1920s. The Living Newspaper was initiated in the United States in 1935 as part of the Federal Theatre Project. One of its major supporters was Elmer Rice, a dramatist and producer who believed in the value of drama as an instrument of social change. It became the most effective new theatre form developed by the Project, vividly dealing, in flashing cinematic techniques, with the realities of agriculture, housing, and economics ... Criticism of the Living Newspaper for alleged communist leanings contributed to the cancellation of the Federal Theatre Project in 1939.[4]

The first Living Newspaper production to open was *Triple-A Plowed Under*. Los Angeles audiences got to see it at the historic Greek Theatre (Chronicle/Alamy Stock Photo).

Through the Living Newspaper productions, the Project had its first major successes. In her introduction to the first volume of three of the scripts published by Random House: *Triple-A Plowed Under, Power,* and *Spirochete,* Flanagan wrote about how they made the idea work.

> The staff of the Living Newspaper was set up like a large city daily, with editor-in-chief, managing editor, city editor, reporters and copyreaders, and they began as Brooks Atkinson later remarked, "to shake the living daylights out of a thousand books, reports, newspaper and magazine articles," in order to evolve an authoritative dramatic treatment, at once historic and contemporary, of current problems. With Arthur Arent as editor and later as playwright, the Living Newspaper from the first was concerned not with surface news, scandal, human interest stories, but rather with the conditions back of conditions.[5]

The first Living Newspaper production was to be *Ethiopia,* but it never opened, and Harry Hopkins "uncensored" theatre was put to lie when the federal government prohibited the impersonation of heads of state onstage. As a result, the first Living Newspaper production came to be *Triple-A Plowed Under* which opened on March 14, 1936, and dealt with the plight of farmers during the dust bowl period and the effect of the Agricultural Adjustment Act of 1933; *Injunction Granted,* an anti-business/pro-union exposé that opened on July 24, 1936; *Power,* which looked at the search for affordable electricity, and was one of the most successful of the productions to date, playing from February 23 to July 10 of 1937; and *One-Third of a Nation,* taking its title and content from President Roosevelt's second inaugural address in which he spoke of "one-third of a nation ill-housed, ill-clad, ill-nourished."

The first Living Newspaper production to open was *Triple-A Plowed Under* (Library of Congress).

President Roosevelt declared that "one-third of a nation [was] ill-housed, ill-clad, ill-nourished." Federal Theatre created a Living Newspaper from that quote. Wherever it played, adjustments were made to the narrative to reflect the problems facing that given area (Photofest).

Another of the more successful productions, it opened in New York on June 17, 1938, and closed on October 22. Unique among the Living Newspaper productions, when *One-Third of a Nation* was playing other cities, it adjusted its narrative to fit each city's challenges. For Roosevelt, "The test of our progress is not whether we add more to the abundance of those who have much; it is whether we provide enough for those who have too little."[6] Federal Theatre took these words to heart by keeping the cost of going to the theatre low and providing numerous productions that could be attended free of charge.

Any number of other plays caused controversy equal to, sometimes exceeding that of the Living Newspaper. One of the best examples was one of Flanagan's biggest success stories, and a foreshadowing of the future of regional theatre in America. *It Can't Happen Here* was a 1935 novel that became a play for the Federal Theatre Project in 1936. With fascism spreading across Europe, it imagines a United States where President Roosevelt was defeated by a fear-mongering politician promising economic and social reforms on a grand and drastic scale, which will lead to the return of patriotism and traditional values. The main character fighting against this is a journalist. On October 27, 1936, 21 productions opened simultaneously in 17 cities across the United States: Birmingham, Boston, Bridgeport, Chicago, Cleveland, Denver, Detroit, Indianapolis, Los Angeles (two productions, the second one in Yiddish), Miami, Newark, New York (also in Yiddish), San Francisco, Seattle (which included a black production), Tacoma, Tampa (which added a production in Spanish), and Yonkers. Other productions followed. Federal Theatre had truly become America's theatre.

On October 27, 1936, 21 productions of *It Can't Happen Here* opened simultaneously in 17 different cities (Library of Congress).

Proving that controversy isn't just for grown-ups, one of the Project's most contentious productions was a play for children that opened in New York on May 20, 1937. *The New York Times*' theatre critic, Brooks Atkinson, dubbed *Revolt of the Beavers*, for old times' sake, "Mother Goose Marx." He ended his review with words that came to haunt the project: "Many children now unschooled in the technique of revolution now have an opportunity, at

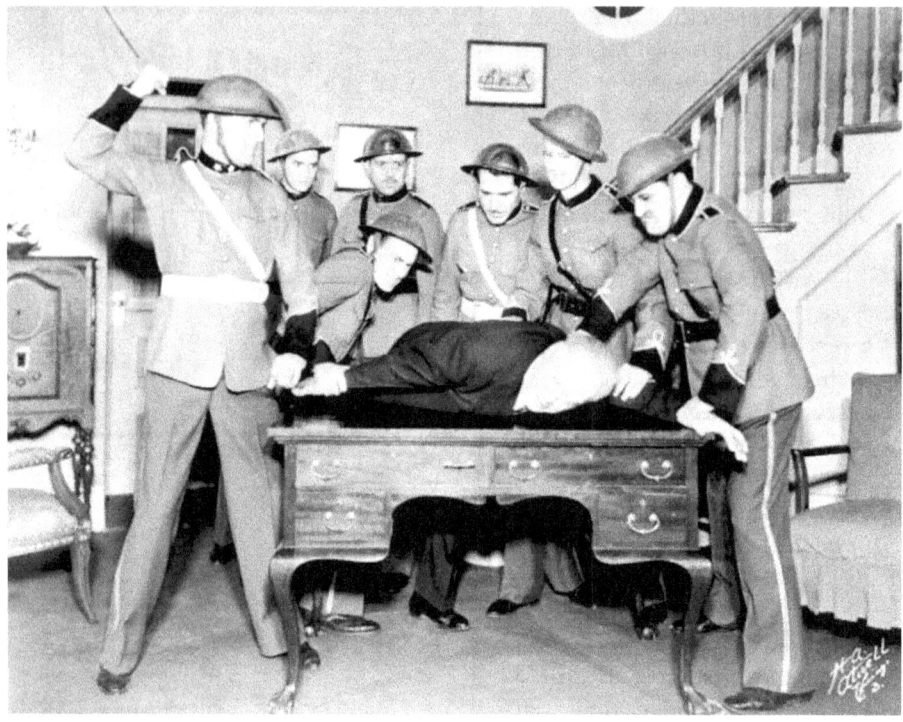

It Can't Happen Here imagines a United States where President Roosevelt was defeated by a fear-mongering politician promising economic and social reforms on a grand and drastic scale, which will lead to the return of patriotism and traditional values (Library of Congress).

government expense, to improve their tender minds. Mother Goose is no longer a rhymed escapist. She has been studying Marx; Jack and Jill lead the class revolution."[7]

John Randolph, then credited as Mortimer Lippman, played one of the bad beavers. As he explained:

> I thought it was a creative thing that the king of the beavers was a son-of-a-gun who was always wretched. Guys like me had roller skates. I was only one of three villains. I've never been in anything like that. We had children hopping onstage and straightening out the actors on where they should go. You saw Julie [future Academy Award nominated director Jules Dassin] running up and down the aisle. There was that kind of variety. The biggest price was twenty-five cents, and if you were poor, then you didn't have to give anything.
>
> It was a wonderful play. It had songs in it. We didn't think it was a communist thing. It was just a good old drama, and we had music. We heard that there were criticisms on the show when it opened at a theatre on Fifty-second Street. The reviews were pretty bad. I couldn't believe that Brooks Atkinson was hurt by whatever reason.

Two. Un-American Theatre

I worked with people that I never worked with after the war. Young people. Old people. There was no question of whether you were black or white. They were part of Federal Theatre.[8]

Revolt of the Beavers closed in New York on June 17, 1937.

June of 1937 was also a month of great controversy, pain, and commotion in the world of the Federal Theatre Project. On June 10, less than two years after its founding, the Project was forced to cut its payroll by 30 percent. June 11, word came down that no new productions would be allowed to open until after July 1.

As a result of this decree, *The Cradle Will Rock,* scheduled to open on June 16, after a month's delay, instantly became the single most famous production that never opened under Federal Theatre. A musical polemic of corruption and corporate greed in 10 scenes with music, lyrics, and book by Marc Blitzstein, the production that did take place on that single day became a thing of theatre lore. It was produced by a young John Houseman and directed by an even younger Orson Welles. The audience and company took a late afternoon stroll from where it was supposed to be opening, the Maxine

The Federal Theatre Project often took the opportunity to engage with the audience in a more direct and engrossing way as illustrated in this photograph from the Chicago Federal Theatre production of *It Can't Happen Here.* Seen (top right) rallying the protestors is the production's star, Glen Beveridge as Berzelius "Buzz" Windrip (Photofest).

Elliott Theatre, 20 blocks uptown to the Venice Theatre where Blitzstein played a single piano from the stage and the actors performed from the audience in order to not break union rules.

Hallie Flanagan spoke of rumors that the play was "dangerous." But more than that, "the stopping of *The Cradle Will Rock*, however, was more than a case of censorship. It marked a changing point of view in Washington..."[9] This seemed to be the true death knell for the free, adult and uncensored theatre that Harry Hopkins had hoped for back in Iowa in the summer of 1935. One of its stars, Howard da Silva, remarked in an interview years later,

> People came up from Washington and raved about it, but certainly it was a direct challenge. It was the "theatre of action." It was some work that said, "Let's go and get them," you know. It was the most susceptible of all of the them, it really was. After all, we're talking about 1937. And again, it has to do also with the vigor of the thirties, the trade union movement.[10]

Theatre is live, and as a result, an audience sometimes sees a moment that will never be repeated in exactly the same way. Such must have been the experience for the 600 audience members who took the walk that day. For her book of interviews, *Voices from the Federal Theatre*, Bonnie Nelson Schwartz found one of those lucky audience members, Lincoln Diamont, who recalled what it was like when the curtain "rose."

The Living Newspaper's *Power* was considered one of the most successful plays in this genre as it looked at the search for affordable electricity (Stocktrek Image, Inc./Alamy Stock Photo).

> Let me try to describe the feeling in the theatre as the play started. There was no curtain pull; there was just this bare piano lit be a single spot. Blitzstein came out and sat down at the piano because he was going to play the musical accompaniment for the entire play, 'cause the musicians' union deserted. The usual level of sound tapers off, and Blitzstein

began to play. He sounded the opening chords of *Cradle Will Rock*, and there was sort of quietness in the theatre that was unlike anything I'd ever seen at that time. He got to the first singing cue, which is "Nickel under My Foot," and as he was singing, a voice came out of the audience. She started singing alongside Blitzstein. He recognized what was happening, and he dropped away and let her continue to sing. It was this girl singing her lines. He gave the follow spot an opportunity to see where she was and pick her up. You can do a play that way. I know because I was there; it happened.[11]

Even if this production didn't open, hundreds of others did. There were new productions, most of which were never heard of again. Companies were formed so that plays could be performed in German, Spanish, and Yiddish. There was dance, children's theatre, musicals, black drama, pageants, spectacles, and puppet shows playing in theatres, parks, and open fields. Audiences were made up of seasoned theatre-goers, and many who never thought they would ever have a chance to see a play.

The New York Times' theater critic, Brooks Atkinson, dubbed *Revolt of the Beavers* "Mother Goose Marx" (Library of Congress).

With all this activity, in no time at all, three years had passed. Fascism was growing across the European continent, and the fear of communist subversion took hold, giving anti–New Deal members of Congress a tool to aid them in their quest to dismantle the New Deal programs. Considered the most vulnerable were the arts programs, and within those programs, the Federal Theatre Project was thought the easiest target.

In May of 1938, Martin Dies, a Democrat from Texas, became the chairman of the reformatted version of the Special House Committee for the Investigation of Un-American Activities, which in no time at all became known as the Dies Committee. The formation of the committee "received little more attention than that usually accorded Congressional investigating committees"[12] until New Jersey Republican representative J. Parnell Thomas "declared that he was determined to have the Federal Theater and Writers' Project investigated. 'It is apparent from the startling evidence received thus far' said Thomas, 'that the Federal Theater Project not only is serving as a branch of the Communistic organization but is also one more link in the vast and unparalleled New Deal propaganda machine.'"[13] Other members of the committee included Democrats Arthur D. Healey of Massachusetts, John J. Dempsey of New Mexico, Joe Starnes of Alabama and Harold G. Mosier of Ohio. The other Republican, besides Thomas, was Noah H. Mason of Illinois.

Three months later, on August 12, 1938, the hearings began. Witnesses included committee investigators, current and former employees of the various projects, as well as Walter S. Steele, the owner of the National Republic Publishing Co., and the managing editor of the *National Republic* magazine representing numerous right-wing organizations, and whose archives at the Hoover Institute at Stanford University include the papers of one Hazel Huffman.

Hazel Huffman appeared before the committee on August 19, 1938, after being prepared extensively by Congressman Thomas. It became apparent

John Randolph, then Mortimer Lippman, was an actor in *Revolt of the Beavers*. His character worked for the boss. Pictured standing left to right: Allen Frank as Ruff, Elena Karam as Gruff and Mortimer Lippman as Tuff. They are attacking Oakleaf played by future director Jules Dassin (Library of Congress).

Two. Un-American Theatre

Howard da Silva as Larry Forman and Olive Stanton as Moll in *The Cradle Will Rock* on January 3, 1938. "Labor speaks to capital. The wistful prostitute laughs" (*Stage Magazine*, vol. 15, no. 5, February. 1938).

quite early on that Thomas used Huffman as his vessel for attacking the Federal Theatre Project. Also apparent in the exchanges that follow is the animus between Thomas and Congressman Joe Starnes, a Democrat from Alabama, which continued throughout these hearings.

> MR. THOMAS: Will you also tell the committee what organization you represent?
> MISS HUFFMAN: The Committee of Relief Status Professional Theatrical Employees of the Federal Theater Project in New York City.
> MR. THOMAS: Miss Huffman, will you, in your own way, tell us about what you know of the Federal Theater Project in New York City; but at the same time the committee would appreciate it if you would confine your remarks to facts, and wherever possible submit whatever documentary evidence you may have.
> MR. STARNES: Mr. Chairman, before proceeding, what is the purpose of this testimony?
> MR. THOMAS: Mr. Chairman, I would like to answer that, if I may.
> THE CHAIRMAN: Yes.
> MR. THOMAS: The purpose of this testimony is to show the communistic activities in the Federal Theater Project in New York City.
> MR. STARNES: I suggest then, if it is an attempt to show that there is any communism in that project that is in question, that her testimony be confined to that

> **Suppressed by the Government!**
> **Acclaimed by the Critics!**
> **Demanded by the Public!**
> **Now on Broadway!**
>
> SAM H. GRISMAN
>
> THE MERCURY THEATRE PRODUCTION
>
> # "THE CRADLE WILL ROCK"
>
> By MARC BLITZSTEIN
>
> "A tingling and stimulating adventure in theatregoing, which, if you are wise, you will take pains not to miss."
> —JOHN MASON BROWN, *New York Post*
>
> "A quality of excitement that gives it genuine imaginative power... worth all the advance discussion it has caused."
> —RICHARD WATTS, Jr., *Herald-Tribune*
>
> **OPENING NEXT MONDAY NIGHT**
> **WINDSOR THEATRE** 48th STREET EAST of BROADWAY · BRyant 9-0178
> Evenings 8:30 · Matinees Wednesday and Saturday at 2:45
> SEATS 50¢ to $2.00 (plus tax) NOW ON SALE

An ad promoting a re-opening of *The Cradle Will Rock* ran in most of the more left-leaning newspapers (author's collection).

>   phase alone. The question that has been asked, as to what she knows about the Federal Theater Project up there is entirely too broad. I think it should be confined solely to anything that would be un–American or subversive.
> MR. THOMAS: I agree with that; but at the same time she will have to bring in certain angles of the Federal Theater Project. I think you will find as she goes along that she will develop the points right along the lines that the committee would desire.
> MR. STARNES: I would very much like to have the testimony restricted to that, because I am not interested in anything except what is un–American or subversive in character.
> Anything beyond that—for instance, an expose of any witness' political background or anything of that sort—I think should be excluded.
> MR. THOMAS: I agree with that. Go ahead, Miss Huffman.
> MISS HUFFMAN: To prove that communism exists and dominates the Federal Theater Project, it might be well to tell when it started and how it obtained its foothold. To correct a disease we must first know what is causing it. Is that satisfactory?[14]

Two. Un-American Theatre

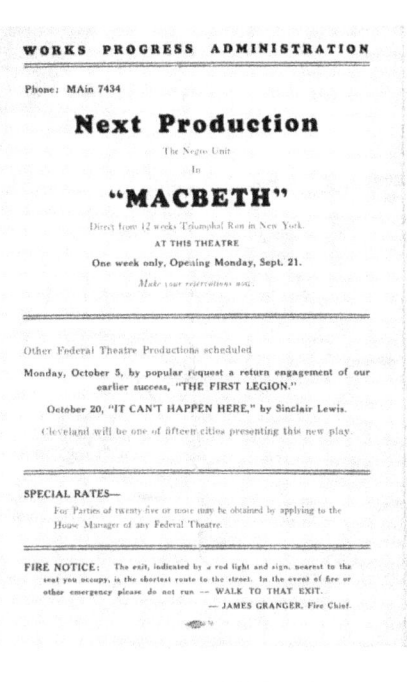

Indeed Federal Theatre kept going all over the country. This program is from the Federal Theatre in Cleveland, Ohio, where the author's father played a robot in Karel Čapek's *R-U-R* (author's collection).

Dies Committee, December 19, 1938: Front row (left to right) : Noah Mason, Chairman Martin Dies, J. Parnell Thomas. Back row: John Dempsey, secretary Robert E. Stripling, unidentified (Harris & Ewing).

Huffman proceeded to name numerous organizations, unions and guilds that worked for or with the FTP, and all of which she painted with the brush of communism. She continued to discuss how pamphlets and flyers were distributed at FTP locations, which led to the first of many comments regarding Hallie Flanagan.

> Mr. Thomas: Do you mean to say that was distributed right on the project itself; right in the buildings on the project?
> Miss Huffman: Yes, sir, on Government property.
> Then we have Mrs. Hallie Flanagan, the national director of the Federal Theater Project. Mrs. Flanagan was known as far back as 1927 for her communistic sympathy, if not membership. Mrs. Flanagan's book, Shifting Scenes—
> Mr. Thomas: (interposing). Who is Mrs. Hallie Flanagan?
> Miss Huffman: Mrs. Hallie Flanagan is national director of the Federal Theater Project. The arts projects are divided into five sections, Mr. Sokolov being head of the music, Mrs. Flanagan head the theater, and so forth.
> In this book Mrs. Flanagan devotes 147 pages of a total of 280 to eulogizing Soviet Russia and the Russian Theater.[15]

Two. Un-American Theatre

Huffman continued to "prove" Flanagan's involvement in all things communist:

> MISS HUFFMAN: It there is any doubt left as to Mrs. Flanagan's active participation and interest in things communistic, let me try to remove that doubt.[16]

Huffman, led by Thomas' questions, goes on for another 50 pages, followed by other disgruntled actors and writers. The next day Sallie Saunders, a naturalized citizen, born in Vienna, Austria, and employed as an actress on a FTP production, *Sing for Your Supper*, explained to the committee how she knows there are communists on the project.

> THE CHAIRMAN: Have you seen with your eyes evidence of communistic or subversive activities on the particular project?
> MISS SAUNDERS: I can only say that literature has been sent around to me personally.
> THE CHAIRMAN: Do you know that Communist literature has been distributed on the premises?
> MISS SAUNDERS: Surely.
> THE CHAIRMAN: On one occasion you were called on the telephone. Will you go into the details of that without going too much into it?

Hazel Huffman appearing before the Dies Committee on August 19, 1938 (Library of Congress).

THE CURTAIN IS UP!

Act I.

Yes, the curtain is up on a tragic Hoax! You can get an INDICTMENT easier than an 'Annie Oakley'. BARNUM labeled us all suckers but we can't afford to be and we won't be suckers!

What's the show all about? It's called "FRAME-UP" — in three acts. The scene of the first act was HOLLYWOOD and WASHINGTON where we saw JOHN HOWARD LAWSON, ALBERT MALTZ, DALTON TRUMBO and the others framed for fighting for their political rights as AMERICANS.

Act II

Now comes the second act! Bigger stuff — on a national scale, the theme based on an idea borrowed from HITLER'S REICHSTAG FIRE. The leaders of the legal COMMUNIST PARTY of the United States are indicted and jailed on the absurd charge that they teach "the overthrow and destruction of the U.S. by force and violence." TRUTH takes a fearful shellacking from the producers of this spectacle. Even their chief playwright, Attorney General TOM CLARK, had been forced to admit to the HOUSE UN-AMERICAN COMMITTEE a month ago that he had not one scintilla of evidence that any Communist was guilty of espionage, force and violence, or service to any foreign power.

But the play goes on. TRUMAN and CLARK don't care if the charges are phony! They want to pull the audience away from a bigger and better show — the new people's party holding its convention in PHILADELPHIA! Yes, the WALL STREET angels are afraid that HENRY WALLACE and GLENN TAYLOR are attracting millions of customers away from their usual donkey-elephant routines.

Truman has to steal the scene from his GOP villain. The "red" issue is hot stuff. Besides, it covers up his bad performances in other shows — the housing shortage, the rising cost of living, and the manufactured hysterics around the BERLIN CRISIS. Now if he does a little yelling, maybe he can whip up a hot war. After all, the boys are in uniform, or getting into one this very day — Why waste all the ammunition? The climax will be the MUNDT POLICE STATE BILL — That is, if — if we, the audience, let him get that far.

Act III

The third act? Well, that's where theatre-workers join the show. Not as active employees — BUT — with gags around their mouths. Congressman THOMAS threatens an "investigation" of BROADWAY. If he gets away with his "indictments" of the COMMUNISTS — who have always defended the economic welfare and democratic rights of the AMERICAN PEOPLE — there won't be any rights left to defend!

We think this is a lousy show! We know you think so too. Let's RING THE CURTAIN DOWN! Yes, before the public is completely hoodwinked into fascism and war. Let's RING THE CURTAIN DOWN!

WIRE YOUR PROTESTS OF THE INDICTMENTS TO ATTORNEY GENERAL TOM CLARK AND PRESIDENT TRUMAN!

READ THE DAILY WORKER FOR THE REAL ISSUE ON THIS AND OTHER VITAL ISSUES OF THE DAY!

ATTEND THE NATIONAL CONVENTION OF THE COMMUNIST PARTY OF THE UNITED STATES AT MADISON SQUARE GARDEN.. MONDAY, AUGUST 2nd, 7:45 PM

Theatre Section of the
Communist Party

An example of a flyer that Huffman says was distributed at the Project. It is signed by the Theatre Section of the Communist Party (author's collection).

Two. Un-American Theatre 35

> Miss Saunders: Yes, sir. On Decoration Day I received a phone call from Mr. Van Cleave.
> The Chairman: This year?
> Miss Saunders: Yes, sir; and he asked for a date. I lived at the Fraternity Club, and there are a great many men there. I thought it was someone I met at the Fraternity Club. I said, "Mr. Van Cleave, I do not remember you; when did I meet you?" He said, I was the gentleman who sketched you in Sing for Your Supper." I said, "There were 289 people down there, and I do not know more than 25 of them." He said, "I am the fellow who was sketching you." I had noticed a Negro making a sketch of me as I was dancing. He shoved the sketch in my face. I did not know his name, and did not know anything about him...

She first reported this to her supervisor Mr. [Harold] Hecht.

> Miss Saunders: He said, "Sallie, I am surprised at you. He has just as much right to life, liberty, and pursuit of happiness as you do."...

After this exchange, Chairman Dies asked if Saunders had reported this to Trudy Goodrich.

> Miss Saunders: She is a secretary of a Workers Alliance division and she came to me of her own accord. She said she felt very sorry that I felt that way about it, because she personally encouraged Negro attention on all occasions and went out with them or with any Negro who asked her to.
> Mr. Starnes: Did she say that it was the policy of the Workers Alliance to do that?
> Miss Saunders: She did not say that; but she is a representative of that party, and they hobnob indiscriminately with them, throwing parties with them right and left.
> Mr. Starnes: Is that part of the Communist program?
> Miss Saunders: Yes, sir; social equality and race merging.[17]

On September 3, an article appeared in *The Chicago Defender* with the headline "Reports of Interracial Parties Shock Probers of Un-American Activities," in which Saunders is referred to as, "the pretty blonde 'expert' on Communism."[18]

Four months later, on December 6, 1938, Hallie Flanagan finally got her turn to come before the committee and tell her side of the story. The brief prepared for that earlier hearing was used once again. After some preliminary questions, Chairman Dies got down to business.

> The Chairman: Now, will you just tell us briefly the duties of your position?
> Mrs. Flanagan: Yes Congressman Dies. Since August 29, 1935, I have been concerned with combating un–American inactivity.
> The Chairman: No. We will get to that in a minute.
> Mrs. Flanagan: Please listen. I said I am combating un–American inactivity.
> The Chairman: Inactivity?
> Mrs. Flanagan: I refer to the inactivity of professional men and women; people who, at that time when I took office, were on the relief rolls; and it was my job to expend the appropriation laid aside by congressional vote for the relief of

the unemployed as it related to the field of theater, and to set up projects wherever in any city 25 or more of such professionals were found on the relief rolls.

MR. THOMAS: Mr. Chairman, I think before her statement is made, we should find out something about Mrs. Flanagan's history. I think it is of great importance that we know something about her history, and that that go in the record—where she went to college and so forth.

THE CHAIRMAN. We are going to get to that, but I wanted to give her an opportunity. I think that you said you are the director of all of these activities?

MRS. FLANAGAN: Yes, thank you. May I add to that fact that the project is national in scope; and that we have projects in Washington, Oregon, California, in Colorado and Michigan, in Ohio and Illinois, in Oklahoma and North Carolina, in Maine and New Hampshire, in New York state and Massachusetts, and New Jersey and Delaware; in other words, in any place where there were a sufficient number of qualified relief applicants. I wanted to say that gentlemen, as a background for the project.[19]

What followed was the beginning of an extensive review of Hazel Huffman's charges and Flanagan's refutations. Ever since Huffman's testimony in August, Flanagan had waited for this opportunity. As questions continued to repeat themselves, Flanagan continued to answer. The committee was unimpressed by the fact that she was the first woman in America to be awarded a Guggenheim Foundation scholarship to study theatre around Europe for 14 months, as they were obsessed by the idea that she spent a good part of that time studying the theatre in Russia.

MR. STARNES: Did you not make the statement that the theaters in Russia are more vital and important?

MRS. FLANAGAN: Yes; I did find that. And I think that opinion would be borne out by any dramatic critic that you cared to call to this chair.

MR. STARNES: What is it about the Russian theater that makes it more vital and important than the theaters of the continent and the theaters of the United States?

MRS. FLANAGAN: I would be glad to do that, but before doing it I would like to say that this is the first time since the Federal Theater started that I have had occasion to answer that question.

I have maintained consistently that we are starting an American theater, which must be founded on American principles which has nothing to do with the Russian theater.[20]

The committee continued to demonstrate how uneducated they were when it came to theatre. Imagine if they had known that since 1931, the Group Theatre had been employing the technique of one Constantine Stanislavski, the acclaimed Russian theatre director and teacher. Fortunately for the Group they were not under the employ of, or receiving any money from, the federal government. Continuing on for the next several pages, Starnes and Thomas banter on what should be asked, what is being asked, and what just might be pertinent to this hearing until Starnes returns yet again to charges leveled by Huffman.

Two. Un-American Theatre

MR. STARNES: Now Mrs. Flanagan, would you go back to this question again of un–American communistic activities on the Federal Theater Project? That charge has been made that the Daily Worker and "red" pins and other communistic propaganda have been disseminated on the project in project time there in the Federal Theater Project. Do you know whether or not that is true, of your own personal knowledge?

MRS. FLANAGAN: Congressman Starnes, I am submitting in this brief administrative orders which absolutely forbid the dissemination of any such literature on project time or money.

I have never seen such literature distributed. I have never seen such notices on bulletin boards.

I know that in the testimony of some of your witnesses these allegations have been made, and I can only tell you that when such an allegation is made, it should be at once followed through the supervisor of that project; and any person who is found guilty of such use, improper use of project time and property, would be dismissed.

MR. STARNES: All right. In other words, if such has been done, it has been done without your knowledge and without your consent?

MRS. FLANAGAN: That is absolutely true.

MR. STARNES: Against express orders on your part?

MRS. FLANAGAN: Against such express orders, Congressman.

MR. STARNES: You don't say, though, it has not been done?

MRS. FLANAGAN: I could not to my own knowledge.

MR. STARNES: But I want to establish the fact, which will clear you of that charge, if such charges are made against you before this committee, that you did not order it done. To the contrary, you said such should not be done?

MRS. FLANAGAN: To the contrary, the specific bulletins are here attached saying that that is absolutely contrary to the work of this project.

MR. STARNES: All right.

Now, you were speaking of the Russian theater a moment ago. Do you believe that the theater is a weapon?

MRS. FLANAGAN: Shall I discuss the American theater or talk about the Russian?

MR. STARNES: No, I refer to the theater generally. Do you believe that the theater is a weapon?

MRS. FLANAGAN: I believe that the theater is a great educational force. I think it is entertainment. I think it is excitement. I think it may be all things to all men.[21]

In the committee's files are copies of the scripts that the committee deemed most offensive, most communistic. One of those scripts was for *Injunction Granted*.

MR. THOMAS: How about Injunction Granted?

MRS. FLANAGAN: Injunction Granted is propaganda for fair labor relations and for fairness in labor courts.

MR. STARNES: In other words, it does teach class consciousness doesn't it?

MRS. FLANAGAN: I am trying to give you my definition of propaganda and just what it teaches.

MR. STARNES: Yes. Well that is what this play teaches, isn't it?

> Mrs. Flanagan: You objected to some of these words, and I agreed with you that they were very trite, and I was trying to explain more clearly and more definitely what I mean by propaganda.
> Mr. Starnes: Yes. But the play, Injunction Granted, was an attack against our present system of courts, wasn't it?
> Mrs. Flanagan: No. I should say that that play was a definite historical study of the history of labor in the courts.
> Mr. Starnes: I know, but don't you believe that it does attack the present system of courts?
> Mrs. Flanagan: I do not believe that it fosters class hatred. No I do not believe so.[22]

Further on Flanagan is asked about the audiences that attended Federal Theatre.

> The Chairman: How many people do you figure you had as audiences in the United States for these plays?
> Mrs. Flanagan: The recorded figure, Congressman Dies, was something like 25,000,000 people.
> The Chairman: In other words, you have reached approximately 25 percent of our population with your plays? …
> Where have your audiences been? What localities have you played mostly?
> Mrs. Flanagan: We have played to, I think I am safe in saying, the widest variety of American audiences that any theatre has ever played before.[23]

A few pages later Congressman Starnes and Mrs. Flanagan have one of the most oft quoted exchanges from this hearing.

> Mr. Starnes: You are quoting from this Marlowe. Is he a Communist?
> Mrs. Flanagan: I am very sorry. I was quoting from Christopher Marlowe.
> Mr. Starnes: Tell us who Marlowe is, so we can get the proper reference, because that is all that we want to do.
> Mrs. Flanagan: Put in the record that he was the greatest dramatist in the period of Shakespeare, immediately preceding Shakespeare.[24]

By Congressman Starnes estimation, Marlowe might well have been a communist while even the Greeks were guilty of "teaching class consciousness." Were Starnes with us today, he would find that artists are still the ones challenging the status quo. Apropos of challenging, the next production to take center stage at these hearings was *Revolt of the Beavers*.

> Mr. Thomas: I have a few questions.
> You heard the testimony yesterday relative to Byrnes McDonald's letter to you in connection with the Revolt of the Beavers?
> Mrs. Flanagan: I did. In fact, I have a complete copy of that in my brief.
> Mr. Thomas: Do you have the answers there that you sent to Byrnes McDonald?
> Mrs. Flanagan: No. I have not. That is, I think, a great oversight on our part. We would like definitely to have that letter written into the record.
> It was a letter in which I simply said that I was sorry that the police commissioner has been disturbed; but all I could say about it was that the play was for children, and that the children had found it pleasant and entertaining.

And may I speak to that point now, because it took up so much of the testimony yesterday, and I really would like to say something about the Revolt of the Beavers. I was very sorry that Mr. Brooks Atkinson, whose skill as a critic and whose learning are valued very greatly, was disturbed by this play, and that the police commissioner was disturbed; but we did not write this play for dramatic critics, nor did we write it for policemen. We wrote it for children; and I wish to write into the record what the children thought about the play.

MR. STARNES: Of course, you know they were criticizing it because they thought that it was not an amusing play for policemen?

MRS. FLANAGAN: They were criticizing it because they said that they thought that it was poisoning the minds of youth.

MR. STARNES: That is correct.

MRS. FLANAGAN: Now I wish to write into the record a survey on Revolt of the Beavers which was conducted under the supervision of Dr. Francis Holder of the department of psychology of New York University, together with 14 honor students of the college on the reactions of the children.

Flanagan went on to read a number of the questions as well as the replies of the nine-year-old students as to their reactions to the play:

The play teaches us never to be selfish; never to be selfish because you don't get anything out of it.

The acting—how to get around on the stage. That is what I like, the acting big people do as small children, and how good they acted as beavers on roller skates.

That it is better to be good than bad. That beavers have manners just like children. To teach that if you are unkind any time in your life, you will always regret it.

To get the beavers to be like children 9 years old, thinking it would be more fun if everyone was 9 years old and a land of talking beavers on roller skates.[25]

The infighting between the congressmen about what direction questioning should take, albeit fascinating and worth a read, adds little more to the debate on whether or not Federal Theatre deserves to continue, and who decides if a play is good or bad. Although asked and answered on a number of occasions, Flanagan's attitude toward communism is asked yet again.

MR. STARNES: The statement has been made in the testimony that you are in sympathy with communistic doctrines.

MRS. FLANAGAN: Congressman Starnes, I am an American, and I believe in American democracy. I believe the Works Progress Administration is one great bulwark of that democracy. I believe the Federal Theater, which is one small part of that large pattern, is honestly trying in every possible way to interpret the best interests of the people of this democracy. I am not in sympathy with any other form of government in this country.[26]

Finally, almost 20 pages later, the committee decides to adjourn for an hour.

MR. STARNES: Have you finished, Mrs. Flanagan?

MRS. FLANAGAN: Just a minute, gentlemen. Do I understand that this concludes my testimony?

THE CHAIRMAN: We will see about it after lunch.
MRS. FLANAGAN: I would like to make a final statement, if I may, Congressman Dies.
THE CHAIRMAN: We will see about it after lunch.[27]

Lunch came and went, and even though the hearings continued until December 14, Hallie Flanagan was never given another opportunity to speak before the committee. Nine days later, December 23, 1938, *Pinocchio* opened at the Ritz Theatre in New York City. It was one of four productions still playing on June 30, 1939, when the Federal Theatre Project ended. In *Arena*, her memoir of the Federal Theatre Project written in 1940, Flanagan recalled that day:

> For the last performance of *Pinocchio* at the Ritz Theatre, New York, Yasha Frank provided a new ending. Pinocchio, having conquered selfishness and greed, did not become a living boy. Instead he was turned back into a puppet. "So let the bells proclaim our grief," intoned the company at the finish, "that his small life was all too brief." The stagehands knocked down the sets in view of the audience and the company laid Pinocchio away in a pine box which bore the legend:
> BORN DECEMBER 23, 1938; KILLED BY
> ACT OF CONGRESS, JUNE 30, 1939[28]

"How was it possible, with such overwhelming [public] support and with a record of accomplishment so substantial, that Federal Theatre was nevertheless ended by an Act of Congress on June 30, 1939?" Flanagan wondered, and then answered:

> It was ended because Congress, in spite of protests from many of its own members, treated the Federal Theatre not as a human issue or a cultural issue, but as a political issue.
> It was ended because the powerful forces marshaled in its behalf came too late to combat other forces which apparently had been at work against Federal Theatre for a long time. Through two congressional committees these forces found habitation and a name.[29]

Sometime between her testimony before the Dies Committee and the end of the project, Hazel Huffman sat down at a typewriter and began what looks like an essay or perhaps even the beginnings of a book: "Why Throw the Baby Out the Window" by Hazel Huffman. Although she quotes liberally from the hearings, she seems to feel the need to explain herself even more.

> There is little question in my mind that in the event the Federal Theater Project closes down that I shall be blamed! Not only by those for whom I have waged a ceaseless [sic] struggle against the maladministration and abuse dealt the professional actor; but by the general public as well. Any credit given me for having been instrumental in bringing the investigation about I am willing to accept. Yes, I most certainly did fight tooth and nail for an investigation into the wanton destruction of a project supposedly set up by congress to give aid to my fellow-men, the people of the theater. It has always been my contention that continuance of these abuses could only result in the eventual collapse of the Federal Theater Project.[30]

Huffman may have thought that Hallie Flanagan was incapable of running the project as she, Huffman, believed it should run, but John Houseman, the then producer of *The Cradle Will Rock*, felt quite differently. Asked to write a forward when Flanagan's book, *Arena*, was reprinted after her death in 1969, Houseman concluded:

> But, by us in the theatre, it is for those [four] frantic and fantastic years that she will be remembered—the years in which she and her collaborators turned a dubious and pathetic relief project into what remains, after forty years, the most creative and dynamic approach that has yet been made to an American national theatre.[31]

The last word, however, goes to Martin Dies, for it was far from over for him. In his self-titled autobiography, he bragged that the committee's "findings were sufficiently impressive to cause a Liberal Congress to abolish these projects." Having already begun looking into work on the other coast, he issued a report on "radical and Communist activities" that were "rampant among the studios of Hollywood."

> From Legionnaires and others, I got a rather clear picture of the Hollywood situation. When Hollywood film producers arranged two luncheons in my honor left-wing actors and screen writers were conspicuously absent. I told the producers we had reliable information that a number of film actors and screen writers and a few producers either were members of the Communist Party, followed the Communist line, or were used as dupes, and that there was evidence that the Hollywood anti–Nazi League was under the control of Communists.[32]

Welcome to the next chapter of our story. Some of the players will be familiar. At least one of the bit players will get a chance to take on a leading role.

Three

Finding Subversives in Hollywood

Welcome to Hollywood, Chairman Dies. Welcome to the land of sunshine, wealth, and fame. Welcome to the world of film, where a movie might be seen in one week by more people than a play that runs for a year on Broadway. Hollywood, where publicity is the mother's milk of fame.

For Martin Dies, the Washington hearings, their success in eliminating the WPA programs, and the attendant publicity left him wanting more, and Hollywood, he opined correctly, gave him more then he ever imagined. Theatre actors came to Hollywood to dip their toes into a world of glamour and riches that a movie career might provide. In Hollywood they found a very different kind of family, where social standing and a person's worth was often determined by the success or failure of a single film. Since one could make a movie with someone and still never even meet them, social and political activities are what brought groups together. Actors from the theatre project Dies had so unceremoniously eliminated were of little interest to him or to the committee that followed unless, and until, Hollywood made them famous and thus worthy of publicity.

Over the course of the next few years, stars like Humphrey Bogart, James Cagney, Fredric March, and his wife Florence Eldridge came before the Dies committee. However, the frenzy of massive public attention that greeted the film industry in 1947 did not take hold at the time, possibly because the concepts of naming names or being cooperative or uncooperative were not part of the conversation. Indeed, the Hollywood types were sandwiched in between aircraft workers, college students and reporters.

In 1945, the Special Committee on Un-American Activities finally was made a standing committee of the House of Representatives: The House Committee on Un-American Activities commonly abbreviated as HUAC (HCUA, the correct acronym has been used in some circles, but is obviously nowhere near as catchy or convenient). Within two years, Martin Dies was

Three. Finding Subversives in Hollywood

Members of the now standing House Committee on Un-American Activities when hearings began in October of 1947. Left to right: Richard M. Nixon, Robert E. Stripling, J. Parnell Thomas (Library of Congress).

no longer a congressman. The Republican Party held a majority in both the House and Senate, and as a result the chairmanship of HUAC fell to former Dies Committee member J. Parnell Thomas. The war had ended, Winston Churchill threw an Iron Curtain across Europe, and the committee now found itself a major publicity outlet in investigating Hollywood, which brought about a radical change for the industry beginning in the fall of 1947.

On October 20, 1947, Congressman J. Parnell Thomas, now the Chairman of the committee, opened the hearings into subversives in the entertainment industry. This is the same Congressman Thomas who led the charge against the Federal Theatre Project and abetted Hazel Huffman's testimony with the goal of ending that project. Sitting on the dais with Chairman Thomas were fellow Republicans Karl E. Mundt of South Dakota, John McDowell of Pennsylvania, Richard M. Nixon of California and Richard B. Vail of Illinois. The four Democrats who joined them were John S. Wood of Georgia, John E. Rankin of Mississippi, J. Hardin Peterson of Florida and Herbert C. Bonner of North Carolina.

Members of the now standing House Committee on Un-American Activities (HUAC), 1947. Left to right: Rep. Richard Vail, Chairman J. Parnell Thomas, Rep. John McDowell, Chief Counsel Robert Stripling, Rep. Richard Nixon (Photofest).

Thomas gaveled the hearing to order stating:

> ... The committee is well aware of the magnitude of the subject which it is investigating. The motion-picture business represents an investment of billions of dollars [quite different from the world of live theatre]. It represents employment for thousands of workers, ranging from unskilled laborers to high-salaried actors and executives. And even more important, the motion-picture industry represents what is probably the largest single vehicle of entertainment for the American public—over 85,000,000 persons attend the movies each week.
>
> However, it is the very magnitude of the scope of the motion-picture industry which makes this investigation so necessary.... We all recognize that what the citizen sees and hears in his neighborhood movie house carries a powerful impact on his thoughts and behavior.
>
> With such vast influence over the lives of American citizens as the motion-picture industry exerts, it is not unnatural—in fact, it is very logical—that subversive and undemocratic forces should attempt to use this medium for un-American purposes.
>
> I want to emphasize at the outset of the hearings that the fact that the Committee on Un-American Activities is investigating alleged Communist influence and infiltra-

Three. Finding Subversives in Hollywood

tion in the motion-picture industry must not be considered or interpreted as an attack on the majority of persons associated with this great industry. I have every confidence that the vast majority of movie workers are patriotic and loyal Americans.

This committee, under its mandate from the House of Representatives, has the responsibility of exposing and spotlighting subversive elements wherever they may exist. As I have already pointed out, it is only to be expected that such elements would strive desperately to attain entry to the motion-picture industry, simply because the industry offers such a tremendous weapon for education and propaganda. That Communists have made such an attempt in Hollywood and with considerable success is already evident to this committee from its preliminary investigative work.[1]

For the next five days, Chairman Thomas and his committee questioned a host of Hollywood luminaries including studio heads Jack Warner, Louis B. Mayer and Walt Disney, as well as actors and future politicians George Murphy and Ronald Reagan. Those first five days introduced us to the concept of cooperative (friendly) and uncooperative (un-friendly) witnesses. For this opening round, only witnesses the committee knew would cooperate testified.

On October 22, the committee called actor Robert Taylor who became the first witness to name a fellow actor.

> MR. STRIPLING: Are you a member of any guild?
> MR. TAYLOR: I am a member of the Screen Actors Guild; yes, sir.
> MR. STRIPLING: Have you ever noticed any elements within the Screen Actors Guild that you would consider to be following the Communist Party line?
> MR. TAYLOR: Well, yes, sir; I must confess that I have. I am a member of the board of directors of the Screen Actors Guild. Quite recently I have been very active as a director of that board. It seems to me that at meetings, especially meetings of the general membership of the guild, there is always a certain group of actors and actresses whose every action would indicate to me that if they are not Communists they are working awfully hard to be Communists. I don't know. Their tactics and their philosophies seem to me to be pretty much party-line stuff.
> The Chair took a short recess and then Taylor's testimony continued.
> MR. STRIPLING: Mr. Taylor, these people in the Screen Actors Guild who, in your opinion follow the Communist Party line, are they a disrupting influence within the organization?
> MR. TAYLOR: It seems so to me. In the meetings which I have attended, at least on issues which apparently there is considerable unanimity of opinion, it always occurs that someone is not quite able to understand what the issue is and the meeting, instead of being over at 10 o'clock or 10:30 when it logically should be over, probably winds up running until 1 to 2 o'clock in the morning on such issues as points of order and so on.
> MR. STRIPLING: Do you recall the names of any of the actors in the guild who participated in such activity?
> MR. TAYLOR: Well, yes, sir; I can name a few who seem to sort of disrupt things once in awhile. Whether or not they are Communists, I don't know.

46 Broadway and the Blacklist

Chairman Thomas (left) conversing with witness Robert Taylor on October 22, 1947 (Photofest).

>   MR. STRIPLING: Would you name them for the committee, please?
>   MR. TAYLOR: One chap we have currently, I think, is Mr. Howard Da Silva. He always seems to have something to say at the wrong time. Miss Karen Morley also usually appears at the guild meetings.
>   MR. STRIPLING: That is K-a-r-e-n M-o-r-l-e-y?
>   MR. TAYLOR: I believe so; yes, sir. These are the two I can think of right at the moment.[2]

Four days later, on Monday, October 27, 1947, a very different part of the hearing commenced. Unlike the group that appeared during the first five days, the next series of witnesses had already, before testimony had even begun, been painted with the brush of potentially, probably, and it turned out most assuredly, being unfriendly when they testified. This group was made up of 19 writers, directors and actors. Four days later, October 30, 1947, the hearings ended. Of the 19, 11 had testified. Number 11 was the playwright Bertolt Brecht, who left the country after testifying. The others became known as the Hollywood Ten: writers John Howard Lawson, Dalton Trumbo, Albert Maltz, Alvah Bessie, Samuel Ornitz, Edward Dmytryk, Ring Lardner, Jr. and Lester Cole; director Herbert Biberman of *Red Rust* fame and the producer Adrian Scott.

Less than one month later, when it became obvious that the Hollywood Ten would be cited for contempt of Congress, Eric Johnston, the president of the Motion Picture Association of America, called a closed-door meeting of the major employers groups and studio heads at the Waldorf Astoria Hotel in New York City. At the conclusion of the meetings that took place November 24–25, they had reached a consensus. A two-page press release that became known as The Waldorf Statement was issued on December 3, 1947.

> Members of the Association of Motion Picture Producers deplore the action of the 10 Hollywood men who have been cited for contempt by the House of Representatives. We do not desire to prejudge their legal rights, but their actions have been a disservice to their employers and have impaired their usefulness to the industry.

Two of the Hollywood Ten: On the left is screenwriter Ring Lardner, Jr., being escorted from the witness stand on the last day of hearings, October 30, 1947. On the right is Lardner's fellow screenwriter, Dalton Trumbo. The photograph is from 1950 just shortly before the Ten began their jail terms for contempt of Congress. Trumbo, who had testified on October 28, 1947, received an Academy Award in 1956 under one of his pseudonyms (Photofest).

We will forthwith discharge or suspend without compensation those in our employ, and we will not re-employ any of the 10 until such time as he is acquitted or has purged himself of contempt and declares under oath that he is not a Communist.

On the broader issue of alleged subversive and disloyal elements in Hollywood, our members are likewise prepared to take positive action.

We will not knowingly employ a Communist or a member of any party or group which advocates the overthrow of the government of the United States by force or by any illegal or unconstitutional methods. In pursuing this policy, we are not going to be swayed by hysteria or intimidation from any source. We are frank to recognize that such a policy involves danger and risks. There is the danger of hurting innocent people. There is the risk of creating an atmosphere of fear. Creative work at its best cannot be carried on in an atmosphere of fear. We will guard against this danger, this risk, this fear. To this end we will invite the Hollywood talent guilds to work with us to eliminate any subversives: to protect the innocent; and to safeguard free speech and a free screen wherever threatened.

The absence of a national policy, established by Congress, with respect to the employment of Communists in private industry makes our task difficult. Ours is a nation of laws. We request Congress to enact legislation to assist American industry to rid itself of subversive, disloyal elements. Nothing subversive or un–American has appeared on the screen, nor can any number of Hollywood investigations obscure the patriotic services of the 30,000 loyal Americans employed in Hollywood who have given our government invaluable aid to war and peace.[3]

It would take another three years for the contempt citations to work their way through the court system of the United States, but for all intents and purposes, this statement was the beginning of what would very soon be thought of as the blacklist era.

In April of 1950, with all their appeals exhausted, the Ten prepared for their jail sentences that began that June. Terms, for no apparent reason, ranged from six months to one year. As the cell doors slammed shut and their sentences began, the worst that had been feared finally arrived as a vindicated HUAC returned to its investigations of Hollywood, resulting in a blacklist that ran rampant.

On March 8, 1951, the hearings resumed. The Democrats now found themselves in control of the House and Senate resulting in a new chairman of HUAC, John S. Wood, a Democrat from Georgia. A side note to this change of chairmanship is that not only was it a change in party power, but it seems that J. Parnell Thomas, like the members of the Hollywood Ten, had gone to jail. The Ten for contempt; Thomas for corruption. Wood's committee was composed of Democrats Francis E. Walter of California, Morgan M. Moulder of Missouri, Clyde Doyle of California, and James B. Frazier of Tennessee. The Republican contingent was Harold H. Velde of Illinois, Bernard W. Kearney of New York, Donald L. Jackson of California, who replaced Richard Nixon as Nixon had been elected to the Senate, and Charles E. Potter of Michigan. Frank Tavenner continued in his role as counsel.

Three. Finding Subversives in Hollywood

The second person called on the second day of the 1951 hearings, March 21, was *The Cradle Will Rock*'s own Howard da Silva. He was accompanied by two of the Hollywood Ten's attorneys, Robert W. Kenny and Ben Margolis. It got to the point, as the years went by, that one knew who would cooperate and who wouldn't based on the attorney(s) the witness brought to the hearing. Da Silva, primarily a theatre actor until 1939, was now called, like a number of others, because of his success in Hollywood. His most well-known role at this point was as Jack Armstrong in *Abe Lincoln in Illinois*. Much like Larry Foreman, his character in *Cradle*, da Silva was no shrinking violet. After several heated exchanges over da Silva's "objections" to what was being asked and how, the subject of the Federal Theatre took center stage.

> MR. TAVENNER: Were you connected at any time with the Federal Theater Project in New York?

The Hollywood Ten (plus two attorneys) (Left to right) Front Row: Herbert Biberman, Attorneys Martin Popper and Robert Kenney, Albert Maltz, Lester Cole. Second Row: Dalton Trumbo, John Howard Lawson, Alvah Bessie, Samuel Ornitz. Third Row: Ring Lardner, Jr., Edward Dmytryk, Adrian Scott (author's collection).

Mr. Da Silva: Yes, I was and I was very proud to be. That was the advent of a magnificent period, and I think some of the greatest work that ever came out came out at that time; truly a people's theater.

Mr. Tavenner: How large an organization was it?

Mr. Da Silva: In the Federal Theater?

Mr. Tavenner: Yes.

Mr. Da Silva: I think it is a matter of record, but there were many hundreds of actors in the Federal Theater all over the country. The audience was many millions of Americans, who for 55 cents could see plays they had never seen before and would not have had an opportunity to see otherwise.

Mr. Tavenner: Was it privately financed, or government financed?

Mr. Da Silva: It is a part of the public record that it was government financed.

Mr. Tavenner: At that time, while you were a member of it, were you a member of the Communist Party?

Mr. Da Silva: Mr. Chairman, it seems to me that the most vital concern of this committee is to really control every concept of free thought throughout the country, to do it by attacking Hollywood, and—

Mr. Wood: This committee is not interested in your opinion. Do you decline to answer the question, or will you answer it?

Mr. Da Silva: It is necessary that I answer it in my own way. It seems vital to say that the object of this committee is a smoke screen. Nobody, either in Washington or Hollywood, thinks there is a group in Hollywood dedicated to overthrow southern California by force and violence.[4]

Howard da Silva testifying before the committee on March 21, 1951 (Photofest).

The barbs back and forth continued. There was even an extended inquiry into da Silva's first wife. As the hearing seemed to be drawing to a close, there was one more exchange regarding another actor from *The Cradle Will Rock* company.

Mr. Tavenner: One further question, if you please. The Daily Worker dated July 8, 1937, at page 5, announced that Howard DaSilva would be a member of the cast of a play to be presented at the seventy-fifth birthday celebration of Mother Bloor. Did you take part in that celebration?

Mr. Da Silva: Your purpose is very clearly indicated, to link me with organizations or people that you find in disfavor. I decline to answer this question for the reasons previously stated.

Three. Finding Subversives in Hollywood 51

MR. TAVENNER: Did you know Will Geer?
MR. DA SILVA: Will Geer? He is a wonderful actor. I have known him for years.
MR. TAVENNER: Did he direct the play on the occasion that I mentioned?
MR. DA SILVA: Which one again?
MR. TAVENNER: The seventy-fifth birthday of Mother Bloor.
MR. DA SILVA: Once again your purpose is to link Will Geer and me through an association that you find in disfavor with you. I will not support that. I decline to answer this question on the grounds previously stated.
MR. WOOD: The answer of the witness is that he declines to answer for the reasons stated.
MR. TAVENNER: I have no further questions.
MR. WOOD: Very well.[5]

On April 11, the aforementioned Will Geer came before the committee, attended by the same attorneys as Howard da Silva. Geer identified himself as "an entertainer, actor, in the theater and screen and in television." He had a PhD in philosophy, but his "main hobby [was] agriculture and horticulture."[6] Geer's testimony was an extended banter with the committee. Unlike da Silva, he was never asked about Federal Theatre, but the program for Mother Bloor did come up. It turned out that Bloor was the grandmother of Geer's wife, Herta Ware.

As the hearings continued, the first member of the Group Theatre was called to testify: Morris Carnovsky. Carnovsky, with his wife Phoebe Brand, settled in Hollywood in 1943, after the Group Theatre had folded. He became one of the go-to actors for character roles, appearing in 19 major motion pictures from 1942 until his appearance before the committee. His films included everything from playing George Gershwin's father in *Rhapsody in Blue* to Le Bret in *Cyrano de Bergerac*. He appeared on April 24. After a review of his background and movie credits the committee's counsel proceeded to ask:

Morris Carnovsky testifying before the committee on April 24, 1951 (Photofest).

MR. TAVENNER: You were describing your activities and experience in New York. Were you a member of the Group Theater at that time?

MR. CARNOVSKY: Mr. Tavenner, there are a number of organizations, all of which have been listed by this committee, of which the organization you just mentioned is one. I feel that I am here under a strong apprehension of chance in saying otherwise than that I now seek the protection of the fifth amendment and avail myself of my privilege to refuse to answer on the grounds that this would tend to incriminate me.

MR. TAVENNER: So on that ground you refuse to answer the question about any alleged association of membership in the Group Theater?

MR. CARNOVSKY: On that ground I refuse to answer.[7]

Elia Kazan was not at all a major player in the Group Theatre, but he was destined to be the most well known of all of them. He made his first appearance in an executive session on Monday, January 14, 1952. By the time of his appearance, Kazan had already directed such films as *Gentleman's Agreement, Panic in the Streets,* and *A Streetcar Named Desire.* When asked by California congressman Richard Nixon, "Were you ever associated with an organization or a group known as the Group Theatre?" Kazan replied:

MR. KAZAN: Yes, I was a member of the Group Theatre. I wasn't a member for the first two years of its existence, but I was a member from the third year of its existence until it dissolved in 1940.

MR. NIXON: Would you describe for the committee what the function or activities of the Group Theatre were?

MR. KAZAN: Well, the functions of the Group Theatre were to present the best plays they could find in a manner consistent with their artistic ideals, which were those of an ensemble company of actors all of whom acted all different kinds of parts.[8]

Elia Kazan, 1950s, one can assume that he dressed this way for the hearing (Photofest).

Nixon went on the ask about the people who were there at the formation of the Group Theatre at which time Kazan answered, "It

Three. Finding Subversives in Hollywood

was formed by Sherrill [sic] Crawford, Lee Strasberg, and Harold Clurman." Later in this hearing, Nixon got to the meat of his interest:

> MR. NIXON: In its report of 1948, the California Committee on Un-American activities described this group as a Communist group whose purpose was to propagandize for the Communist Party. Was there anything in your experience, in your association with the Group Theatre that would conform to that description of it?
>
> MR. KAZAN: I would say that that description was erroneous. I would say the men [actually two men and one woman] who founded the Group and who guided its policies were not at any times fronting for anybody. I think anything they produced or came out for was their own choice, and they would be responsible for it.[9]

Kazan then proceeded to discuss his own membership and separation from the Communist Party. According to Kazan, the cell he joined was one for theatre professionals and not a cell within the Group. Still, Nixon was finally prompted to ask:

> MR. NIXON: Now, were there other individuals to your knowledge who were members of the same cell of the Communist Party, who were also members of the Group Theatre at the same time?
>
> MR. KAZAN: I don't want to answer that question. I don't take any refuge in anything, and I am not hiding behind any immunity of any kind. It is a matter of personal conscience.[10]

During the course of the balance of Kazan's testimony, Nixon was unable to get him to add to names the committee already had, even when questioning him directly about them. As the hearing was drawing to its conclusion, Representative Kearney tried to cajole Kazan one last time.

> MR. KEARNEY: I think the committee will agree with me that there have been instances of that here in the past when men have come here and testified under oath that they were members of the Communist Party and still working in the profession. I have in mind several of the Hollywood witnesses we had here, who have not been penalized because they came here and made a clean breast.
>
> MR. KAZAN: Well, I may be wrong, but I feel if this were an open meeting instead of the one we are having now, the plans I am working on as director of a picture in Hollywood would be off tomorrow. I may be wrong about it. But it is just that the pressure groups are so strong and I understand everyone is [anxious]. God knows, I think you should investigate, and what you are doing is right. But I feel, myself, if this were known, if this were an open meeting, I would be out of a job so to speak.[11]

It seems that Kazan was correct in his analysis. As a result, he returned to testify in another executive session three months later, April 10, 1952, when his extended statement was placed on the record and his testimony released to the public the next day. His statement read in part:

> I, Elia Kazan, being duly sworn, depose and say
> I repeat my testimony of January 14, 1952, before the House Committee on Un-American Activities to the effect that I was a member of the Communist Party from sometime in the summer of 1934, until the late winter and early spring of 1936, when I severed all connections with it permanently.
> ... For the approximately 19 months of my membership, I was assigned to a "unit" composed of those party members who were, like myself, members of the Group Theatre acting company. These were—
> Lewis Leverett, co-leader of the unit
> J. Edward Bromberg, co-leader of the unit, deceased.
> Phoebe Brand (later Mrs. Morris Carnovsky) I was instrumental bringing her into the party.
> Morris Carnovsky
> Tony Kraber, along with Wellman (see below), he recruited me into the party.
> Paula Miller (later Mrs. Lee Strasberg). We are friends today. I believe that, as she has told me, she quit the Communists long ago. She is far too sensible and balanced a woman, and she is married to too fine and intelligent a man, to have remained among them.
> Clifford Odets. He has assured me that he got out about the same time I did.
> Art Smith
> These are the only members of the unit whom I recall and I believe this to be a complete list. Even at this date I do not believe it would be possible for me to forget anyone.[12]

Kazan went on to list what the group was asked to do. Their duties were fourfold with number (4) being "To try to capture the Group Theatre and make it a Communist mouthpiece."[13] He went on to describe this in more detail:

> ... I want to repeat emphatically that the Communist attempt to take over the Group Theatre failed. There was some influence and a great deal of talk, the members of the Communist unit consumed a great deal of time at group meetings, they raised some money from the non-Communist members for Communist causes and they sold them some Communist pamphlets: they brought the prestige of the group name to meetings where they entertained as individuals, but they never succeeded in controlling the Group Theatre.
> This was because the control of the group stayed firmly in the hands of the three non-Communist directors, Harold Clurman, Lee Strasberg, and Cheryl Crawford. (In 1937 Clurman became sole director and remained so until the theater broke up in 1940).[14]

After an extensive review of his credits and a few more mea culpas for joining in the first place, the final line of his statement reads, "I have placed a copy of this affidavit with Mr. Spyros P. Skouras, president of Twentieth Century Fox."[15] Elia Kazan returned to work on the film *Viva Zapata!*

The committee was not quite finished with the Group Theatre members. On May 20, 1952, Clifford Odets came before the committee. He had done some work in the film industry at this point, most notably the screenplay for

Humoresque, but he was still best known as a playwright. After the usual opening questions, the committee got down to business, and that business went on for two days. Fortunately, Odets added to an understanding of why this party joining might occur.

> MR. TAVENNER: Will you relate to the committee the circumstances under which you joined the Communist Party?
> Let me put it this way: How were you recruited into the Communist Party and by whom?
> MR. ODETS: As has been testified here before, there were a number [of] small group[s] of Communist Party members in this Group Theater, of a total Group Theater membership of perhaps 35 there were four or five people who were connected with the Communist Party. Literature was passed around, and in a time of great social unrest many people found themselves reaching out for new ideas, new ways of solving depressions or making a better living, fighting for one's rights, whatever those were.
> MR. KEARNEY: What were those rights?
> MR. ODETS: Those rights would be to have steady employment.
> MR. KEARNEY: Beg your pardon?
> MR. ODETS:. The rights to be steadily employed for instance. I believe at that time there were perhaps 15 or 16 million unemployed people in the United States, and I myself was living on 10 cents a day. Therefore, I was interested in any idea which might suggest how as an actor I could function as a working actor who could make a living at a craft he had chosen for his life's work. These were the early days of the New Deal, and I don't think that one has to describe them. They were horrendous days that none of us would like to go through again.
> On this basis there was a great deal of talk about amelioration of conditions, about how should one live, by what values should one work for, and in line with this there was a great deal of talk about Marxist values. One read literature: there were a lot of penny and 2-cent and 5-cent pamphlets. I read them along with a lot of other people, and finally joined the Communist Party, in the belief, in the honest and real belief, that this was some way out of the dilemma in which we found ourselves.
> Does that answer the question?
> MR. TAVENNER: I think it does except that you have not told us the exact circumstances under which you were recruited into the party. What was the process of recruitment in your case?
> MR. ODETS: Well, it went that you read some pamphlets; you listened to some one talk, and finally a person would ask you if you didn't want to join the Communist Party. In my case it happened, "No; I don't. When I am ready, I will." I was not ready that month, I was ready a month or two later.
> MR. TAVENNER: Who was the individual who made that suggestion to you?
> MR. ODETS: This would be an actor friend of mine named J. Edward Bromberg.
> MR. TAVENNER: Was he a member of the Group Theater?
> MR. ODETS: Yes; he was.
> MR. KEARNEY: Was he the actor who died a few months ago?
> MR. ODETS:. Yes, sir; he was.

MR. TAVENNER: Who actually recruited you into the party?
MR. ODETS: My best memory would be that Mr. Bromberg did.
MR. TAVENNER: When you were recruited into the party were you assigned to a particular cell or group?
MR. ODETS: Yes; it would be to be connected with those few people who were in the Group Theatre.
MR. TAVENNER: Who were the other persons who were members of the same cell of the Communist Party to which you were assigned?
MR. ODETS: Well, they have been mentioned here as Lewis Leverett, a young actress named Phoebe Brand, and an actor about whom you refreshed my memory the last time I was here [in executive session] named Art Smith.
MR. TAVENNER: That is Art Smith?
MR. ODETS: And then from my reading of the New York Times, a couple of other members were mentioned that I have no memory of, as I told you.
MR. TAVENNER: Elia Kazan. Was he a member of that group?
MR. ODETS: Yes, Mr. Kazan.
MR. TAVENNER: Did you meet with all of those persons as members of the Communist Party; that is, those you have named up to the present time?
MR. ODETS: Yes, sir.
MR. TAVENNER: Tony Kraber?
MR. ODETS: He, too.[16]

Mr. Odets' testimony continued with details on Communist Party officials who perhaps visited the members, how the organization functioned, and how dues were collected. In addition, time was spent on petitions he signed, organizations he may have joined and ultimately his plays that were produced. It is far and away one of the most detailed testimonies of any of the actors whose testimony appears in these pages. By the afternoon session, the committee had Odets go into great detail about his theatrical productions and, in particular, about their reception critically, especially by critics who wrote for publications like *The Daily Worker* or the *New Theater Magazine*, identified as the official publication of the New Theater League, another organization that was suspect. Odets' first day of testimony ended at 4:30 p.m.

At 10:30 a.m. the next day, the interrogation of Clifford Odets continued along the same lines as the day before. As the morning session was finally drawing to a close, Congressman Velde asked,

> Mr. Odets, would you, if you had this to do over again—that is, join all of these Communist-Front groups—would you do it at the present time? Would you sponsor the same things that you call liberalism and so forth?

To which Odets replied,

> I do not think I would sponsor many of them. I would pick very carefully and would be careful where I put my signature.[17]

Kazan and Odets continued to work in film. Da Silva, Geer, Carnovsky, and many of the others named, whether or not they appeared as uncooperative witnesses, found the doors leading to film work slammed shut. Many packed their bags and returned to the East Coast and theatre. Being the creative folks that they were, they found a way to practice the profession they so adored.

Four

Making Work While Blacklisted

The streets of Hollywood may have been paved with gold for those seeking fame and fortune in the movies, but quickly, and with little notice, the streets retuned to their original asphalt for the entertainment professionals who found themselves on the "blacklist" of the early 1950s. They returned to the streets of New York City, which could now boast being the home of television and radio and, by extension, the business of commercial advertising, which (financially) supported the media. Television was live at this time and desperate for product. Valuable was the stage actor who could learn lines and perform a scene live. Sadly, if the émigrés from Hollywood thought television or commercials might help pay the bills, they were mistaken. While they were facing off against HUAC in Hollywood, any path to those lucrative areas back in New York City was being closed to them as well.

On June 22, 1950, television producers and advertising executives arrived at work and found on their desks a 213-page paper-covered booklet entitled *Red Channels: The Report of Communist Influence in Radio and Television.* It was the brainchild of three former FBI agents: Theodore Kirkpatrick, Jack Keenan, and Ken Bierly. They had formed an organization they called American Business Consultants and put together a staff, including Vincent Hartnett, whose sole purpose was to ferret out information on potential subversives in television and radio. The files they compiled were reminiscent of the files compiled by HUAC. The booklet contained an alphabetical list of 151 members of the various performing arts professions followed by almost as many (130) entries, also alphabetical, of "organizations, unless otherwise indicated," that had been "prepared and released by the Committee on Un-American Activities, U.S. House of Representatives, December 18, 1948."[1]

As a performer one could find oneself on the list in the form of a single entry of what the trio considered subversive activity, or as pages of entries. It made little difference to those availing themselves of the information. And thus, the people charged with putting together much of the work in New York City now had in their hand the first formally printed "blacklist." On that list were any number of the players in the pages of our story of theatre and blacklisting: Luther Adler, his sister Stella Adler, Marc Blitzstein, J. Edward Bromberg, Morris Carnovsky, Howard Da Silva, John Garfield, Will Geer, Jack Gilford, Lillian Hellman, George Keane, Adelaide Klein, Tony Kraber, Madeline Lee, Arthur Miller, Zero Mostel, Anne Revere, Pete Seeger, Gale Sondergaard, Elliot Sullivan, Orson Welles, and Martin Wolfson.[2]

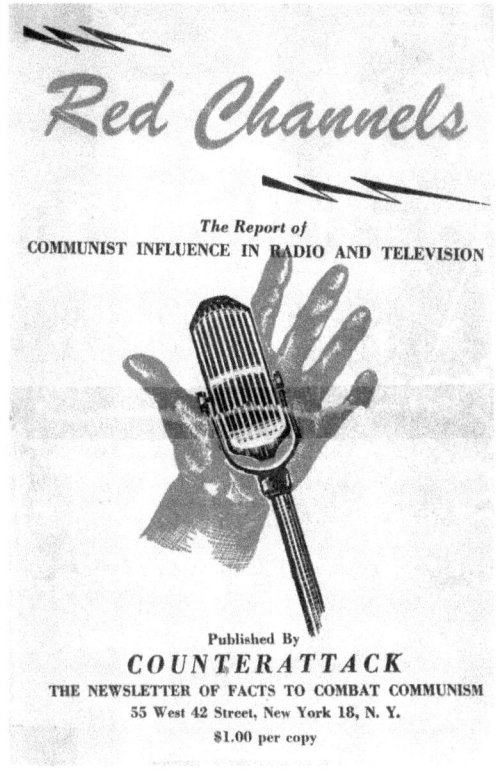

The cover of a well worn copy of *Red Channels* (author's collection).

The organizations they were "accused" of either belonging to or supporting included the Abraham Lincoln Brigade, the Actors Laboratory (and Theatre), the American League Against War and Fascism, almost anything with the word "peace," "democracy," "citizen," or "international" in its title, the Book Find Club, the Motion Picture Artists' Committee, the Musicians' Congress Committee, the National Lawyers Guild, the Negro Cultural Committee, the New Theatre League, People's Artists, Inc and People's Songs, Stage for Action, the Theatre Arts Committee, United American Artists, and Young People's Records.[3]

Hot on the heels of the publishing of *Red Channels* came Laurence Johnson, a grocer from Syracuse, New York. Johnson launched a "Campaign for Americanism" that virtually brought the television industry to its knees. His threat, which he carried out in his own four stores while implying that it could go national, was to post a "do not buy/support" notice by any product that was advertised on any show that supported any purported communists or their supporters by hiring them as performers, writers, or directors. For a time, Johnson was actually invited into the major production offices before hiring was completed. He was eventually brought down by an anti-blacklisting lawsuit filed by the humorist John Henry Faulk and his attorney Louis Nizer.[4]

MASTER INSTITUTE
310 Riverside Drive (103rd Street), New York City

PRESENTS

"ROUND TABLE REVIEW"

AN UNUSUAL SERIES PROVIDING A CRITICAL DISCUSSION OF
THREE PROVOCATIVE AND CONTROVERSIAL MODERN NOVELS
HIGHLIGHTED WITH READINGS BY PROFESSIONAL ACTORS

PRODUCED BY PHOEBE BRAND AND JOHN RANDOLPH
COMMENTARY BY DR. FREDERIC EWEN

PARTICIPATING ARTISTS:

PHOEBE BRAND · SARAH CUNNINGHAM · RUBY DEE
LUDWIG DONATH · JOHN RANDOLPH
PAUL SPARER

Three Tuesday evenings, 8:30 P.M.
October 15 - November 12 - December 17, 1957
Master Institute Lecture Auditorium

—o—

PROGRAM

October 15—"THE LAST ANGRY MAN" by Gerald Green
November 12—"COMPULSION" by Meyer Levin
December 17—"THE MANDARINS" by Simone de Beauvoir

Open Discussion from the Floor
Tuition: Single — $1.50.   Series of Three — $4.00.

Subscription Blank

Round Table Review: Master Institute
310 Riverside Drive
New York 25, N. Y.

I enclose check for $............for............series subscription (s) to "Round Table Review" at $4 each. (Checks payable to Round Table Review.)

Name..

Address..

....Phone...........

MASTER INSTITUTE
OF UNITED ARTS, INC.

310 Riverside Drive, New York 25, N. Y.
(103rd St.)   UN 4-1700

Nettie S. Horch, Director

Art · · Dance · · Opera · · Drama

(Transportation: 5th Ave. Bus, No. 5;
B'way IRT Subway)

The flyer from the Master Institute for the "Round Table Review" one of the many programs designed by Frederic Ewen, Phoebe Brand and John Randolph (author's collection).

Four. Making Work While Blacklisted

The Revolt of the Beavers' Mortimer Lippman, now John Randolph the actor, as he introduced himself, often remarked that it was theatre that kept a roof over his head and fed his family during the years when film and television jobs were unavailable to him and so many others like him.[5] Reunions of many of the theatre families of the thirties and forties started to take place. Some got work in summer stock and at theatre summer camps while others played on Broadway and on tour. And it wasn't only the theatre folk who made this work possible.

Frederic Ewen had been an English professor at Brooklyn College from 1930 until 1952. Forced to resign after refusing to cooperate with the House Committee on Un-American Activities' investigation of communism in higher education, he organized lectures that included performances of adaptations of literary classics: classic materials in the public domain requiring no payments of royalties. Ewen gathered a team of blacklisted actors who were also in need of work, including John Randolph, Ossie Davis, Ruby Dee, Phoebe Brand, and Sarah Cunningham. They performed in theatres, union halls, and Jewish community centers. Ewen provided the commentary on literature and drama, and the actors read excerpts from the selected works.

At the Master Institute of United Arts, a tall art deco building on Riverside Drive, they put together a series they called, "Round Table Review" which they described as "an unusual series providing a critical discussion of three provocative and controversial modern novels highlighted by professional actors." The "tuition" was $1.50 for a single performance or the series of three for $4.00. They were doing this work from the late 1950s into the early 1960s. In the union hall at Local 1199 of the United Healthcare Workers, John Randolph and his wife Sarah Cunningham performed scenes from the works of Sean O'Casey. "Each performance [was] followed by an informal discussion with the guest stars plus free refreshments." As part of the Jewish Center Lecture Bureau they worked under the title of Quartette Productions, presenting "For your club, party or organization—A group of outstanding actors in a delightful program in English from the wealth of Jewish Folklore including the best loved stories of Sholom Aleichem, the great Yiddish humorist."

The success of this venture, among others of a similar nature, led to a more complete professional theatrical production in 1953, *The World of Sholom Aleichem*, produced by Howard da Silva and Arnold Perl, dramatized by Perl and directed by da Silva. The cast was a who's who of blacklisted actors. Some of the actors had already appeared before HUAC. Some were names familiar from the lists in *Red Channels*, while others made appearances before the committee when it came to New York City to investigate Broadway in 1955 and 1958. The list included Phoebe Brand and her husband Morris Carnovsky; Ruby Dee, whose husband, Ossie Davis, got a contract as stage

Labor unions often had great auditoriums. This flyer is for a performance at SEIU1199 (author's collection).

Four. Making Work While Blacklisted 63

QUARTETTE PRODUCTIONS

Presents:

For your club, party or organization — A group of outstanding actors in a delightful program in English from the wealth of Jewish Folklore including the best loved stories of Sholom Aleichem, the great Yiddish humorist.

Directed by:
MARJORIE DA SILVA

JOHN RANDOLPH

SARAH CUNNINGHAM

AMELIA ROMANO

ALBERT OTTENHEIMER

ADDITIONAL MEMBERS OF
QUARTETTE PRODUCTIONS

JANET WARD

WILL KULUVA

MAURICE SHROG

VINCENT GARDENIA

Among the distinguished Broadway plays in which the actors of Quartette Productions have appeared are:
The Shrike · *Middle of the Night* · *Inherit the Wind*
The World of Sholom Aleichem · *Three Penny Opera*
Guys and Dolls · *Come Back Little Sheba* · *Volpone*
Paint Your Wagon · *Peer Gynt* · *House of Flowers*

For further information and booking arrangements contact

MR. SAMUEL FREEMAN   Jewish Center Lecture Bureau   145 E. 32nd. St.   LEhigh 2-4949

This outing by Quartette Productions laid the ground work for *The World of Sholom Aleichem* (author's collection).

BARBIZON-PLAZA THEATRE

PHILIP C. ROGERSON, Director

HOWARD DA SILVA and ARNOLD PERL
present

The WORLD OF SHOLOM ALEICHEM

Dramatized by
ARNOLD PERL

Directed by
HOWARD DA SILVA

Music by
SERGE HOVEY
ROBERT DE CORMIER

Costumes by
ALINE BERNSTEIN

Lighting by
BERNARD GERSTEN

CAST
(in order of appearance)

A Tale of Chelm — Folk Story

The Melamed, a teacher	Will Lee
Rifkele, his wife	Phoebe Brand
Rabbi David	Gilbert Green
The Angel Rochele	Marjorie Nelson
Stranger (from Lithuania)	Jack Banning
Rifkele's friend	Warren Logan
Dodi	Vincent Beck
The Goatseller	Sarah Cunningham

Bontche Schweig — based on the story by I. L. Peretz

First Angel	Jack Banning
Second Angel	Marjorie Nelson
Third Angel	Phoebe Brand
Fourth Angel	Warren Logan
Fifth Angel	Vincent Beck
Sixth Angel	Sarah Cunningham
Father Abraham	Will Lee
Bontche Schweig	Jack Gilford
Presiding Angel	Morris Carnovsky
Defending Angel	Ruby Dee
Prosecuting Angel	Gilbert Green

INTERMISSION

The High School — based on the story by Sholom Aleichem

Aaron Katz	Morris Carnovsky
Hannah, his wife	Sarah Cunningham
Moishe, their son	Jack Banning
Men at the list	Jack Gilford
The Tutor	Vincent Beck
Woman at the list	Marjorie Nelson
The Principal	Gilbert Green
Uncle Maxl	Will Lee
Aunt Reba	Phoebe Brand
Kholyava	Warren Logan

Mendele, the Book Seller	Howard Da Silva

Staff for Rachel Productions

General Manager	Bernard Gersten
Promotion Manager	Louise Craig
Press Representative	Merle Debuskey
Stage Manager	Ossie Davis
General Understudies	Hesh Bernardi, Osna Palmer
Master Electrician	Arthur Dignam
Master Carpenter	Edgar Dignam

Special thanks to B. Z. Goldberg and the Sholom Aleichem Family, to Myron Ehrenberg, Carol Sylbert, Paul Sylbert, Tony Schwartz and Ben Shahn.

Credits

Lighting equipment by Century Lighting, Inc.
Costumes by Brooks.

For theater parties and reservations write
Rachel Productions, 756 Seventh Ave., New York 19, N. Y., or call CIrcle 6-4434

After the theatre, visit the Café Continental—lower lobby level
SMOKING POSITIVELY FORBIDDEN IN THE ORCHESTRA AND BALCONY

The original program from the first run of *The World of Sholom Aleichem* at the Barbizon-Plaza Theatre (author's collection).

manager; Elliott Sullivan; Sarah Cunningham; Will Lee; and Jack Gilford; with Bernard Gersten as general manager and lighting designer.

The evening consisted of three short plays. Act one opened with "A Tale of Chelm," a traditional Jewish folk tale of a village's foolishness as it tells the story of a local joke about a teacher who can't tell the difference between a billy goat and a nanny goat. The second piece, "Bonche Schweig," was based on a story by I. L. Peretz. It tells the tale of a man who, on Earth, lived a wretched life, expecting nothing. Now he is in heaven and, after hearing his life defended by an angel, he is offered anything he wants as a reward for living such a humble life. Bonche's request, like his life, is quite simple: "In that case, if it's true, could I have, please, every day, a hot roll with butter." The third piece was based on a work by Sholom Aleichem, "The High School," or "Gymnasium." The story is set in Russia, where there is a Jewish quota on boys who want to attend a regular (non-religious) school. It is the story of Aaron and Hannah Katz, who want their son Moishe to receive nothing less than the best education they can find for him. Of the play, Vernon Rice of the *New York Post* wrote,

The second piece in the evening was *Bontche Schweig*. When the production toured to Los Angeles, da Silva hired local actors for smaller roles. In this picture Jacob Ben-Ami is Bontche and the third angel from the right is the author's mother (author's collection).

SEPTEMBER 11 THROUGH NOVEMBER 1
SEVEN WEEKS ONLY
The World of SHOLOM ALEICHEM

Morris Carnovsky, Howard Da Silva, Ruby Dee, Jack Gilford, Will Lee
Directed by HOWARD DA SILVA, Dramatized by ARNOLD PERL, Costumes by ALINE BERNSTEIN, Music by SERGE HOVEY and ROBERT DE CORMIER

Howard Da Silva in the role of Mendele, the Book Peddler. (Mendele Mocher Sforim).

Phoebe Brand, Marjorie Nelson, Will Lee, Morris Carnovsky, Sarah Cunningham, and Jack Banning in a scene from "The High School" ("Gymnasium") by Sholom Aleichem.

Morris Carnovsky as The Presiding Angel in Isaac Loeb Peretz' "Bontche Schweig."

"The acting, staging, costuming and music are first rate. Bontche Schweig is a gem." —ATKINSON, New York Times.

"Humor and spirit are punctuated to make it a warm and exhilarating experience." —RICE, New York Post.

"Thoroughly engaging time." —SHAEFFER, B'klyn Eagle.

"Replete with irony, drollery and pathos; it is chucklesome and rewarding." —Women's Wear Daily.

"Every scene, every character is presented in a Jewish but also in a universal spirit. You leave the theater feeling uplifted." —B. Z. GOLDBERG, Jewish Day.

BARBIZON-PLAZA THEATRE
58TH STREET AND 6TH AVE.

Tickets now available for this limited seven week engagement.

EVENINGS AT 8:30 (EXCEPT MONDAY) MATINEES, SATURDAY AND SUNDAY AT 2:30.

PRICES: (EVENINGS) $3.60, $3.00, $2.40, $1.80. (MATINEES) $2.40, $1.80, $1.20.

MAIL ORDERS PROMPTLY FILLED. THEATRE PARTIES ACCOMMODATED. CALL OR WRITE

RACHEL PRODUCTIONS, 756 Seventh Ave. • Circle 6-4434

(please make checks payable to Rachel Productions)

The success of the production found it reopening at the Barbizon. Now they had the reviews to make a snazzy flyer (author's collection).

> Humor and spirit are punctuated in "The High School" and the closeness of Jewish family life are emphasized in such a way to make it a warm and exhilarating experience ... it is a play which will bring pride to its specialized audience and understanding and tolerance to all others.... IN THE WORLD OF SHOLOM ALEICHEM the da Silva-Perl tribe show how theatre-wise imagination with long experience can make so much out of so little.[6]

Critical praise was quite universal. A three-week run in the spring was followed by a re-opening at the end of summer and a production that ran for a year in New York City, toured across the country, was recorded and ultimately filmed. There was also hate mail.

The September 25, 1953, issue of *Counterattack,* an American Business Consultants vehicle for updating *Red Channels,* took four single-spaced typed pages to excoriate anyone and everyone involved with the production of *The World of Sholom Aleichem,* as well as any critic who liked it. Perl and da Silva may not have saved their hate mail, but Brooks Atkinson did. In many cases it was obvious that the writer of the missive had not seen the play.

> From Wilton, Connecticut: "Your treatment of 'The World of Sholom Aleichem' has caused me an especial pain. When one communist sneaks into a cast, it can be overlooked. When the cast is predominantly communist, even you must recognize that fact. When you Fail to mention this in your column, You are plainly dishonest. You must necessarily suffer to that degree in one's consideration.
>
> Now wrestle with your conscience."[7]

This undated photograph shows, left to right, director/actor Howard da Silva who played Mendele, the Book Seller in *The World of Sholom Aleichem,* and Ruby Dee who was the Defending Angel in *Bontche Schweig*; Ossie Davis was the stage manager (Photofest).

From Chattanooga, Tennessee: "At least you are living up to the public's idea of a typical drama critic—a fuzzy-brained dope who know not what goes on more than two blocks east or west of Broadway.

I doubt that an American would help such SOB's as are connected with 'The World of Sholom Aleichem,' so I'm wondering what your real name is. Bernstein?"[8]

And from Milton, Massachusetts: "This is a protest against your fulsome praise of a group of actors and actresses with Communist records appearing in 'The World of Sholom Aleichem.'

Doesn't the fact that these people have been proved to be supporters of Communist fronts and in some cases have been identified as Communists fill you with any contempt at all?...

Would it not have been more fair to your readers had you shown that side of the picture too?...

For my money, the case that you praise so highly will get no support from me in any way whatsoever."[9]

The scene Ring Lardner, Jr., was referring to in his letter was *The High School*. The actors who played the roles Lardner so joyously praised were Sarah Cunningham and Morris Carnovsky (Wisconsin Center for Film and Theater Research).

On any number of occasions, Atkinson wrote a reply. However, his most cogent answer to all of this he saved for a book that was published in 1970. He looked back on this production while at the same time acknowledging the period in which it was performed, and the intelligence of the theatre-going audience. Atkinson wrote:

In this barbaric era, a few actors who had belonged to radical organizations in the thirties produced a tender, imaginative, wholesome folk program called, "The World of Sholom Aleichem." It became the focal point of McCarthyites all over the nation. They stigmatized the actors as traitors; they excoriated the critics who had praised the production. They tried to make a national scandal out of it. Externally the feud looked alarming. But Broadway theatergoers liked "The World of Sholom Aleichem" so much that it had to be revived the next season. As usual, they went to see what interested them.[10]

Ring Lardner, Jr., one of the Hollywood Ten, attended a performance on Saturday, October 17, 1953. Three days later he wrote a fan letter to da Silva. It said in part:

> Then, during The High School, I realized fully what nothing I had heard about the production had prepared me for: that the total effect—the message or whatever you want to call it—of The World of Sholom Aleichem is one of much greater significance than that of many plays which deal more directly with the struggles of our time. The Katzes, so wonderfully recreated by Morris and by Sarah Cunningham, are true heroes of the irrepressible masses, and their development from one level of struggle to another makes for people's theatre at its best.[11]

This was written by the same Ring Lardner, Jr., who in 1947 challenged HUAC when he was asked about his union membership.

> MR. STRIPLING: Mr. Lardner, the charge has been made before this committee that the Screen Writers Guild which, according to the record, you are a member of, whether you admit it or not, has a number of individuals in it who are members of the Communist Party. This committee is seeking to determine the extent of Communist infiltration in the Screen Writers Guild and in other guilds within the motion-picture industry.
> MR. LARDNER: Yes.
> MR. STRIPLING: And certainly the question of whether or not you are a member of the Communist Party is very pertinent. Now, are you a member or have you ever been a member of the Communist Party?
> MR. LARDNER: It seems to me you are trying to discredit the Screen Writers Guild through me and the motion-picture industry through the Screen Writers Guild and our whole practice of freedom of expression.[12]

Lardner was one of the first witnesses to challenge the committee's negative attitude toward union membership before the committee. How the various unions responded to the blacklist plays a major role in this examination of theatre and blacklisting. The life of a professional play such as *The World of Sholom Aleichem* owes a debt to Actors' Equity, the one union that chose not to brook the blacklisting of its members. The actors in *The World of Sholom Aleichem* had been denied work in radio, television and film owing in no small part to the lack of support from their other unions, the Screen Actors Guild and the American Federation of Television and Radio Artists.

FIVE

What Has My Union Done for Me?
SAG, AFTRA and Blacklisting

A plaint so often heard by the staff and elected officials of unions from the automobile assembly plant to the janitor in a high-rise building, from the chorus dancer in a Broadway show to the bit player on a long running soap opera, is, "What has my union done for me?" Unions are expected to fight for the rights of their members; to create a safe and sanitary working environment while attaining a living wage and benefits. Performing on stage or in film or television, however, is often perceived as working in a "glamorous" industry, one in which an actor or actress is thought to be of a different breed with different needs than most workers. Indeed, in the early days of Actors' Equity Association (Equity), the first performing arts union, something as simple as being paid for rehearsals had to be fought for. The Screen Actors Guild (SAG) was founded on the idea of bettering working conditions that were far removed from any idea of glamour. The concept of a benefits package for a performer seemed virtually impossible until the American Federation of Television and Radio Actors (AFTRA) made it their single issue in contract negotiations and won. Indeed, the performing arts unions have fought for their members to be considered workers like any other workers, with all of the associated rights and privileges. For all intents and purposes they won that battle. Then one day the issue became something much greater than a safe surface to dance on—it became a question of whether or not the dancer would be allowed to set foot on that floor at all. These two unions dealt with this new situation, the idea of the blacklisting of their members, in ways not always in concert with one another. What follows is how SAG and AFTRA dealt, or didn't deal at all, with the issue.

To understand the framework in which these unions confronted this situation it becomes necessary to look back and place their actions in the context of the decade. It is now time for a little history review.

Five. What Has My Union Done for Me?

The 1950s was a time of unrivaled American prosperity. Real wages rose dramatically. Working conditions improved. Despite some occasional economic blips, there were no real hard times, and, when necessary, the government intervened to ameliorate difficult conditions. More and more Americans left a decaying urban life behind them, moving to the expanding suburbs and the mass-produced Levittowns. For minorities the benefits came slower, but a hard push through the courts for integration of the races in the South resulted in decisions and legislation eventually ending decades of legal segregation everywhere in the U.S. (although the major actions came in the 1960s). Television grew exponentially as it became the American mass medium, bringing the country closer together and challenging regional cultures.

During the 1950s, as the journalist Dan Wakefield recalled, there was a "whole lotta shakin' goin' on."[1] Certainly by the beginning of the decade, Americans justifiably could be concerned about the personal impact of developments in the latter 1940s. In 1948 the Communists had taken over Czechoslovakia in a well-planned coup. During 1948–1949 Berlin had been blockaded by the Soviets in an attempt to drive the Western Allies from the former German capital, and only an innovative and costly "airlift" had kept the city from falling under Russian control. In 1949 the Soviets exploded their first atomic bomb, and the Communists won control of China. The "iron curtain" that former British Prime Minister Winston Churchill, in an address to an American college audience, had so eloquently described being dropped across the European continent in 1946 seemed by 1950 to be pulling tight everywhere.

Historian Howard Zinn—a major critic of American foreign and domestic policy during those years—argues that President Harry Truman presented "the Soviet Union as not just a rival but as an immediate threat."[2] The speechifying of the President and other American politicians, as well as the actions of the Communists everywhere in the world, coupled with domestic developments created a mood in the U.S. that one perceptive media historian has accurately described as "unsettled and uncertain"; both at home and abroad he asserts "the situation ... seemed grim and sinister."[3]

Despite the general prosperity marking the first years of the 1950s, they were often referred to as more an era of fear than of fun. This fear built on the uncertain public mood of the later 1940s. People were concerned about how the Cold War turned into a hot war in Korea that ended inconclusively. They were concerned with the revelations about Alger Hiss and the Rosenbergs, who were presumed to be only the tip of the iceberg in terms of Communist penetration of the government, and concerned about what "Senator Estes Kefauver's televised criminal investigations ... dramatically revealed about the extent and power of organized crime."[4]

In response to a Republican sponsored Internal Security Act which called for the registration of groups presumed to be Communist front organizations, some liberal senators, anxious not to be tarred as less than security conscious, proposed a substitute measure which included the setting up of detention centers for suspected subversives. Instead of substituting for the initial proposed legislation, this measure was added to the original bill, and both provisions became law. According to Jean Rouverol Butler, then the wife of blacklisted writer Hugo Butler, it was rumored in California that the camps used during World War II as relocation centers for the Japanese were being readied to receive suspected subversives and fellow travelers.[5]

The fear that led to such legislation ultimately permeated American life. Despite the prosperity most Americans enjoyed, a great many were also scared. In part because the conditions of daily life had become so attractive, many Americans came to unrealistically fear international Communism and unreasonably fear internal subversion. Such fears put a premium on conformity and led to a reassertion of a certain kind of value system "which would have pleased a Twenties fundamentalist" as particular brands of "domesticity, religiosity, respectability, security through compliance with system became the essence of the Fifties."[6]

In its attempt to maintain itself and to demonstrate its commitment to the trends of the times, the movie industry also hewed to a kind of fearful conformity both on-screen and off. By 1950, industry product became what many considered bland, and remained so for most of the decade with a few notable exceptions. Already by the end of 1947, the industry's response to the Hollywood Ten from Chapter Three resulted in the establishment of a blacklist, which the historian David Thomson aptly defined as "an option for false security over real thinking and a preference for money over ideas or openness."[7]

In the spring of 1950, jail, in addition to blacklisting, became a reality for the Hollywood Ten as the cell doors slammed shut and their sentences began. Other members of the Hollywood community were concerned about the threat of jail if they failed to cooperate with Congressional committees or government agencies such as the FBI, and they started to make plans for their own futures. As a result, a significant number chose to leave the country for Europe or Mexico and make "a home somewhere else" for however long might be necessary.[8] For Hollywood the worst came to pass as HUAC returned to its investigations into the politics of the industry in 1951. In an atmosphere of suspicion and repression, which saw sister pitted against brother, husband against wife, colleague against colleague, lovers against each other, and friend against former friend, the blacklist ran rampant. The manner in which SAG, and subsequently AFTRA and Equity, dealt with blacklisting would have an effect that still reverberates today.

Five. What Has My Union Done for Me?

The Screen Actors Guild was conceived in 1933 by a group of six Equity actors working in Hollywood. Legend has it that although Equity was doing whatever representing of actors was happening at the time, it did not pursue representing members of the film community, as the organization's leaders, and much of its membership, considered movie acting to be far less serious than stage work. Indeed, it has been opined that stage actors were against the formation of SAG, but that some silent screen stars and many of the early sound actors recruited from Broadway for the new-fangled talkies were in favor of organization. Initially SAG had problems, especially as important film executives such as Irving Thalberg were strenuously opposed to the fledgling organization and actively fought it. Indeed, Thalberg swore he would die before accepting SAG. But as the union's website boasts, "In 1936 Thalberg died and in 1937 the studios accepted defeat and signed a contract with the Guild that, for the first time in Hollywood, gave actors a sense of empowerment." By 1940 SAG was considered "the strongest and most prestigious union in Hollywood."[9]

Being the face of the industry that during the 1930s and World War II attained an enormous following, with millions going to the movies every week, it should come as no surprise that the publicity-seeking congressmen involved with HUAC attempted to use Hollywood for their own ends. Martin Dies, whom we first met in Chapter Two, as chairman of HUAC's precursor attempted this in 1940 to very little effect on the industry. As we learned, the committee (now officially HUAC) set out again in 1947, taking advantage of increasing public fears about Communist subversion and resulting in the formulation of a basis for a blacklist. Although those union members attacked were members of the Screen Writers Guild (SWG) and the Directors Guild of America (DGA), it would be another four years before members of SAG and AFTRA came before the committee.

There were, however, stars that voluntarily came before the

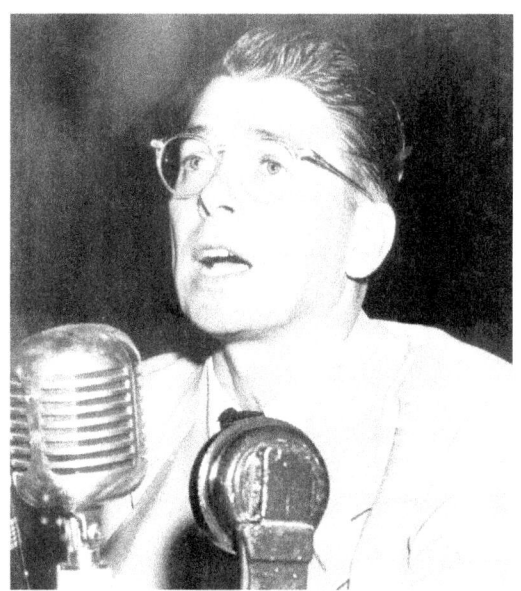

As President of the Screen Actors Guild, Ronald Reagan made a statement on the union's behalf during the early part of the 1947 hearings (Photofest).

committee in 1947, adding luster and added media coverage. There was the loquacious Adolphe Menjou, the somewhat diffident Gary Cooper, and Robert Taylor, who we already know named names. And then, on October 23, 1947, the President of the Screen Actors Guild, Ronald Reagan, appeared before HUAC and assured the committee that when it came to communists in the Guild,

> Well, sir, ninety-nine per cent of us are pretty well aware of what is going on, and I think, within the bounds of our democratic rights and never once stepping over the rights given us by democracy, we have done a pretty good job in our business of keeping those people's activities curtailed. After all, we must recognize them [Communists] at present as a political party. On that basis we have exposed their lies when we came across them, we have opposed their propaganda, and I can certainly testify that in the case of the Screen Actors Guild we have been eminently successful in preventing them from, with their usual tactics, trying to run a majority of an organization with a well-organized minority. In opposing those people, the best thing to do is make democracy work. In the Screen actors Guild we make it work by insuring everyone a vote and by keeping everyone informed…. I happen to be very proud of

The Academy Award winning actress Gale Sondergaard was called before the committee on March 21, 1951. As the wife of one of the Hollywood Ten, Herbert Biberman, her husband had only recently finished serving his sentence for contempt of Congress. The strain is evident in this photograph (Photofest).

the industry in which I work; I happen to be very proud of the way in which we conducted the fight. I do not believe the Communists have ever at any time been able to use the motion-picture screen as a sounding board for their philosophy or ideology.[10]

The 1947 hearings might have become legendary because of the uncooperative witnesses, who quickly became known as the Hollywood Ten, but the subsequent hearings which began in early 1951 were damaging to many more famous and not-so-famous Hollywood people. Bolstered by the successful contempt citations, which had resulted in prison terms for the Ten, HUAC called in and worked over a wide array of people. It was at this point, very early in the proceedings, that SAG was asked to take a stand in support of its subpoenaed members.

On March 13, 1951, just eight days before she was scheduled to appear before HUAC, Gale Sondergaard, the star of Chapter One's *Red Rust*, the winner of the first ever Academy Award for Best Supporting Actress (for her performance in the 1936 Warner Brothers blockbuster *Anthony Adverse*) and the wife of the director Herbert Biberman, who was one of the Hollywood Ten and had only recently gotten out of jail, wrote a letter to SAG which she had published in the trade paper *Daily Variety* on March 16:

Dear Board Members:

I am addressing you of the Board not only as the directors of our union but also as fellow actors. I am addressing you because I have been subpoenaed, together with other members of our union before the Un–American Activities Committee. I will appear next Wednesday.

I would be naïve if I did not recognize that there is a danger that by the following day I may have arrived at the end of my career as a motion picture actress.

Wishing to place my position and my request of my union before both Board and membership before I take the stand next Wednesday, March 21st, I am having this letter published in the Friday, March 16th issue of *Daily Variety*.

Surely it is not necessary for me to say to this Board that I love my profession and that I have tried to bring to it honesty of feeling, clarity of thought and a real devotion. Surely it is also un-necessary for me to state that I consider myself a deeply loyal American with genuine concern for the welfare and peace of my own countrymen and humanity.

Today I read that this particular inquisition is not directed against the industry but is directed at individuals. This would seem to imply that any number of individual actors could be destroyed without injuring the industry—and that the employers, having been guaranteed that they would not be personally involved, have given the committee carte blanche to attack individuals to their own purposes.

Employers have been known to do this before and members of unions have, in just such times, come to know the comfort and the dignity of belonging to a union and of seeking its strength and its higher moral dedication.

I believe in freedom of speech and religion and association as described in our first amendment. Unfortunately our present Supreme Court has not seen fit to spell out its legal availability to us in our own days. But it has done so in respect to the oldest right of the individual in recorded history—the right of silence—the right under the fifth amendment.

I intend to avail myself of this right before the committee.

Many Guild members, called before the committee, will not agree with my choice. They will take other roads looking to their protection from the attacks, insinuations, and sneers of the committee. But surely no one will believe that the economic well being of our members or the security of our union or the welfare of the industry is being served by the committee.

I most earnestly and fraternally ask the Board to consider the implications of the forthcoming hearing. A blacklist already exists. It may now be widened. It may ultimately be extended to include any freedom-loving non-conformist or any member of a particular race or any member of a union—or anyone.

For my own security—for the security of all our members, I ask our Board to weigh this hearing carefully—to determine whether it can afford to witness its approach with passivity.

I must especially appeal to the Board, to my fellow actors, to consider whether it will not be proper and necessary for it to make a public declaration that it will not tolerate any industry blacklists against any of its members who see fit to act upon a unanimous decision of the Supreme Court and avail themselves of the privilege against self-incrimination which is once more available for the purpose for which is was originally established—as a barrier to political and religious persecution.

I can find no reason in my conduct as an actress or as a union member why I should have to contemplate a severing of the main artery of my life—my career as a performer—because I hold to views for which during the last war I was an esteemed member of the Victory Committee and the recipient of the thanks of my government, industry and union.

With appreciation of the Board's consideration of this request,
I am,
fraternally yours,
Gale Sondergaard[11]

On March 20, the day before she was scheduled to appear, the Board of the Screen Actors Guild issued a reply:

Dear Miss Sondergaard:

The Board of Directors of the Screen Actors Guild has received and carefully considered your letter of March 13th, which you saw fit also to publish in the press. The Guild's answer should be equally available to the public and will be published.
Your letter (1) attacks as an inquisition the pending hearings by the House Committee on Un-American Activities into alleged Communist Party activities by a few individuals and (2) asks that the Guild protect you against any consequences of your own personal decisions and actions.

The Communist Party press also has attacked the hearings as a "warmongering, labor and freedom-busting ... witch-hunt ... by Congressional inquisitors." The Guild Board totally rejects this quoted typical Communist party line. We recognize its obvious purposes of attempting to smear the hearings in advance and to create disrespect for the American form of government.

The deadly seriousness of the international situation dictates the tone of our reply. This is not the time for dialectic fencing. Like the overwhelming majority of the American people, we believe that a "clear and present danger" to our nation exists. The Guild Board believes that all participants in the international Communist Party conspiracy against our nation should be exposed for what they are—enemies or our country and of our form of government.

It is not the province of the Guild Board to decide what is the best method of carrying out this aim. It is our hope that the current House Committee hearings will help to do so, in an objective and intelligent manner. We are informed that the Committee will guard against smearing of any innocent individuals. We will watch with extreme interest the way in which the hearings are conducted and any and all developments stemming therefrom.

The Guild as a labor union will fight against any secret blacklist created by any group of employers. On the other hand, if any actor by his own actions outside of union activities has so offended American public opinion that he has made himself unsaleable [sic] at the box-office, the Guild cannot and would not want to force any employer to hire him. That is the individual actor's personal responsibility and it cannot be shifted to his union.

Board of Directors
Screen Actors Guild[12]

Gale Sondergaard testified, did not cooperate with the committee, and was indeed blacklisted. She appeared for a second time in 1956 and again did not cooperate. She would not make another movie until 1969.[13]

Anne Revere, thrice nominated for an Academy Award for Best Supporting Actress (she won for her role in the 1944 MGM Elizabeth Taylor vehicle *National Velvet*), was called before HUAC in April, took the Fifth Amendment (until the end of her life she maintained that the unsigned CP membership card "used as evidence of her Party membership was a fake"), and resigned from her position as the Guild's Treasurer. Like Sondergaard before her, she sent a letter to the Guild Board, which she had published in *Daily Variety*:

You, the Board of the Screen Actors Guild point with pride to your seven-year fight against the Communist conspiracy. What have you accomplished? You have sanctioned the blacklist of 23 of your fellow members because they chose to defy an unconstitutional investigation into their thoughts and beliefs. Have you given strength to the industry by depriving those artists of their art and bread? Or have you further incapacitated the industry and the art which you profess to nourish? For seven years you have purged the screen of "dangerous ideas." With what results? The obliteration of all ideas. And people. Behold an industry that once bestrode the envious pinnacle of world leadership, now so paralyzed with fear that the screen is now inhabited solely by three-dimensional spooks and men from Mars. But there is still hope. The invalid is sick but not dead. Unlock the dungeon doors. Given him fresh air and sunshine. Take off the strait-jacket and let him move about with freedom. But above all, return his conscience which you have filched from him.

For years, Revere too was blacklisted. She did not return to movie-making until 1970, but thanks once again to Actors' Equity, she had some success in the theatre, winning the 1960 Tony Award for Best Supporting Actress in Lillian Hellman's *Toys in the Attic*.[14]

On July 1, 1953, the Screen Actors Guild sent the following to its membership for a vote:

> No person who is a member of the Communist party or of any other organization seeing to overthrow the Government of the United States by force and violence shall be eligible for membership in the Screen Actors Guild. The application for guild membership shall contain the following statement to be signed by the applicant: "I am not now and will not become a member of the Communist party nor of any other organization that seeks to overthrow the Government of the United States by force and violence."[15]

The referendum passed by a vote of 3,769 in favor; 152 opposed.[16] The oath was made optional in 1967 when the Grateful Dead refused to sign it, and it was removed from the by-laws in July 1974.[17]

Acknowledging that Reagan's strong stand had grown partially from being closely involved with a union battle waged by two groups representing the behind-the scenes film workers (one tagged as allegedly Communist), he would for the duration of his public life fight Communism, and would be credited by some as responsible for the collapse of the Soviet Union.[18] At the time he appeared before HUAC, he "and his wife [had] sat down with FBI agents ... and explained what they were facing." Reagan's secret role as an informant for the Bureau had begun.[19] This was a role thought possible but never proven during his tenure as SAG president. According to the blacklisted director, Martin Ritt, Reagan always insisted that there never was a blacklist.[20]

The 1950s are often seen as the Golden Age of Television. At the beginning of the decade on the first broadcast of *See It Now*, highly regarded then and there-

Like Sondergaard, Anne Revere had also won an Academy Award a number of years before her appearance before HUAC on April 17, 1951 (Photofest).

after, veteran broadcaster Edward R. Murrow, showing viewers simultaneously pictures of the Atlantic and Pacific oceans, told his audience, "For the first time in the history of man we are able to look out at both ... coasts of this great country at the same time," and asserted that such a capacity meant that "no journalistic age was ever given a weapon for truth with quite the same scope as this fledgling television."[21]

For the virulently anti–Communist Senator Pat McCarran (a Democrat from Nevada), television was also a weapon, but one that could be used by subversives against American values, and therefore those "responsible" for its development "must also accept responsibility for its character and the type of programs it channels into the homes of America." McCarran warned against those "strategically placed" individuals who, whether Communists or very active pro-Communists, were in a position "to take advantage of television's progress."[22]

For many children and adults in the 1950s, neither point of view seemed to matter. Television just magically came out of nowhere. There it stood, a box that looked almost exactly like a radio except this one produced images on a strange little screen. If that box was in a neighbor's house, that was the place to be at the beginning of the decade. A few years later, almost everybody in any given neighborhood had a much improved box with a larger screen. Soon there would be color and other enhancements. Television seemed literally, as Murrow had indicated, to bring the world into anyone's living room.

From television we learned to love Lucy and were assured that Father knew best. The imagination required to "picture" something as had been the case with radio was no longer necessary. Black counterparts, for example, replaced the white actors who had played Amos and Andy and the Kingfish on radio as the show began a successful run on television in 1951. Old movies no longer disappeared but were shown endlessly on TV.

It was to be on television that a rapt audience watched the hands of organized crime kingpin Frank Costello in 1951. The television audience saw Costello's "hands drumming on the table; hands gripping a water glass, fingers tightly clenched; hands tearing paper into little shreds; hands sweating"[23] while being questioned by Senator Estes Kefauver. When black students defied a hostile mob and attempted to reach the front door of Central High School in Little Rock, Arkansas, television was there. When Richard Nixon was plagued with a scandal that might derail his 1952 bid for the vice-presidency, television was there to show you his tears and Checkers, his cute little puppy.

From October 20, 1953, to March 16, 1954, Edward R. Murrow and Fred W. Friendly ran a series of programs on their CBS program *See It Now* that led directly to a confrontation with Senator Joseph R. McCarthy. When challenged as to the possibility that this might appear to be slanted reporting, Murrow is credited as saying, "There are not always two equal sides to every story." Prior to this time, many had heard or read McCarthy's words; now they were able to see them delivered by the man himself. When heightened awareness caused by television coverage combined with the political frustration simmering in the United States Senate, McCarthy found himself censured by that body before the close of 1954.

By the middle of the 1950s, the television commercial had overtaken all other forms of advertising, and because of television's dependence on the advertising dollar, McCarran's point of view now became the dominant one, and the industry became an easy target for the blacklisters. Their weapon of opportunity was the afore discussed *Red Channels*, which for red-baiters made the elimination of the reviled liberals and their progressive causes even easier targets.

Television was ripe for attack by the compilers of *Red Channels*. Thanks to them, Philip Loeb was forced off *The Goldbergs* (despite the attempts of its star/creator Gertrude Berg to retain him), while the producers of *The Aldrich Family* terminated Jean Muir's contract before she could appear. The response of these individuals, like the dozens of others who were blacklisted, varied considerably. Loeb, unwilling to say what the blacklisters wanted him to say, and faced with financial hardships which compromised his support of an ailing child, killed himself. Muir became a cooperative witness before HUAC. However, as they and others responded to the blacklist, one thing was certain: they received no support from their union, the American Federation of Television and Radio Artists (AFTRA).

The story of AFTRA begins in 1952, when the American Federation of Radio Artists (AFRA) and the multi-guild Television Authority (TVA) merged.[24] Under the leadership of George Heller, the TVA made inroads in helping minorities, and because Actors' Equity was one of the more dynamic components of the TVA, there was even an active Blacklisting Committee from which members could seek help. It was a major regret of Heller's that he was unable to carry some of the TVA initiatives into the newly formed union he also came to head.[25]

In 1954, while in the midst of becoming the first industry union to win employer-funded health and retirement plans for its membership, AFTRA was also getting ready to take a stand against members who went before HUAC and didn't cooperate. At that time AFTRA was divided into two main locals: one in Los Angeles and one in New York. Los Angeles led the way in this situation by instigating disciplinary action against its members who did not cooperate.[26] In June, they suspended three members, Libby Burke, Shimen Ruskin, and Murry Wagner, for "their alleged failure to tell a Congressional investigating committee whether they are or ever have been Communists."[27] The three would remain suspended unless they "voluntarily purge[d] themselves before the House committee and before the AFTRA directors within a year."²⁸ They appealed, their appeals were denied, and although the New York local had not yet formally adopted such a position, the suspension of the three members was ultimately upheld on a national level.²⁹

SAG may have had a president in Ronald Reagan who was working with the FBI, but there was no indication that members actually were aware of the fact. This was one way in which the AFTRA situation was different insofar as at the New York local, members of the governing board turned out to also be executives of AWARE, one of the organs of the burgeoning blacklist, and the members knew it. Jack Gould of the *New York Times* defined AWARE as a "privately constituted organization that has been applying its own standards as to whether a performer is a Communist or Communist sympathizer."³⁰ Active in blacklisting activities in radio and television, the group at AFTRA included Vincent Hartnett, one of the authors of *Red Channels* and *Counterattack*. Imagine wanting to speak up at a meeting of your own union and having the very people you want to speak up against sitting in attendance taking notes. This uncomfortable situation was what it was like at AFTRA membership meetings in New York in 1955.

In June 1955, by the narrowest of margins, the New York local's membership passed a resolution, presented by actor George Ives at a membership meeting, to take a vote of the full New York membership on whether to condemn AWARE and its activities.³¹ The campaign was led by a group which became labeled as the "middle," and included a CBS television personality from Texas, John Henry Faulk. It is important to note that AWARE was, among other things, one of the groups to which members of unions could "apologize" for past Communist affiliations. By a vote of 982 in favor, 514 opposed, AWARE was condemned by the New York local in July 1955. The *Times'* Jack Gould noted that "the vote is one more reflection of the changing public temper that has come to recognize that truly effective anti-communism need not necessitate sacrifice of fundamental legal principles and basic American tenets."³² "It was so funny," George Ives said of an event that followed his involvement with the motion:

> ... I was up for a Kraft [television episode] one day and Marion Dougherty was the casting director, and there was a fellow there who was a friend of mine, Mike Dreyfus, who was working in the office. I later got the call [to do the job], and I talked to Mike, and I said, "What happened?" I got the job. And he said, "Well, you'd have loved it. After you left Marion said, 'Oh gosh, I can't remember what it was but George is somehow involved with AWARE Incorporated. Well, that's a good idea in a way, that way it will shut them up. So we can use him.'"... I turned away so nobody could see my face, because it made as much sense that you got the job for the wrong reason as if you lost the job for the wrong reason.³³

However, any joy locally was soon to be erased, as nationally AFTRA chose not to reflect "the changing public temper."³⁴ In August of 1955, a rule was adopted by a vote of 3,967 to 914. It read:

> If any member of AFTRA is asked by a duly constituted committee of the Senate or House of Representatives of the United States whether or not he is or ever has been a member of the Communist Party, and said member fails or refuses to answer that question, said member shall be subject to the charge that he is guilty of conduct prejudicial to the welfare of AFTRA.
>
> The accused may be investigated and the charges may be heard by the board of the local of which the accused is a member. The local board may, in its discretion, fine, censure, suspend or expel the accused from membership, in accordance with the constitution and by-laws of the local, subject to such appeals as are provided in the local and national constitutions.[35]

It was in that same August that HUAC, having subpoenaed a group of theatre and live entertainment personnel to appear before them, came to New York City. Of the 30 witnesses subpoenaed for these hearings, 20 were members of Actors' Equity, and the majority of those also belonged to AFTRA. Anyone involved with these unions at the time was not surprised to read that "One actor who received a subpoena said last night it was his information that all the performers summoned thus far had signed the petition [that led to the vote] urging condemnation of AWARE, Inc."[36]

Fortunately for those Equity members, their union had taken a stand with regard to blacklisting that was very different from that of SAG and AFTRA. The union's support of its members during the heyday of the Red Scare in the early 1950s stands in strong contrast to the other entertainment industry unions and thus markedly changed the tone of the 1955 hearings.

Six

Actors' Equity Association
The Chronicle of an Anti-Blacklisting Resolution

The initial impetus for the creation of Actors' Equity Association lay in the chaotic, sometimes ruthless, treatment performers received at the hands of the producers who employed them. Discharge without notice was possible, and oftentimes took place without back wages being paid. There was no pay for rehearsals, which sometimes dragged on for months. It was not uncommon practice for a show to be closed far from home, with cast members stranded.

In May 1913, 112 actors met in New York City to form a union. In July 1919, the American Federation of Labor chartered the Associated Actors and Artistes of America (commonly referred to as the Four A's), an umbrella group of entertainment unions of which Equity was the largest constituent. A strike for recognition of the union as the actors' bargaining agent followed in August. Bitterly contested by management, the strike closed 37 plays and prevented 16 additional productions from opening.

The strike ended in October 1919 with a five-year contract between the union and the organization representing the producers, the Producing Managers Association.[1]

Gains in the following years included bonding provisions guaranteeing salaries and transportation (1924); restrictions on actors from other countries working on the American stage (1928 and still a major issue today); the franchising of agents setting, among other things, the cap of a ten percent fee on negotiated salaries (1929), and minimum wage guarantees (1933).[2]

The governing body of Equity is Council, which in the 1950s was composed of 50 members of the union elected to 5-year terms. Each year one-fifth (i.e., ten members) stood for election or re-election, the candidates being presented for election by a nominating committee made up of Councilors and members. Those opposed to this slate could choose to run by petition. In discussing the Equity election process, a study prepared for the union in

1947 noted that "there seems to be a desire ... on the part of many Equity members ... to split votes so that 'liberals' and 'conservatives' will both be represented on the Council."[3] The study concluded that this factionalism actually contributed to Equity as a democracy.

To fully understand the operations of Equity during the years of the Red Scare, it is important to note that Equity was a union centered in New York City with branches in Los Angeles, Chicago, and San Francisco. These branches did not work autonomously; any motions passed by a regional office had to meet approval by Council in New York. It was not until the 1990s that Equity became restructured so that regional decisions were left in the hands of the regional branches.

It was this structure that determined Equity's involvement in things political such as the desegregation of theatres. Equity has consistently worked to better the treatment and working conditions for its members irrespective of color. Over the years, Council formed committees to deal with issues that directly affected its minority members, from housing on the road to expanded opportunities in casting. In 1947 Equity took a stand against the segregation of audience members who attended the theatre when Council voted to refuse to allow its members to perform at Washington, DC's National Theatre until such time as the audience was integrated.[4]

Of those active in support of this action, many were among those blacklisted in film and television over the next five years, including any number of those who are a part of our story: J. Edward Bromberg, Phoebe Brand, Morris Carnovsky, Cliff Carpenter, Eda Reiss Merin, Jeff Corey, Mark Lawrence, Lloyd Gough, Karen Morley, Lee J. Cobb, John Randolph, Philip Loeb, Sam Wanamaker, and John Garfield.[5] As a result of this boycott, the National Theatre closed its doors. It reopened in 1952 as a fully integrated example for the country.[6] For its leadership in this area, Equity was presented with the National Brotherhood Award by the newly formed Labor Council of the National Conference of Christians and Jews.[7] With the help of the League of American Theatres, this Equity policy spread throughout the country's theatrical venues as the integration of theatres became the order of the day.

The HUAC investigations of the entertainment industry had been dormant since the 1947 hearings. When the committee once again opened its investigations to include the entertainment industry in 1951, Christopher O'Brien, Assistant Executive Secretary in charge of the West Coast office of Equity, wrote to Council in New York on March 5:

> The West Coast Advisory Committee wishes to call attention to the fact that the House Committee on Un-American Activities has already subpoenaed a number of West Coast Equity members to appear before it in its current investigations, and to the danger that members so subpoenaed may be damaged professionally by the tendency of theatrical employers to accept the fact of such subpoenas as grounds for blacklist discrimination.

of Equity Library Theatre until January 1, 1951. Dorothy Davies, Marjorie Hildrith, Irene Marmein, Phoebe McKay, Elizabeth Parrish, Walter Reimer and Henry Scott.

Fund Raising

Members who have not yet returned the books containing contributing membership cards, are urged to return them, with all funds received, IMMEDIATELY. To date the receipts are disappointingly far from our goal of 25,000 dollars. There is strong possibility of paid employment for numerous E. L. T. productions next season, IF we have the funds to do the job! Please Help!

Special Meeting Backs Contract Demands

(Continued from Page 8)

Briggs explained his vote in the negative had been due not to lack of sympathy to the purpose of the resolution, for he was as much against segregation as anyone, but because it would jeopardize accommodations for companies on tour. he was met by calls for a point of order.

These calls were legally correct. Mr. Derwent conceded, but it had always been the tradition of Equity to permit members to state their points of view. And so Mr. Briggs was permitted to finish although it was apparent that the membership was opposed to the chair's decision.

For a Special Contract Meeting

Eli Wallach now presented the final resolution on which the meeting acted. It was that a special meeting should be called to consider contract demands only. There was not, he said, time at the Annual Meeting for such consideration.

Mr. Simon agreed that this was so and said that the executives were considering asking the Council for such a meeting in advance of the Annual Meeting.

Mr. Francis proposed that this recommendation be amended so that at the meeting preceding the Annual Meeting a Contract Committee should be elected, not appointed by the Council, which should not report back to the Council but to the membership. This amendment was acceptable to Mr. Wallach, and the recommendation was adopted.

Attacks on Alleged Subversives

Elliott Sullivan now referred to a list of alleged subversive actors which had been published in "Counterattack" which he said would hamper Equity in its current negotiations. There was also a book which had been sent to producing managers with similar lists and he wanted Equity to join AFRA and other organizations in fighting such publications.

Mr. Wallach brought up a resolution which he had presented to the Annual Meeting which had requested Equity to take a stand against blacklists for political views. It had asked Equity to make this fight a part of its contract negotiations and that the Council instruct Equity's delegates on Television Authority to make it a part of TvA's contract demands as a violation of fair labor practices. This resolution had just plain gotten lost in the debate at the Annual Meeting and no action had been taken on it. Now Mr. Wallach demanded that it be made part of the negotiations for it was, in his opinion, just as important as a pension fund or the six day week.

Edith Meiser pointed out that the Council could not instruct its TvA delegates as they had been given a completely free hand in their work on that Board.

And Mr. Simon declared that it could not now be included in the contract negotiations. There had to be a time limit for the introduction of new matter in these negotiations or added demands from either side would prolong them for months.

Robert Earle Jones demanded that Equity take a stand in opposition to the Mundt-Nixon Subversive Control Act now before Congress. Clay Clement replied that the Council had voted to support the American Federation of Labor, which had recorded its opposition to the Bill. Michael Lewin declared that this was not enough, that the Bill might come out to the floor of Congress any day and he asked for a vote on opposing the bill by this meeting and that Equity should express its views publicly.

But before this could be brought to a vote a motion to adjourn was made and carried and the meeting stood adjourned.

The Guild Had a Heart

Burton Mallory, of the Theatre Guild production of "As You Like It," wrote to the Council from a full heart, and the Council, feeling that credit should be given where earned, suggested that Mr. Mallory's letter be presented to the membership through the pages of the EQUITY MAGAZINE. On May 30th, then, Mr. Mallory wrote:

"So many sins of omission, etc., have been charged to the Theatre Guild that I should like to bring to your notice their very fine treatment of me. After playing Adam, in 'As You Like It,' all season, I was rushed to City Hospital on the morning of May 8th with a ruptured peptic ulcer which necessitated an emergency operation.

"On my third day there, Katherine Hepburn came down herself to tell me that the Theatre Guild was paying me full salary for the entire time I should be out, even if it were right through to the closing date, June 3rd.

"Fortunately I was out of the hospital May 19th and went back into my part on Monday, the 22nd. For the two weeks I was out I did get my full salary.

"I am grateful to the Theatre Guild for this generosity and hope that you will set it down on the credit side of your accounts with the Theatre Guild."

Equity, too, recognizes it as a kind and generous action and assures the Guild of its appreciation.

Lockers at CBS

George Heller, National Executive Secretary of Television Authority, has notified Equity that he has been advised by the Columbia Broadcasting System that it is installing lockers for individual performers at their studios. While it may take a little while to secure and install them all, they are, at least, on the way and, Mr. Heller feels, will help solve a difficulty which has annoyed members working for CBS for some time.

Although HUAC had not started back yet in the summer of 1950, it was the time that the Hollywood Ten went to jail. With *Red Channels* in print, things were starting to get rough when the actor Eli Wallach wrote an editorial for the August 1950 issue of *Equity*, the union's magazine (author's collection).

In This Issue

Special Meeting Backs Contract Demands

Why Do We Say Yes?
By Cornelia Otis Skinner

Kind Hearts and Gentle Hands
By Alfred Elting

Catching Up With the Calendar

AUGUST 1950

25¢ a Copy

As debate raged on about the wording of the anti-blacklisting language that had been voted for at an Actors' Equity membership meeting, and as Council was working to make it into contract language, members were kept up to date in the November 1951 issue of *Equity* (author's collection).

We urge that Council consider action to protect its entire membership and ultimately the Association itself from this danger and from this discrimination.[8]

Council determined that it would "watch with interest and concern the manner in which this (Congressional) Committee manages its current investigation and the actions of employers in the engagement of Equity members who may have appeared before this Committee."[9]

The statement was purposefully evasive as councilors felt it was an issue primarily for SAG. As we now know, Hollywood seemed to be HUAC's major target at the time. Equity even borrowed from a letter written by SAG's Board of Directors and, like that union, concluded:

> ... as a general statement of principle, this Council believes that the deadly seriousness of the international situation is responsible for our decision that this is not the time for dialectic fencing. Like the overwhelming majority of the American people, we believe that a 'clear and present danger' to our nation exists. This council believes that all participants in the International Communist Party conspiracy against our nation *should* be exposed for what they are—enemies of our country and of our form of government.[10]

In response to the ever-darkening landscape, the membership at Equity's quarterly meeting in New York on Friday, September 28, 1951, passed a strong resolution against blacklisting.[11] Being passed at a membership meeting meant that a resolution had to be considered by Council. It came before Council at its October 2 meeting. On the recommendation of the executive, Louis Simon, Council moved to make it a Special Order of Business for two weeks later, with the text of the resolution being sent to members of Council.[12] The resolution they received read as follows:

> WHEREAS the Council of Actors' Equity Association, in July of 1950, concerned with the spread of Blacklisting in the Entertainment industry, passed a resolution which declared that, quote, 'the use of the so-called Blacklist is contrary to some of the most fundamental purposes for which the Actors' Equity Association and Chorus Equity Association were formed, as herein set forth, and in order to protect themselves and their members they must vehemently denounce such practice and take action to eliminate it,' end quote; and
>
> WHEREAS, in September of 1950, the membership of Actors' Equity Association, moved by our failure to be effective in the Jean Muir case and the threat of Blacklisting in the Legitimate Theatre, passed a resolution almost unanimously reaffirming Council's previous declaration; and
>
> WHEREAS, in spite of all these declarations, the practice of Blacklisting has not abated, but in fact has spread to such an extent that more and more of our members find themselves on one or another blacklist which jeopardizes their employment in all entertainment fields, so that we men and women of the theatre are becoming increasingly aware of the fact that Blacklisting of one actor in any area of the Entertainment industry threatens the security of all actors and, indeed, jeopardizes the very existence of our Association; and

Form NLRB-1081
(6-51)

UNITED STATES OF AMERICA
NATIONAL LABOR RELATIONS BOARD

AFFIDAVIT OF NONCOMMUNIST UNION OFFICER
(See instructions on reverse)

The undersigned, being duly sworn, deposes and says:

1. I am a responsible officer of the union named below.

2. I am not a member of the Communist Party or affiliated with such party.

3. I do not believe in, and I am not a member of nor do I support any organization that believes in or teaches, the overthrow of the United States Government by force or by any illegal or unconstitutional methods.

_____
(Full name of union, including local name and number)

_____
(Full name of national or international union of which it is an affiliate or constituent unit)

Signature _____

Residence _____
(Number and street)

_____
(City and State)

(The notary public or other person authorized by law to administer oaths must fill in completely all blank spaces below.)

Subscribed and sworn to before me this _____ day of _____ 19 ___

A notary public or other person authorized by law to administer oaths and take acknowledgments in and for the county of _____, State of _____

My commission expires _____

_____
(Signature)

[SEAL]

WARNING.—The attention of persons filing this form with the Board is directed to U. S. Code, Title 18, Sec. 1001 (formerly Sec. 80), which provides that any person willfully making or causing to be made any false or fraudulent statements or representations in any matter within the jurisdiction of the Board shall be fined not more than $10,000 or imprisoned not more than 5 years, or both.

Above and opposite: In May of 1951 the National Labor Relations Board sent out for signature an Affidavit of Noncommunist Union Officer. Statement number 2 stated quite simply, "I am not a member of the Communist Party or affiliated with such party." There was no mention of the "...have you ever been" part of the statement. This gave many former party members the ability to sign (author's collection).

Six. Actors' Equity Association 89

INSTRUCTIONS FOR THE USE OF THIS FORM

WHO MUST FILE.—This affidavit must be filed by each officer of a labor organization before that organization may receive the help of the National Labor Relations Board. An affidavit must be on file for each officer listed in your constitution and by-laws.

WHERE TO FILE.—NATIONAL AND INTERNATIONAL LABOR ORGANIZATIONS must file this affidavit with the Affidavit Compliance Branch, National Labor Relations Board, Washington 25, D. C.

LOCAL LABOR ORGANIZATIONS must file this affidavit with the Regional Office of the National Labor Relations Board with which they usually file cases.

WHEN TO FILE.—This affidavit is good for only one year from the time it is signed and must be renewed each year. Each time a new officer is elected or appointed, he must file this affidavit. If an officer is reelected, it is not necessary to file a new affidavit unless the affidavit on file with the National Labor Relations Board is more than one year old.

HOW TO PREPARE THIS AFFIDAVIT:

a. Read carefully items 1, 2, and 3 of this affidavit.

b. Fill in the full name of your labor organization, including the local name and number.

If your organization is affiliated with a national or international organization, give the full name of the national or international.

(EXAMPLE)

Plastic, Button and Novelty Workers Union, Local 506
(Full name and local number)

International Ladies Garment Workers Union--AFL
(Full name of national or international)

c. The officer must sign his name in the presence of a notary or other person authorized by law to administer oaths.

d. The officer must give his full home address; be sure to give the street address, city and State.

WHEREAS we recognize that this overall Blacklist against our members, Negro and White, constitutes a double Blacklist, an added burden for our Negro members, as they have always been discriminated against in term of employment;

THEREFORE: in the spirit of our tradition in the Theatre of our Association of—ONE FOR ALL AND ALL FOR ONE,'

BE IT RESOLVED: that Actors' Equity Association declare that Blacklisting of it members for color, race, religion, political belief, or union activity, is hostile to the fundamental purposes of this Association, and that Actors' Equity Association will act to the fullest of its capacities in defense of its members.

TO THESE ENDS WE FURTHER RESOLVE: that Actors' Equity Association take the necessary steps with the League of New York Theatres to secure the inclusion in our basic agreement of a clause declaring Blacklisting of members of Actors' Equity Association for color, race, religion, political beliefs or union activity an unfair labor practice and a violation of our basic agreement.

WE FURTHER RESOLVE: That Actors' Equity Association declare that Employer usage of 'Red Channels,' 'Counterattack,' and any other published and/or unpublished list constitutes an unfair labor practice; and

WE FURTHER RESOLVE: that Actors' Equity Association act to secure mutual cooperation with the 4 A's and/or any member union thereof, T.V.A. and any other union in the entertainment field for the purpose of eliminating Blacklisting in the entertainment industry, and specifically to inform our Equity Representative in T.V.A. of our position against Blacklisting; and

WE FURTHER RESOLVE: that a Committee be formed, composed of equal numbers of Council members and members-at-large, said members-at-large to be elected from the floor, to implement the foregoing "Resolve."[13]

The debate at the Council meeting two weeks later on October 16 was fierce and varied. An illustration of the stands taken by various Council members is demonstrated by the following examples:

> The ten communications which were received [from Councilors] via mail and telegraph were read by Mr. Simon and were, in effect, as follows:
>
> MR. [Clarence] DERWENT—Stating his unalterable opposition to blacklisting of all sorts but doubting the advisability of making the subject an issue in negotiations with the League.
>
> SIDNEY BLACKMER—Registering strong opposition to the Resolution; questioning the sincerity of the origins of the Resolution and opposing the principle of blacklisting of any person because of race, color, creed, or union activities.
>
> MARGALO GILLMORE—Opposing the Resolution and advising that the Association stand on the position adopted in 1950 [supporting the government, decrying the blacklist, and taking no action].
>
> BARBARA ROBBINS—Opposing the practice of blacklisting but strongly opposing the proposed Resolution as being unable to correct the evils of blacklisting and in the long run not being beneficial to the welfare of the Equity membership.
>
> BILL ROSS—Supporting the Resolution and stating that he would vote for it.
>
> LEE TRACY—Unalterably opposed to the Resolution for the principal [sic] reason that it is unworkable and unenforceable and might lead to the Association finding itself involved in hopeless litigation based, perhaps, on wholly [sic] imaginary charges.
>
> MAURICE EVANS—Registering strong opposition to departure from Council's already declared policy and specifically opposed to the formation of the Committee advocated in the Resolution.
>
> KENT SMITH—Violently opposing the Resolution, both for reasons of principle and practicality.
>
> *PHILIP OBER—Expressing the opinion that the Resolution is Communist-inspired

RESOLUTION RE BLACKLISTING AS REVISED AND ADOPTED BY COUNCIL NOV. 13, 1951

WHEREAS, This Association now, as in the past, is unalterably opposed to Communism, Fascism and any and all other forms of subversive acts and ideologies, and has repeatedly gone on record to this effect, and

WHEREAS, It is against the declared policy of this Association to aid or defend any person who has been duly proven to be subversive, and

WHEREAS, It has repeatedly been brought to the attention of this Association that certain employers within the entertainment industry have used a form of anti-union discrimination, commonly known as "blacklisting", which practice this Association deems to be to the detriment of its members, and

WHEREAS, This Association, through its Council and its Membership, has heretofore gone on record that the United States Government, by and through judicial process, is amply capable of determining who is subversive and who is not, and has declared itself with great vigor and emphasis in protest against the practice of certain employers within the entertainment industry who are allowing themselves to be intimidated by private individuals, organizations and publications, who, in the irresponsible manner of vigilantes have improperly assumed the functions of government and are thereby injuring some of its members by publicly branding them as disloyal without giving them an opportunity to be heard and are thus depriving such members of the pursuit of their chosen profession and ability to earn a livelihood therein, and

WHEREAS, This Association is also against the blacklisting of any members who suffer because of their opposition to duly proven subversive activities and ideologies.

WHEREAS, The aforementioned practice of "blacklisting" is, by its very nature, based on secrecy and prejudiced judgment and results in conviction by accusation without an opportunity given to the accused person to be heard and to defend himself, and

WHEREAS, This Association deems the aforementioned practive of "blacklisting" and the detriments necessarily arising therefrom to innocent persons as a practice diametrically opposed to the time-honored American principle that an accused person has the inherent and vested right to a just and fair hearing.

NOW, THEREFORE, BE IT RESOLVED, That this Association again condemns the practice of "blacklisting" in all its forms, and that this Association will act to aid its members in their right to obtain a fair and impartial hearing of any charges that may be brought against them. To this end, BE IT FURTHER

RESOLVED, That this Council appoint from among its members a Committee of five persons for the purpose of recommending a course of action to this Council. The Committee shall have no power to enter into any commitments or to take any action other than to investigate, but this Committee shall specifically be empowered to:

(1) Create such working Committees composed of other members of the Council or of the membership as in its discretion it may deem advisable; such working Committees to function as directed by the Committee and solely within the provisions of this Resolution.
(2) Contact such unions and organizations as may be helpful in its work.
(3) To interview such actors, and other persons as it may deem advisable for the purpose of gathering information to the Council in their endeavor to stop blacklisting.

The final resolution was handed out to the members in November of 1951. In 1952 Equity succeeded in getting anti-blacklist language into its contracts (author's collection).

and as a member of AEA being opposed to it, but as an American registering himself in favor of the principle which the Resolution 'pretends' to represent and urging a referendum on the issue. (*Mr. Ober requested that his expression be spread on the Minutes. The Council did not act specifically on his request; therefore, as of the moment Mr. Ober's opinions are being summarized as are the opinions of all others who sent in written communications).

MATT BRIGGS—Registering strongest protest against the adoption of the Resolution and declaring it to be 'a piece with the Stockholm Petition for Peace and, therefore, utterly Communistic.' Further, protesting Mr. Derwent's reading of John Randolph's letter at the Quarterly Meeting and sharply criticizing the Executive Secretary's Report as 'a piece of unwarranted rabble rousing' and calling for the removal of Mr. Simon.[14]

[Equity President] Mr. [Ralph] Bellamy warned against over-emotionalism and asked Council to analyze the intent of the Resolution. The only weapon at our means to fight proven blacklisting would be for our entire membership to strike," he said.[15]

Other speakers followed, and numerous attempts were made to amend the current resolution. Suffice it to say, the resolution as originally written was rejected, while the following resolution passed:

WHEREAS, Upon examination and consideration of Council, the present Resolution is found unacceptable in the endorsement which might be inferred from it of all political beliefs and/or activities including those which are subversive; and

WHEREAS, There are other objections to the Resolution in its current form, and

WHEREAS, It is clear the innocent may be convicted without due process and injustices to our membership have occurred and will continue to occur.

NOW, THEREFORE, BE IT, RESOLVED:
1. The proposed resolution is rejected, but
2. Council reiterates its stand on blacklisting and
3. Council appoints a committee to:
    a) Draft an acceptable resolution for Council's approval
    b) Set up means to protect the unjustly accused, including but not limited to seeking the assistance of other performer unions.[16]

The committee was formed and the meeting adjourned.[17] At the Council Meeting of November 13, 1951, the committee that had been selected to redraft the membership resolution made their final report. The minutes of that meeting reflect the numerous amendments proposed with only the occasional comment. Finally, in more diplomatic language and with no record of the vote in the minutes, the resolution that passed looked like this:

WHEREAS, this Association now, as in the past, is unalterably opposed to Communism, Fascism and any and all forms of subversive acts and ideologies, and has repeatedly gone on record to this effect, and

WHEREAS, it is against the declared policy of this Association to aid or defend any person who has been duly proven to be subversive, and

WHEREAS, it has repeatedly been brought to the attention of this Association that certain employers within the entertainment industry have used a form of anti-union discrimination, commonly known as 'blacklisting,' which practice this Association deems to be to the detriment of its members, and

WHEREAS, This Association, through its Council and its membership, has heretofore gone on record that the United States Government, by and through judicial process, is amply capable of determining who is subversive and who is not, and has declared itself with great vigor and emphasis in protest against the practice of certain employers within the entertainment industry who are allowing themselves to be intimidated by private individuals, organizations and publications, who, in the irresponsible manner of vigilantes have improperly assumed the functions of government and are thereby injuring some of its members by publicly branding them as disloyal without giving them an opportunity to be heard and are thus depriving such members of the pursuit of their chosen profession and ability to earn a livelihood therein, and

WHEREAS, this Association is also against the blacklisting of any members who suffer because of their opposition to duly proven subversive activities and ideologies, and

WHEREAS, the aforementioned practice of 'blacklisting' is by its very nature, based on secrecy and prejudiced judgment and results in conviction by accusation without an opportunity given to the accused person to be heard and to defend himself, and

WHEREAS, this Association deems the aforementioned practice of 'blacklisting' and the detriments necessarily arising there from to innocent persons to be a practice diametrically opposed to the time-honored American principle that an accused person has the inherent and vested right to a just and fair hearing.

NOW, THEREFORE, BE IT RESOLVED: That this Association again condemns the practice of 'blacklisting' in all its forms, and that this Association will act to aid its members in their right to obtain a fair and impartial hearing of any charges that may be brought against them. To this end, BE IT FURTHER

RESOLVED, that this Council appoint from among its members a Committee of five persons for the purpose of recommending a course of action to this Council. The Committee shall have no power to enter into any commitments or to take any action other than to investigate, but this Committee shall specifically be empowered to:

(1) Create such working Committees composed of other members of the Council or of the membership as in its discretion it may deem advisable; such working Committees to function as directed by the Committee and solely with the provisions of this Resolution.

(2) Contact such unions and organizations as may be helpful in its work.

(3) To interview such actors, and other persons as it may deem advisable for the purpose of gathering such information as may be helpful to the Council in their endeavors to stop 'blacklisting.'[18]

In 1952, once again in concert with the League of New York Theatres, a paragraph regarding blacklisting became standard language in Equity's basic agreement, making Equity the first and only performing arts union to do so. Over the course of each new contract negotiation, this paragraph would be added:

> The Manager and Actor admit notice of the anti-blacklisting provision contained in the basic agreement between Equity and the League of New York Theatres, and agree to abide by and to be governed by all the terms and conditions thereof with the same

force and effect as if each were party signatory to said basic agreement; the parties further admit notice and agree to abide by and be governed by all the rules and regulations of Actors' Equity now or hereafter adopted, and which may, from time to time, be adopted and/or amended pertaining to anti-blacklisting pursuant to said provisions of the basic agreement.[19]

There would be no blacklist on Broadway or in any theatres outside this major market due in no small part to the efforts of Actors' Equity Association. Thanks to Equity, many actors finding themselves unemployable in film and television returned to the stage. It was at those stages that many were served their subpoenas to appear before HUAC in August of 1955.

Seven

Investigating Broadway
The 1955 HUAC Hearings

Knowing that subpoenas were being issued in the summer of 1955, actor Stanley Prager worked assiduously to avoid being served. He told his friend, actor George Ives,

> "I'd been watching out because I didn't want to get served, and I was careful getting to the theatre," and he said, "you know what happened? I came off stage [after the curtain call for the July 6, 1955, matinee performance of *The Pajama Game* at Broadway's St. James Theatre] and this man was there smiling at me, and he said, 'Mr. Prager,' and I said yes, what can I do for you, thinking it was a fan."

At that point, committee investigator Frank Bonora served him with a subpoena to appear before the House Committee on Un-American Activities (HUAC) on August 15, 1955.[1]

Over the next few weeks, Bonora, Dolores Faconti Scotti, and their colleagues visited stage doors, dressing rooms, hotels, and apartments, serving subpoenas on 29 members of the New York performing arts community. Shortly thereafter, the time came for the subpoenaed actors to prepare to give their all in a production scheduled to open on Monday, August 15, 1955. True to the tradition of professionals in theatre, most of them got together to rehearse.

"We were all rehearsed by [blacklisted writers] Abe Polonsky and Arnie Manoff," Madeline Lee Gilford commented in one of our interviews. "Abe Polonsky was also a lawyer so that he was a tremendous help to us. We were all good actors, and by encouraging us we could [use those skills]."[2] About half of those subpoenaed came to rehearse if they were in town, and according to Lee, Stanley Prager was made the monitor for the group. They were encouraged to "use up as much time" as they could in the hopes that they would run out the clock and other witnesses would not be called, and it was made clear that if they didn't take the Fifth Amendment, they could be held in contempt.

"He [Polonsky] encouraged us all to play our own characters." As a result, Madeline decided that since she "was a cute little blond who played a lot of dumb blonds and a lot of youngsters" she would wear "this cute little borrowed organza dress, and I had flowers in my hair because Lillian Hellman had said 'we aren't romping through this with flowers in our hair,' so I did." At the same time, Sarah Cunningham Randolph returned to her roots and decided she would appear as the quintessential Southern Belle, complete with wide-brimmed hat and Southern drawl.[3] Noted folk singer Pete Seeger did not join this group for their rehearsals, but "I put on my best suit of clothes because my lawyer said, 'dress neatly. Don't come in your usual blue jeans,' and I even brought a banjo with me because I knew they would question me about music,"[4] which they did. His wife Toshi also arranged for Seeger to meet with friends who had already appeared so he would know what to expect. Seeger's way of rehearsing was to jot down answers to possible questions.[5]

Rehearsals being over, the hearings began on August 15, 1955, in the Foley Square Courthouse. The courthouse is an intimidating building that sits on one edge of what was once the gang-ruled "five-corners" neighborhood in lower Manhattan. Climbing the wide concrete steps that lead to the entrance must have been especially daunting to a generation not raised on *Law and Order*. Once inside, the witnesses took the elevator to the 17th floor of the tower and went to room 1703. As much as the committee often appeared to be a court, albeit without the rules of procedure such as cross-examination of accusers, its rules did allow that everyone could be in the room and listen to the other witnesses. As a result, witnesses were in the hearing room along with their supporters, provided the supporters were not also scheduled to appear that day. George Ives recalled attending the hearings:

> I went down. I remember going down and John [Randolph] came by and he goes, "Chaps, you're all here," because there was a whole bunch of us who went to watch the hearings.
> It was just chilling because the attitude was so adversarial. Before anybody opened their mouth you knew they were all just going to try and see if they couldn't get some of these people, and the idea of any of them talking about other people was just so awful. I mean, because they knew these people and they knew there was nothing about them that was subversive. That was just a ridiculous idea.[6]

Chairman Francis E. Walter, a Democrat from Pennsylvania, opened the hearings by explaining why the committee had come to New York:

> During the course of numerous hearings conducted in Los Angeles between 1951 and 1955, it was learned that many individuals alleged to have knowledge of Communist party activities within this field came to Hollywood from the city of New York, and in some instances returned from Hollywood to the city of New York. The conclusion was reached by the committee several years before I became its chairman that the hearings begun in the general field of entertainment should be extended to the New York area.

Besides Chairman Walter, the other two members of the committee present on this day were Gordon H. Scherer, a Republican from Ohio, and Edwin E. Willis, a Democrat from Louisiana. Also present each day of the proceedings were committee investigators Donald T. Appell and Frank Bonora, who had served many of the subpoenas to those in attendance, along with Thomas W. Beale, Sr., chief clerk.[7]

The first witness called was actor George Tyne.

The Committee for the August 1955 hearings: left to right: Edwin Willis (Democrat, Louisiana), Francis Walter, Chairman (Democrat, Pennsylvania), Gordon Scherer (Republican, Ohio) (author's collection).

During the course of his testimony, Tyne had the opportunity to lay out all six of what became the major recurring themes prompted by questions over the next four days: the blacklist, prior relationships, legislative purpose, investigation of theatre, the First Amendment freedoms, and the always popular union affiliation.

Theme one was blacklisting: Like many actors before him, Tyne started in the New York theatre before going to Hollywood to find a career in film. Counsel Frank Tavenner inquired, "Then, what was your next work in Hollywood?" Tyne replied, "As I said before, because I was blacklisted out of the motion picture industry, I came to New York to seek employment."[8]

Theme two was prior relationships: Tavenner inquired, "Were you a member of the group of the Communist Party in 1943 of which Mr. Lee J. Cobb was a member?" Tyne answered, introducing along the way the third and fourth of our major themes: legislative purpose and investigation of theatre.

> Mr. Tavenner, I would like to say that I see no legislative purpose in this committee and its inquiry into the theater, and I would like to voice my responsibility to the Constitution and say that this committee has no right to invade my inner beliefs and my conscience or my associations.[9]

With the committee continuing along this same line of questioning, Tyne attempted to make himself clearer in the following exchange, forcibly presenting the fifth major theme of First Amendment rights:

> MR. TYNE: I say, again, that I stand on the basic rights, the Bill of Rights, of the Constitution, which says that Congress has no right to make inquiries or interfere or

question my private beliefs, and the invasion of my associations and of my conscience. There is no legislative purpose in this committee making an inquiry into the theater. This is an area of ideas.

CHAIRMAN WALTER: Just a minute. You are not the theater. You may think you are, but you are not the theater.

MR. TYNE: I am a proud member of this theater.[10]

As his testimony continued, the committee introduced the sixth and final recurring theme of these hearings: union membership. Tyne was asked whether he was a member of Actors' Equity, and then if he was a member of AFTRA. He refused to answer either question, claiming once again, "this committee has no right to inquire into my associations, my beliefs, and my conscience."[11]

At no time during his testimony did Tyne take the Fifth Amendment. Near the end of his testimony, he reiterated, "that there is no legislative purpose in making inquiries into the theater" at which point Chairman Walter interrupted to explain:

> We made it abundantly clear that we are not making any inquiry into the theater. We are just finding out, if we can, what elements there are in the theater which might at some time or other bring criticism upon decent and innocend [sic] people.[12]

The next witness was the actor John Randolph who had appeared in the Federal Theatre's *Revolt of the Beavers* as Mortimer Lippman. His testimony echoed the issues presented by Tyne. Randolph had the opportunity to expand on the theme of blacklisting when Tavenner asked, "To what extent has your acting been on television?" Randolph replied:

> It was quite good, and I did a lot of television work up until 1952 when I was blacklisted by Mr. Johnson of Syracuse, as I understand, then later by Counter-Attack, and then later by Aware, Incorporated, and I never knew what the accusations were, or what reasons, but they were anonymous phone calls, and you know the kind of stuff. There were little hate letters and so on and so forth, and not many, but enough to make me quite disturbed about it, and find out that I was being blacklisted on television and I never could find out who did the accusations or any

John Randolph (right) talking to Chairman Walter (author's collection).

of that sort, and I never had a chance to answer any of that. That happened about 1952.

Ever since that time I have devoted my entire time to fight blacklisting, and Aware, Inc., and all of those little outfits that unfortunately bring so much fear and terror into our industry.[13]

Randolph was excused shortly after this statement, having sought protection under the Fifth Amendment.

Stanley Prager appeared next, and judging from his testimony, the questioning was arduous in its repetitiveness. He followed along on the themes presented by the first witnesses, adding, "I cannot involve myself with you in a discussion about the theater or about the theater's ideas, because this is an attack on the theater and something I won't be a party to."[14] Prager took the Fifth Amendment and later talked to George Ives about his experience before the committee:

I remember Stash [Stanley Prager] telling me [that] when he was testifying, which I did see, his description of it was, "You remember I was answering, I was refusing to answer, I was answering, I was refusing to answer and all of a sudden that chairman [actually Representative Scherer] said, 'I think Mr. Prager has lost his right to refuse' and my heart sank." And he [Prager] said, "At that moment fighting Marty Popper, my attorney leaned over to me and he said 'bullshit,' and it was such a wonderful word to hear. I was so relieved."[15]

The afternoon session included four more actors: Martin Wolfson, Lou Polan, Phil Leeds, and Sarah Cunningham. The four continued along the lines established by the morning's witnesses. Attention once again fell on the theatre when Tavenner asked Martin Wolfson, "Were you a member of the Communist Party at the time that you were in Russia [on a cultural exchange]?" Wolfson replied,

> Mr. Chairman, I think that the purpose of this committee is to throw fear into the theater. I think that it is no accident that you come here at this time, just when productions are being planned for the fall, actors are being engaged, and plays are being read. You are trying to throw fear into the theater, and I don't think the purpose is a correct one or valid.[16]

Sarah Cunningham [Randolph] on her way to the August hearings (author's collection).

Lou Polan's experience before the committee was astonishing in two ways: first, because he actually got to read his prepared statement under the guise of listing his theatre experience. Polan began his statement by simply stating, "I think I can save a lot of time." He listed his credits and continued:

> All of my adult life and a good part of my youth has been dedicated to the theater, and my name is hardly important to you for the purpose of our inquisition, and your subpoena naming Lou Polan might just as well have named, "Mr. Theater."
>
> I wish to put this committee on notice that I will not assist you in your lawless efforts to censor the legitimate theater or control the entertainment field which, in my opinion, are the real aims of this committee. I challenge the legal authority of this committee to conduct this star-chamber proceeding. I am going to take an unequivocal position here, and I am going to give the reasons for not answering and I am not going to answer any questions of this committee, and I wish to state the reasons.[17]

Second, the committee was not interested in hearing his reasons, thus, astonishingly, he never was asked or had the opportunity to claim the protection of the Fifth Amendment. He was also never found in contempt.

Phil Leeds followed Polan and found numerous amusing ways to talk about the rights protected by the First Amendment:

> I believe that it is the privilege of an American citizen to believe in Yogi Berra if he so desires, or that lanolin will save the world. I do not believe that it is your right to ask me any question concerning my politics, how I worship, and how I think, and

Actor Phil Leeds (left) testifying before the committee at the Foley Square Courthouse in New York City (Photofest).

what I read, and if I wear suits with narrow lapels or if I use an underarm deodorant. I think you are intruding on the privacies, or my privacy as an American citizen and as such I refuse to answer that question on the grounds previously stated.[18]

Leeds continued taking the Fifth Amendment and was excused.

The final witness on the first day of hearings was actor Sarah Cunningham, wife of John Randolph, and a member of the original company of *The World of Sholom Aleichem*. Having taken the privilege of the Fifth Amendment from the beginning of questioning, she finally got to explain her stand in an exchange with Counsel Tavenner:

> MR. TAVENNER: Will you tell the committee, please, what knowledge you have, if any, of the existence within the Actors Equity of a group of persons organized by the Communist Party as a Communist Party group?
> MISS CUNNINGHAM: Do you really expect me to answer that question?
> MR. TAVENNER: I am very much in hopes that you will answer it. I hope that you will have enough courage to tell the committee what you know about communism in the field in which you are a specialist.
> MISS CUNNINGHAM: I see. Well, I would like to use my courage in the way that I feel it takes more courage, and that is to tell you that I do refuse to answer this question because my folks signed the Declaration of Independence, and they fought in the American Revolution and settled this country, in the early 1770's in the South, and the tradition of my family has been that we do not defy—I am sorry, would you strike that from the record?
> CHAIRMAN WALTER: You can read it, it is here.
> MISS CUNNINGHAM: What I am trying to say is, because this is what I consider a very foul question, that we do not talk about any of our association. My mother taught me that I had the freedom to think as I pleased and to go where I pleased, and to talk with whom I pleased, and to have any friend that I wished, and that no one had the right to question me about it.
> I believe that I am carrying out the tradition of my ancestors by saying that I refuse on the basis of the first amendment, and I invoke the privilege of the fifth amendment.[19]

The first day was over. The six major themes that were to be carried throughout the majority of the testimony had been established and demonstrated. It was now time for day two.

On Tuesday, August 16, actor Elliott Sullivan, accompanied by his counsel Bella Abzug, was the first to take the stand. His testimony lasted

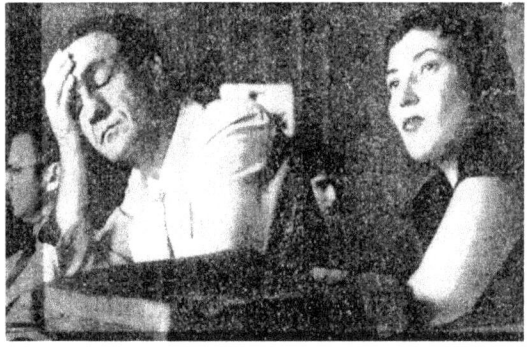

Elliott Sullivan, with his lawyer Bella Abzug, testifying before the committee (author's collection).

the entire morning. When asked about his theatrical credits, Sullivan made it clear to the committee that he "got these jobs because of talent and ability and not because of my political reasons." This prompted Tavenner to ask, "What do you mean when you say 'political reasons'?" to which Sullivan replied, "What I mean by that is that I think that this committee has changed the qualifications for acting, and I think they have substituted good standards of talent and ability with some sort of political test."[20]

This was Sullivan's second committee appearance. The first time he appeared, he took the Fifth Amendment. He promised himself that, given a second appearance, he would say what he wanted and not seek the protection of the Fifth Amendment.[21] As a result he was brought up on contempt charges.[22]

After the lunchtime recess, the committee called folk singer and composer Lee Hays. They were interested in the songs Hays had written and under what circumstances the songs were performed. According to Pete Seeger, before Hays even entered the room, he had decided that "he wouldn't bother with anything other than the Fifth Amendment," and that is exactly how he performed. At one point in his testimony, Congressman Scherer offered Hays the possibility of immunity if he answered their questions. Hays declined to discuss it and was excused.[23]

Composer Irma Jurist followed Hays and took the Fifth. She found the committee "scary but pompous."[24] Susan d'Usseau, painter and wife of blacklisted writer Arnaud d'Usseau, followed Jurist to the stand. D'Usseau protested that the committee had "made a mistake in calling me to this committee. I have nothing to do with the theater."[25] According to Madeline Lee, this had been d'Usseau's well-rehearsed response. Day two drew to a close.

August 17, 1955, day three of the hearings in Foley Square, started out differently from the others. The first witness called was actor George Hall. The first thing that distinguished Hall's arrival was the absence of legal counsel. When this absence was noted by committee counsel Frank Tavenner, Hall replied, "I am satisfied with my

George Hall, the only cooperative witness at these hearings, testifying on August 17, 1955 (Photofest).

own opinion, sir."²⁶ George Hall was to be the first, last, and only cooperative witness to appear before the committee during these hearings.

Hall admitted membership in the Communist Party. When Tavenner asked the inevitable question, "Will you tell the committee, please, the circumstances under which you were recruited or became a member of the Communist Party?" Hall replied,

> I would like to make it very clear, if I may, that no one, and I would like to specify, no one specifically influenced me or persuaded me or cajoled me or talked me into becoming a member of the Communist Party. This blunder was mine, and I take full responsibility for it.²⁷

Hall continued to answer the committee's questions, and over the course of his testimony he named eight people he knew to be Communists: Alan Manson, David Kanter, John Randolph, Sarah Cunningham, Josh Shelley, George Keane, Keane's wife Betty Winkler, and Irma Jurist. All those named, except Winkler, had testified or would be testifying at these hearings. Hall also confirmed the committee's fear that the communists had influence at Actors' Equity Association:

> MR. TAVENNER: Did you receive any directions from the Communist Party as to how you should vote in business affairs of Actors Equity?
> MR. HALL: Not from the Communist Party, specifically, but from individuals whom I knew to be Communists, at a couple of Equity meetings I recall when election time came around, I would be handed a piece of paper, and I would be told that was the slate, and I would vote the slate which they specifically wanted me to vote for.²⁸

Having at last heard from a cooperative witness, Chairman Walter seized the opportunity to thank Hall before he excused him:

> Yes, I will take the responsibility [of thanking Hall on behalf of] the whole Congress, for what you have done here today. It is not easy, and it is not any easier on you than it has been on these other brave people who have come forward in an attempt to preserve the institutions that are so sacred to America and so necessary for the preservation of the stability of the world. It is not easy. I should not like to be called a stool pigeon, and I am sure that that appellation will be applied to you.
> But let me tell you something: Every patriot in the history of America has been proud of the enemies that he has made, and I am sure that you will be proud as you go along in life of the enemies that you have made. Your contribution here cannot be appraised. It may well be that it is equal to that of a division of infantry, and nobody knows in this cold war to what extent this sort of a revelation has contributed to ultimate victory—and the victory will be ultimate.
> As we go along we are going to run into all sorts of impedimentia [sic], and we are going to run into witnesses who would like to testify but who have not the courage, and other witnesses who have indicated that they intend to testify but have been dissuaded by Communist lawyers, and other witnesses who cannot testify because of pressures that are being applied [a probable indication that Walter was expecting

more cooperation at these hearings than he got]. But nonetheless there is going to come the day when we are going to be out of this [sic] woods and all of this haziness that you have experienced will be dissipated.

When that day arrives, and you will live to see it, you can feel very happy of the contribution that you have made.

The committee will stand in recess for 10 minutes.[29]

The committee might not have realized it at the time, but they needed that recess. Upon their return they brought forward an uncooperative witness with an agenda: to keep talking and to keep the committee constantly guessing about what she would do or say.

Madeline Lee Gilford had plenty to say about her experience testifying, and even though she added a little extra drama, her memories matched up quite well with the government's transcript:

> Representative Scherer was a very impervious little puppy, congressman from Ohio, Cleveland, I think, who was deciding to become the next Nixon. He was going to find someone [to make his reputation as Nixon had with Hiss].
>
> [During Lee's questioning] Scherer kept jumping up like a little puppy and saying, "Direct her to answer. Direct her to answer," and instead of answering him directly, Walters waved him down with his hand so nothing appears in the record. You just see him saying, "Direct her to answer." Walter is waving him down because he doesn't want anymore 1st Amendment cases and I had not taken the 5th yet, so he's like waving him down you know, like shut up you dope I'll direct her to answer when I'm ready. Here was Tavenner questioning me; a very fancy Southern gentleman who had questioned Brecht and Ring Lardner, Jr. and all of the Hollywood 10. He showed me a picture of a May Day parade where I was marching next to Pete Seeger. Pete Seeger was in his army uniform which technically you're not allowed to wear in a parade without permission. They were trying to get him on that technicality. He [Tavenner] kept asking me about the May Day parade in which I was pushing my daughter who was in a carriage.

Madeline Lee Gilford testified before the committee in her borrowed organza dress, and yes, those are flowers in her hair. She went on to evoke four separate Amendments: the First, Fourth, Fifth and Eighth (Photofest).

[Tavenner] is asking about this picture and I told him that I would not discuss anyone else. I wouldn't let anyone else get blacklisted and we had this long quarrel and then Walter directed him to direct me to answer and Tavenner says, "I forgot the question." So I did it I think Jewish style in that I answered every question as much as I could with a question. Is a May Day parade illegal? Was it illegal at the time? Could anyone march in it? Tavenner then asked me the question I forgot now, but that's how we used up the time. They knew I'd be a strong witness. I think they placed me after George Hall because they thought it would all go down. Well, I took a deep breath, and I'm very proud of my testimony. I kept stopping to ask [her attorney Leonard] Boudin advice and taking quite a long time with it because [that's] what Polonsky had instructed us to do.

At one of these points I said I wish to consult with my attorney and Walter said, "We know Leonard Boudin and we know what he is going to tell you." Boudin got up and told him that he [Walter] should be disbarred for saying that; how dare he decide what he was going to give me advice about or what. They had a quarrel and it went on for quite some time. Walter said that "advice from an attorney was a courtesy from the Committee and not a right." I finally had to tug Leonard Boudin's coat to say, "I'm testifyin' you know." I whispered it to him.

Then I took 12 or 13 [actually four: the First, Fourth, Eighth, then Fifth], amendments at different times and finally the 5th. One of times when I stopped to ask his [Boudin's] advice I asked him if I could take the amendment about drinking, and I hiccuped in his ear. But then, you know, this is [how] I stalled.[30]

At the end of Lee's testimony, Tavenner showed how obviously tired and frustrated he was. When Chairman Walter encouraged him to proceed, he stated, "I doubt that it would be of any value to question this witness further. She has indicated she is not going to answer any questions relating to the matter of communism."[31] Lee fired back, "I am perfectly willing to answer all of your questions about subversive and infiltration in the entertainment industry, and the answer is that there is none."[32] Two sentences later, the witness was excused.

Producer and former stage manger Peter Lawrence (not the one currently working on Broadway) was the next witness called.

Peter Lawrence [the current Broadway stage manager is no relation] arriving to testify before the committee (Photofest).

The committee was hoping to continue what they had begun during George Hall's testimony: exposing communist infiltration of AEA. When asked about an Equity meeting Lawrence was purported to have attempted to hold soliciting support for the 12 members of the Communist Party national committee who were on trial in New York City in 1949, Lawrence replied:

> I won't answer that question on the grounds previously stated [the First and Fifth Amendments] but it seems to me to be a complete outrage, your talking about discussion of questions by adult members of a union and if they are not entitled to discuss it if they choose to, that is their choice and if they don't wish to discuss this question, again that is their choice, and I think the inference here that the union is having anything put over on them is again an insult to the union and there are questions which can be debated, and discussed, and if they were, this again is a union province, and if they are not interested, the members of the union can refuse to discuss it and they are perfectly capable of discussing unions if they so choose to discuss them, and if you are saying that they can't discuss questions, then it is subversion to discuss questions and I think that this is something that should be examined.[33]

Peter Lawrence was excused. Actor Joshua Shelley was their next witness.

Shelley did not spend a very long time in front of the committee. After a brief discussion about how blacklisting affected his career, Shelley refused to answer the next series of questions "under my privilege in the Fifth Amendment, and the First Amendment."[34] Not giving up quite yet, Tavenner asked, "Did you ever attend a caucus within Actors' Equity, composed of members of the Communist Party?" The exchange continued:

> MR. SHELLEY: I feel this question is an attack on Actors Equity, and it attempts to bring a climate of fear in the union so that any caucus if it meets to defeat such publications as Aware, will be frightened to meet, and I feel this is a smear on my union.
> MR. TAVENNER: No; it is not a smear on your union at all, you know that.
> MR. SHELLEY: I feel that it is, sir. You are trying to bring fear into members of unions who have fought against blacklisting, who have fought for good things in the unions when you ask questions like that.[35]

Shelley was excused, clearing the way for actor George Keane. The closing witness on day three was actor Albert M. Ottenheimer. Both gentlemen took the privilege of the Fifth Amendment, and the committee agreed they would "stand in recess" until the following day.

On day four the first witness called was actor Alan Manson. When Manson said that he "cannot" tell the committee what they want to hear, Chairman Walter fired back, "Just a minute. You say, 'I cannot,' by that you mean that you will not? You could." Manson replied, "I cannot because I am devoted to the principles on which this country is founded, sir."[36] Manson took the Fifth and was excused.

Actor, folksinger, and former executive director at CBS television Tony Kraber, a member of the Group Theatre, was the next witness to be heard.

Seven. Investigating Broadway

Near the end of his testimony, it was his position as an executive director/producer that intrigued the committee most.

> MR. TAVENNER: As executive producer was one of your duties that of employment of talent?
> MR. KRABER: Yes, sir.
> MR. SCHERER: You wouldn't blacklist at that time any talent who were members of the Communist Party, would you?
> MR. KRABER: I loathe the blacklist, and I think of the reasons for the blacklist is, if I may say so, this committee. When I was called into the [network] president's office, after the old smears had appeared in the Journal American, he opened the interview with me by saying "You have one of the finest records of any young executive in the company," and then he proceeded to demand my resignation because he said they had reason to believe that I was about to receive a subpoena from the un–American committee. This was in 1951, and since 1951, and it is now 1955, I have been denied my income which I should be earning, and furthermore the public of the United States has been denied the use of my trained talents.
> CHAIRMAN WALTER: Now here is a great opportunity for you to clarify the atmosphere for all time to come. Are you now a member of the Communist Party?[37]

Tony Kraber took the Fifth and was excused. The committee took a 10-minute recess.

When the committee returned, they called Pete Seeger to the witness stand. Seeger had already decided that, unlike his colleague, Lee Hays, "I was in a stronger position, a much stronger position, and that's why I didn't bother using the Fifth Amendment."[38] Seeger's singing talents were of great interest to the committee. They wanted to know where he sang and for whom. They advised him that earlier George Hall had admitted that he, Hall, "was to use his talents by entertaining at Communist Party functions." This prompted Counsel Tavenner to ask Seeger if he had been "engaged in a similar type of service...." Seeger, after consulting with his counsel, replied:

> I have sung for Americans of every political persuasion, and I am proud that I never refuse to sing to an audience no matter what religion or color of their skin, or situation of life. I have sung in hobo jungles, and I have sung for the Rockefellers, and I am proud that I have never refused to sing for anybody. That is the only answer I can give along that line.[39]

Not at all satisfied by this answer, the committee continued to question Seeger, and he, without taking the Fifth, continued declining to answer their questions. Since, as stated earlier, not taking the Fifth can earn one a contempt citation, the Chairman wanted to be sure of what he was hearing.

> MR. SEEGER: My answer is the same as before.
> CHAIRMAN WALTER: What is that?
> MR. SEEGER: It seems to me like the third time I have said it, if not the fourth.
> CHAIRMAN WALTER: Maybe it is the fifth, but say it again, and I want to know what your answer is.

MR. SEEGER: (after consulting with counsel): I decline to discuss, under compulsion, where I have sung, and who has sung my songs, that I have helped to write as well as to sing them, and who else has sung with me, and the people I have known. I love my country very dearly and I greatly resent this implication that because some of the places that I have sung and some of the people that I have known, and some of my opinions, whether they are religious or philosophical, or I might be a vegetarian, making me any less of any American. I will tell you about my songs, but I am not interested in telling you who wrote them and I will tell you about my songs, and I am not interested in who listened to them.[40]

If Congressman Scherer was keeping score, Seeger had definitely earned the contempt citation that he went on to receive. The committee continued to question Seeger for an extended period of time. When he was finally excused, the committee took their lunchtime recess.

The last three witnesses that Thursday were publicist Ivan Black, film importer and translator Harold Salemson, and stage manager David Kanter. Ivan Black refused to answer the committee's questions, and in doing so bested Madeline Lee's refusal by one amendment:

Sir, on that question [as with several others] I will assert the privilege of the first amendment, freedom of association and beliefs and thoughts. Until it is legal to have thought police in the United States, I don't think that is a proper question. I will assert and assume and embrace the privilege of the fifth amendment, and the sixth amendment, and the tenth amendment, and for the benefit of the committee, the fourteenth amendment.[41]

Pete Seeger arriving at the 1955 hearings with his banjo. In an interview he told the author it made him feel good to have it with him. He famously played it on the courthouse steps after the hearing (Everett Collection, Inc./Alamy Stock Photo).

The committee continued questioning Black and, in doing so, learned a great deal about the career of a press agent, but little else. Black continued to refuse to answer and was excused.

Harold J. Salemson, upon request from Counsel Tavenner,

described his current employment situation: "I am employed by a company that imports foreign films and I handle general problems, straightening out of contracts, translations of the contracts from Italian into English, French into English, and general administrative and executive work of that kind."[42]

The committee was more interested in an earlier position that he had held with the Newspaper Guild. Salemson informed the committee that he had decided he would only answer questions, including whether or not he was a Communist, for the seven years after July 1, 1948.

> I feel that it is my right as an American citizen to state to you that I will reasonably cooperate with you for a period of the 7 years, which I think is quite adequate, and beyond that I stand on the fifth amendment.[43]

The committee kept asking and Salemson kept refusing. They learned nothing about the Newspaper Guild from this witness.

The final witness of the day was David Kanter, accompanied by his counsel, Harry Schwimmer. Kanter, with his former attorney Paul Ross, had appeared in an executive session on August 1, 1955. It was during that appearance that Kanter was first offered immunity if he would testify fully about his beliefs and associations. He refused. Also during that appearance, the committee was told that when Investigator Frank Bonora served Kanter, Kanter had been more forthcoming. Kanter denied that was the case, and there is no memo from Bonora in Kanter's committee file to back this claim.

Representative Scherer had been among those present for the earlier testimony. As the August 18 session drew to a close, Scherer hoped that time, and a different attorney, might make Kanter more forthcoming. After reading into the record a good portion of Scherer and Kanter's earlier exchange, Counsel Tavenner presented the offer again:

> MR. TAVENNER: Now, Mr. Kanter, from what I understand, that offer of the committee stands good today, and I want to ask you this question:
> If proper application is made to the Federal court to secure immunity against prosecution, will you testify as to the facts within your knowledge?
> MR. KANTER: (consulted with [new] counsel): Sir, I must tell you that I must take the same position today as I took when I was first called before the subcommittee in Washington, because I am advised again by counsel that this law is in a highly debatable state.

Not one to give up so easily, Scherer engaged Kanter in the final exchange of the afternoon:

> MR. SCHERER: You mean then, Witness, that if there was no question about it—you base your refusal now to answer on the ground that this law is debatable.
> Now, my question was, if that question was resolved, and it was no longer debatable [the same argument he tried earlier with Lee Hays], and we granted you immunity, would you then answer the questions?

MR. KANTER: (consulted with counsel): I don't recall saying that I would have changed my opinion if the decision was changed or if the Supreme Court issued a new decision on it.
MR. TAVENNER: In other words the debatability [sic] of the act has nothing to do with your decision. In any event you are just not going to testify?
MR. SCHERER: That now becomes obvious. And I was in error in my judgment of this witness.
MR. KANTER: That is about right.
MR. TAVENNER: I have no further questions.
CHAIRMAN WALTER: The witness is excused.[44]

Although the committee had scheduled, and indeed had subpoenaed witnesses for five days' worth of hearings, day four would be the committee's last August day at Foley Square in 1955. This was a surprise for at least one witness, Angers Wooley, whose subpoena called for his appearance on Friday, August 19. Writer/director Jerome Chodorov, most well known for the play *My Sister Eileen* that then became the musical *Wonderful Town,* was expecting to testify, as was the actor Sam Jaffe, who had received his first subpoena in 1951. Ultimately, none of these gentlemen appeared before the committee.[45] Madeline Lee commented that they left early because witnesses they believed would cooperate did not, and much the same behavior awaited them if they continued. During the testimony of the final witness, David Kanter, the committee's frustration was evident. There is no indication in the record or in any of the files that this was planned. Without commenting on the change, Chairman Francis Walter simply announced, "The committee is adjourned."[46]

On August 19, 1955, major newspapers reporting on the hearings made no reference to the committee's early departure, with the *New York Times* and the *Los Angeles Times* referring to the hearings as being a "four day" affair.[47] Only the *Daily Worker*'s David Platt seemed to remember that the original subpoenas had been issued for five days of hearings when he wrote, "The Un-American witchhunt (sic) into the New York theater folded its tents prematurely and got out of town yesterday after being thoroughly trounced by the score of 22–1 in its attempt to find stool pigeons and informers in show business."[48]

Eight

After the 1955 HUAC Hearings
A Life in the Theatre Goes On

Of the 23 witnesses who appeared in the first four days, 22 refused to cooperate, and those with theatre jobs returned to their stages. The actor John Randolph, one of the 22, would remark of the day he testified, "I was feeling good when I went in front of the committee. I knew I was finished [in film and television], it didn't make any difference. At least I said what I had to say." He continued, "My wife [Sarah Cunningham] was called too, and she was wonderful."[1] Upon completing his testimony, Randolph returned to the Brattle Summer Theatre in Cambridge, Massachusetts, to finish his run in *Much Ado About Nothing*.[2] Randolph had one of the most successful postblacklist careers of the witness pool at these hearings. He continued to work in theatre for the rest of his professional life, winning a Tony Award in 1987 for Best Performance by an Actor in a Featured Role in a Play for Neil Simon's *Broadway Bound*. His career in television and film started again in 1960 and then took off. His face is familiar to most movie and television watchers. His many credits include Angelo "Pop" Partanna in *Prizzi's Honor* and Mr. Brockelman in the TV series *Richie Brockelman, Private Eye*. He died in 2004 at the age of 88. Although his wife's list of credits is not as impressive, she also continued to work in theatre and then in film and television. Sarah Cunningham died on March 26, 1986, while attending the Academy Awards with her husband. She was 68 years old.[3]

The majority of the others in this group seemed to have picked up where they left off before climbing those courthouse stairs. Ivan Black continued to work as a press agent for Broadway, Off-Broadway, and nightclubs. He is best remembered in the community as the man who gave Sam Mostel the name Zero. He died in 1979 at the age of 75.[4] Susan d'Usseau continued her career as a painter. She had her first "one-man show" in 1971 at the age of 71. She died two years later.[5]

It is unclear whether or not the one cooperative witness, George Hall,

One of many blacklisted actors, John Randolph won the 1987 Tony Award for his role in Neil Simon's *Broadway Bound*. First row (left to right): Linda Lavin, Jonathan Silverman, and John Randolph; second row: Phyllis Newman, Philip Sterling, and Jason Alexander (Photofest).

was in the Broadway production of *The Boy Friend* at the time he appeared. He is listed as a replacement in the company, which ran from September of 1954 through November of 1955, but as he did not discuss, nor was he asked about his current employment during his appearance, we have no way of knowing. He did continue to work on Broadway as well as in film and television. He died October 21, 2002, at the age of 85. His obituary in the *New York Times* makes no reference to his HUAC appearance.[6]

On the Christmas Eve following the hearings, Lee Hays and the other members of the Weavers (including Pete Seeger) reunited for a concert at Carnegie Hall. They continued as a group until 1963. In 1981, one year prior to his death, Hays and the Weavers returned to Carnegie Hall. This performance was captured in the 1982 documentary *Wasn't That a Time?* which is also the title of one of several songs co-written by Hays.[7]

Irma Jurist continued to compose music and perform both as a solo artist and with her trio. At the time I interviewed her, she was still living in the same apartment she was in at the time Dolores Scotti served her with a subpoena. She played the piano with little or no coaxing and would rather discuss religious concepts than politics.[8]

David Kanter, like George Hall who named Kanter as the person who introduced Hall to the Communist Party, is also listed as a replacement in the company of *The Boy Friend*, which was playing at the Royale Theatre on 45th Street in New York City. He started the job, according to his executive session transcript, the week he testified in New York.[9] The *Chicago Daily Tribune* wrote of Kanter's testimony, "For a few moments, a dramatic climax impended as the last witness, David Kanter, 46, a Broadway stage manager, appeared uncertain about accepting an offer of immunity in return for frank testimony."[10] As demonstrated in his testimony in August, Kanter was not as uncertain

Irma Jurist was quite the character and that made her quite the entertainer. After she played the piano for the author at our interview she gave me this flyer to add to my collection.

as the committee had hoped. Kanter continued stage-managing on Broadway until 1961.

George Keane had been appearing in the Broadway production of *The Seven Year Itch* that closed the Saturday before his appearance. In the fall he opened in the short-lived *The Heavenly Twins*, and he had some television credits before he died on October 10, 1995, at the age of 78. His *New York Times* obituary noted, "Mr. Keane left acting for the business world in the 1970's, becoming a successful pension adviser and financial planner."[11]

Tony Kraber continued to work as an actor on stage. There is no indication that he had any career in radio or television, although his obituary indicated that he held "executive positions" prior to being named before HUAC by fellow Group member Elia Kazan in 1952. The obituary continued: "Mr. Kraber went on to make films, including the prize-winning documentary 'Boundary Lines.'" I have found no record of that film. Kraber's last credit cited was in 1977, when "he appeared as the old man in the New York production of 'Nobody Heard the Lions Roar.'" He died in September of 1986 at the age of 81.[12]

Peter Lawrence continued to produce for the theatre. His last known credit has him returning to his roots as a replacement production stage manager for the Broadway production of *A Raisin in the Sun*, which closed June 25, 1960.

Albert M. Ottenheimer was the only witness appearing at these hearings who had already served jail time for refusing to answer questions before the Washington State's Un-American Activities Committee, the Cantwell Committee. His summation letter in the HUAC files makes it clear that he was found again because of a positive review in the *Daily Worker*, and because he had publicly advocated for the AFTRA anti–AWARE resolution.[13] Ottenheimer occasionally appeared both on and off Broadway over the next 20 years, including in the role of Doc as a replacement in the original production of *West Side Story*, as well as in film and on television in the 1970s. He died in Cincinnati, Ohio, on January 25, 1980, at the age of 76.

When he was subpoenaed, Lou Polan was appearing in the original production of *Bus Stop* at the Music Box Theatre in New York City. He returned to work after completing his testimony. The production ran until April of 1956. Primarily a man of the theatre, he returned to film work in 1960 and television in 1961. He was 71 when he died on March 3, 1976.[14]

Although there is no material in the committee files of an exchange of correspondence regarding Martin Wolfson's appearance before the committee, he indicates in his testimony that he gave up work in order to appear. At the time he appeared, Wolfson had already had one of the most extensive stage careers of any of his fellow witnesses, a career which continued to flourish. Martin Wolfson died on September 12, 1973, at the age of 69.[15]

Eight. After the 1955 HUAC Hearings

Madeline Lee Gilford left the hearings and headed straight back to her children on Fire Island. She had not been working as a performer recently, so not being able to get that type of work did not surprise her. When her husband, Jack, returned from doing summer stock, he continued working in theatre while she worked towards helping him return to film and television in her continuing role as an activist at AFTRA. In the 1970s, she did some work on television and in film and produced for the Broadway theatre in the 1980s and 1990s.[16] She performed both for the camera and as herself, as one of the few living raconteurs of this event in history until her death in 2008.[17]

If there is one witness whose credits outnumbered John Randolph's in the ensuing years, it was Phil Leeds. Just three months after the hearings, he landed a role in *The Matchmaker*, which ran for over a year on Broadway. With only one television episode to his credit prior to his appearance, he began working again in 1962 and never stopped. His hang-dog face graced many major television shows including *Ally McBeal*, *Murphy Brown*, and *Cagney & Lacey*. He worked right up until his death on August 16, 1998, at the age of 82.[18]

When Alan Manson told the committee, "I feel that these matters lie within a province that is hallowed, that I spent 5 years in the Army for..." he was speaking as a man who not only served in the Army but began his professional career as one of the group of soldiers chosen during World War II to appear in the Irving Berlin musical *This Is the Army*, both on Broadway and in the film. He continued to work in the theatre, although he did have to take odd jobs "like a position as a tour guide with the Circle Line." A charter member of AFTRA, he appeared in television and film as the blacklist began to fade. Manson was 83 when he died in 2002.[19]

There is no indication as to whether Harold Salemson's employment continued. When he died in 1988 at the age of 78, his obituary identified him as "a former film and book critic who translated biographies of Pablo Picasso, Salvador Dalí and Georges Simenon."[20]

Joshua Shelley had just completed a run in *Phoenix 55* when he was scheduled to appear before the committee. Not long after his appearance, he began to direct, and his last Broadway credits are as a director. His film and television careers stopped until the 1960s, when he worked as both an actor and director in those fields until his death in Los Angeles on February 15, 1990, shortly after turning 70. Although he had an impressive list of credits, his death was not announced in any of the major newspapers or in the industry publication *Variety*. According to Internet sources, "He became a well-known teacher during the 1970s, and ironically, given the years of blacklisting, was given responsibility for training new acting talent at Columbia Pictures."[21]

Stanley Prager, another one of the 22, continued to appear on Broadway in *The Pajama Game*. Fearful of possible repercussions from his testimony, he returned to his theatre where he "had his contract torn up—and was given a new one at higher pay and for a longer period of time." His producer was the legendary George Abbott. Prager "was not being rewarded for his 'unfriendliness,' he was being rewarded for his professional ability. And it is ability that still counts on Broadway."[22] Stanley Prager continued to work in the theatre as an actor and then as a director until his death in 1972 at the age of 54. He never acted in films or television again but did gather a few credits as a television director.

The remaining three witnesses from these hearings, George Tyne, Pete Seeger, and Elliott Sullivan, faced a slightly different future than the others. Because they did not protect themselves by taking the Fifth Amendment, they each received a contempt citation. Tyne returned to his role in the Broadway production of *Lunatics and Lovers,* Seeger soon began working with the Weavers again, while Sullivan, "Refusing to 'lay low' during the 1950s ... appeared at many progressive and leftwing occasions as a performer."[23]

The citations for Tyne and Seeger were issued on July 25, 1956. With his case pending in the United States District Court for the Southern District of New York, the resolution on Sullivan passed the House on September 16, 1961. Sullivan and Tyne "were acquitted of contempt in 1961 when the district court found their indictments to be 'fatally defective' because the government had not submitted the Committee's resolution ordering the hearing."[24] Seeger was convicted, but his case was overturned on appeal.

After his appearance before the committee, George Tyne continued to work in the theatre both in New York and on tour. When his film and television career picked up again in the mid–1960s, he moved back to the West Coast and worked as both an actor and a director. He died in 2008 at the age of 91.[25] Pete Seeger continued to write and perform, and although in his later years he no longer sang, he continued to play the banjo and call out the words with the enthusiasm he demonstrated in the earliest days of his career. Pete left us in 2014 at the age of 94, only six months after the death of his beloved Toshi.[26] In 1962 Elliott Sullivan began working in Europe. He became a member of British Actors' Equity. He died on June 2, 1974, at the age of 66, while on a visit to Los Angeles.[27]

As for the members who made up this committee in August of 1955, these hearings seem to have had little effect on their lives or careers. Chairman Francis Walter, who had served in Congress since 1933, continued to serve and remained in his post as chairman of HUAC until his death on May 31, 1963, at the age of 69.[28]

Gordon H. Scherer stayed in the House of Representatives until 1962 when he went back to his private law practice. He was a delegate from Ohio to the Republican National Conventions in 1964 and 1968 and served as chairman of the Hamilton County Republican Party from 1962 to 1968. President

Nixon appointed him the U.S. Representative to the United Nations where he served from 1972 to 1973. Scherer died in Cincinnati, Ohio, on August 13, 1988, at the age of 82.[29]

Elected to the House in 1949, Edwin E. Willis remained there until 1969. He became the chairman of HUAC when Francis Walter died and served in that capacity until he left the House. Willis died in St. Martinville, Louisiana, on October 24, 1972, at the age of 68.[30]

The House Committee on Un-American Activities continued to investigate.

In 1969 it was renamed the Internal Security Committee. Six years later it was completely abolished with its functions transferred to the House Judiciary Committee.[31]

Above all else, these 1955 hearings were defined by the fact that in many ways it was theatre that was on trial. For all intents and purposes, theatre was an afterthought in the tale that was blacklisting in the entertainment industry. Nonetheless, Chairman Walter was, furious when he brought HUAC to New York City. Since 1951, the Committee had felt so superior in their ability to assure that those they had accused who had not cooperated were now bereft of work. One could say they were justified in their feelings for, as you will see, the theatre, even the mainline Broadway theatre, was indeed a place where a disenfranchised artist could find his or her own name featured prominently on the theatre's marquee.

The members of this community stayed involved with issues that they found important well after the blacklist was over. This program was put together in January of 1967 to protest the war in Vietnam (author's collection).

In a 1956 report sponsored by the Fund for the Republic with the purpose of defining the presence of a blacklist in the various entertainment media, the theatre was virtually a footnote. Without probing the table of contents of both volumes of the report, a researcher might miss the fact that over 200 pages into Volume II—Radio-Television there is a report on theatre. With the extraordinary access John Cogley was afforded into the workings of the various forms of media, it is well worth searching out. In his report on blacklisting, Cogley wrote of these hearings:

> The experience of the 22 uncooperative witnesses in the New York Theatre probe illustrates the tremendous difference between the legitimate stage, and the movies and radio-tv. The basic difference between these media lies in the fact that the American legitimate theatre is the only entertainment medium still entrepreneurial in its methods of production.[32]

Bernard Gersten, managing director of Lincoln Center Theatre and himself a witness in 1958, agrees with Cogley's assessment. When asked why there was no blacklist on Broadway, he remarked:

> If I had to say it in one word, I'd say no advertisers. There were no advertisers. *Red Channels* was able to put the fear in advertisers, and find natural allies among those who placed ads, and those who owned companies who were certainly anti-communist if you were to generalize. But the theatre community was mom and pop stores. Certainly the audience didn't care. Who believes that Arthur Miller's *Death of a Salesman* say or *All my Sons* failed to sell tickets because Arthur didn't testify ... certainly no one failed to go see Lillian Hellman's plays because she testified. And certainly it wouldn't have mattered to the audience who went to see *High Button Shoes* if Jerry [Robbins, the choreographer] was a communist or from Timbuktu.
>
> I think the economics of the theatre was so much different from radio and television and movies. Essentially it wasn't that the theatre doesn't have, didn't have at that time producers who were Republicans or producers who were anti-communist, but self-interest was governed in a stronger way, so if there was an actor you wanted you hired the actor.[33]

Echoing what Brook Atkinson wrote about the audience that attended 1953's *The World of Sholom Aleichem*, John Cogley also admitted that "such a situation [no blacklist on Broadway] could not exist were it not for the peculiar nature of the theatre audience in New York."[34] In 2005, George Ives also gave credit to the audience when asked why he thought there was no blacklist on Broadway.

> If people were interested enough to go to the theatre, they were not the kind of people who could be terrified by thought and argument. They were people who were interested in it. The fact that somebody had a viewpoint that was different than yours, they wanted to hear it, and they wanted to argue it just like I did. [Theatre] audiences just weren't ready to be put into a mass kind of hysteria. They were more interested in hearing the ideas.[35]

Eight. After the 1955 HUAC Hearings

Dorothy Thompson, one of the premier commentators and news reporters of the radio broadcasting age, author of *Romancing the Soul* and *Let the Record Speak*, wrote a commentary on these hearings for her syndicated column, "On the Record," which appeared in the *Daily Press* of Newport News, Virginia. In the column titled "All The World's a Stage," Thompson spoke of the hearings not as a trial but as a show.

> The Committee gives these "known Communists" an audience. The public is asked to believe that they are subverting America via "The Pajama Game," "The Seven Year Itch," and "Much Ado About Nothing." Several things can result. They can be sent to jail for contempt of Congress—and what an act that would be. Or they can be dropped by producers, creating another uproar. (That is far less likely than it would have been two years ago.) Or they will go on making audiences laugh, cry, and otherwise emote, with the mental reservation, "They say he's a Communist. And he is so wonderful."

Thompson ends her commentary with words decidedly appropriate for the conclusion of this, or any, chapter on members of the New York theatre community: "Give the actor a stage, without which he simply does not exist. Not a stage in a court room. A stage in a theater. His judge will never be a Congressional Committee. It will always be the audience."[36]

In spite of all the efforts of that congressional committee, the audience continued to come, and the plays continued to be produced.

NINE

The Name on the Marquee
Working on Broadway in the Shadow of the Blacklist

Broadway and working on Broadway was the gold standard for every theatre professional followed closely by a major tour of a hit Broadway play or musical. It was the theatre's equivalent of a blockbuster movie, or a recurring role on a popular television show. Since the 1947 HUAC hearings, the courts holding up the contempt citations of the Hollywood Ten, and the publishing of *Red Channels*, theatre was also the only form of work available. Although Arthur Miller had been named in *Red Channels*, his work continued unabated. Miller was already a Tony Award winner for his 1947 play *All My Sons*, and the Broadway theatre community was ready to welcome his next production opening in February of 1949. *Death of a Salesman* was a big hit and won not only a Tony Award, but the Pulitzer Prize as well. For its producers, Kermit Bloomgarden and Walter Fried, sending it out on tour just made sense.

Unbeknownst to the principals involved, as *Death of a Salesman* began its tour, one of the authors of *Red Channels* who now also sent out a biweekly newsletter called *Counterattack* whose purpose was to "update," "amend," and add names to the original *Red Channels*' entries, also went on tour. Vincent Hartnett, arriving a week or two before a given production, met with members of a given city's American Legion posts as well as anyone else who might be interested. His goal was a boycott of the production when it arrived. Hartnett made sure that everyone knew Arthur Miller had been named in *Red Channels,* that the actor playing the lead, Albert Dekker, made the pages of a report on un-American activities in California, and that the producer, Kermit Bloomgarden, had allowed people like this to thrive.

One of those cities was Peoria, Illinois, where *Death of a Salesman* was due to play on October 27 and 28, 1950. More than a week before the opening, Hartnett met not only with the American Legion, but with the Junior Chamber of Commerce as well. In the *Peoria Journal* a week before the opening, one

Jaycee member challenged the decision to boycott in a letter to the editor concluding,

> The action of the J.C. board of directors is, I submit, inadequately supported by evidence. Peoria area theater fans, already suffering from malnutrition on the thin diet of stage attractions available here, need not deny themselves the chance to feast on "Death of a Salesman" because of the ill-considered action of [the] Junior Chamber of Commerce.[1]

This letter was then followed by "another Jaycee and Legionnaire" who wrote,

> You [the prior Jaycee Member] are unaware of the fact that a Communist-fronter, such as Arthur Miller, whose record you seem to be familiar with, is in accord with the principles of Communism, and that he supports the Communist party by his contributions to Communist-front organizations. Party members turn over on the average 10 per cent of their earnings to the Communist conspiracy, while Communist-fronters turn over about 5 per cent of their earnings for this game purpose.
>
> Although you are aware of Miller's record, you are not cognizant of Albert Dekker's [the lead actor] record. Dekker is a product of the Group Theater, which was the spawning ground for many notorious Communist-fronters.[2]

Albert Dekker as Willy Loman in the national tour of Arthur Miller's *Death of a Salesman*. Dekker was the star when the show played Peoria (Wisconsin Center for Film and Theater Research).

In the *Daily Variety* of October 23, 1950, "Hartnett further put the finger on [the] play's co-producer Kermit Bloomgarden," charging that he was also "allied with front organizations."[3] Unlike Miller, Dekker and Bloomgarden had not made the original *Red Channels* list.

Death of a Salesman ran the two days it was scheduled. The attendance was, not unexpectedly, down, and in later correspondence the tour stop was referred to as "the Peoria incident." The Broadway production which had opened February 10, 1949, ended its run on November 18, 1950. Over the ensuing years, four more award winning revivals played on Broadway and toured around the world. Miller himself directed a production in China. The month after *Salesman* closed, Miller was again on Broadway with an adaptation of an Ibsen play, *An Enemy of the People*.

Another playwright and screenwriter featured prominently in *Red Channels* was Lillian Hellman, a fixture of the Broadway theatre since her 1934 hit, *The Children's Hour*. She was preparing to stage a revival to be produced by one of Miller's producers, Kermit Bloomgarden, when she received a subpoena to appear before HUAC.

On Wednesday, May 21, 1952, in Washington, D.C., Hellman came before HUAC in a public hearing. Born in New Orleans, she had been a student at both New York and Columbia universities before taking up residence in New York City. By the time of this hearing she had had nine plays produced on Broadway, four of which had been turned into movies. The chairman, now a familiar face, was the same John S. Wood who had reopened hearings in 1951. The only other committee member present was Francis E. Walter, familiar to the reader from the 1955 hearings.

Soon after receiving her subpoena, Hellman carefully crafted a letter to Chairman Wood. Known for her well-documented ferocious temper, she was duly proud that she had exercised such impressive restraint in her letter. As she said to Mr. Tavenner,

> ... I would like at this point to refer you to my letter.... To be fair to myself I think I have worked very hard over this letter, and most seriously. I would like to ask you once again to reconsider what I have said in the letter.[4]

After some discussion between Mr. Tavenner, Chairman Wood, and Ms. Hellman's attorney Joseph Rauh, Mr. Tavenner read her letter, dated May 19, 1952, into the record:

> Dear Mr. Wood: As you know, I am under subpoena to come before your Committee on May 21, 1952.
>
> I am most willing to answer all questions about myself. I have nothing to hide from your Committee and there is nothing in my life of which I am ashamed. I have been advised by counsel that under the Fifth Amendment I have a constitutional privilege to decline to answer any questions about my political opinions, activities and associations on the grounds of self-incrimination. I do not wish to claim this privilege. I am ready and willing to testify before the representatives of our Government as to my own opinions and my own actions, regardless of any risks or consequences to myself.
>
> But I am advised by counsel that if I answer the Committee's questions about myself, I must also answer questions about other people and that if I refuse to do so, I can be cited for contempt. My counsel tells me that if I answer questions about myself, I will have waived my rights under the Fifth Amendment and could be forced legally to answer questions about others. This is very difficult for a layman to understand. But there is one principle that I do understand: I am not willing, now or in the future, to bring bad trouble to people who, in my past association with them, were completely innocent of any talk or any action that was disloyal or subversive. I do not

like subversion or disloyalty in any form and had I ever seen any I would have considered it my duty to have reported it to the proper authorities. But to hurt innocent people whom I knew many years ago in order to save myself is, to me, inhuman and indecent and dishonorable. I cannot and will not cut my conscience to fit this year's fashions, even though I long ago came to the conclusion that I was not a political person and could have no comfortable place in any political group.

I was raised in an old-fashioned American tradition and there were certain homely things that were taught to me: to try to tell the truth, not to bear false witness, not to harm my neighbor, to be loyal to my country, and so on. In general, I respected these ideals of Christian honor and did as well with them as I knew how. It is my belief that you will agree with these simple rules of human decency and will not expect me to violate the good American traditions from which they spring. I would, therefore, like to come before you and speak of myself.

I am prepared to waive the privilege against self-incrimination and to tell you anything you wish to know about my views or actions if your Committee will agree to refrain from asking me to name other people. If the Committee is unwilling to give me this assurance, I will be forced to plead the privilege of the Fifth Amendment at the hearing.

A reply to this letter would be appreciated.

Sincerely yours,
Lillian Hellman.

The answer to the letter, also read into the record, is as follows:

Dear Miss Hellman:

Reference is made to your letter dated Mar 19, 1952, wherein you indicate that in the event the committee asks you questions regarding your association with other individuals you will be compelled to rely upon the fifth amendment in giving your answers to the committee questions.

In this connection, please be advised that the committee cannot permit witnesses to set forth the terms under which they will testify.

We have in the past secured a great deal of information from persons in the entertainment profession who cooperated wholeheartedly with the committee. The committee appreciates any information furnished it by persons who have been members of the Communist Party. The committee, of course, realizes that a great number of persons who were members of the Communist Party at one time honestly felt that it was not a subversive organization. However, on the other hand, it should be pointed out that the contributions made to the Communist Party as a whole by persons who were not themselves subversive made it possible for those members of the Communist Party who were and still are subversives to carry on their work.

The committee has endeavored to furnish a hearing to each person identified as a Communist engaged in work in the entertainment field in order that the record could be made clear as to whether they were still members of the Communist Party. Any persons identified by you during the course of committee hearings will be afforded the opportunity of appearing before the committee in accordance with the policy of the committee.

Sincerely yours,
John S. Wood, *Chairman*[5]

COMMUNIST INFILTRATION OF THE HOLLYWOOD MOTION-PICTURE INDUSTRY—PART 8

HEARINGS

BEFORE THE

COMMITTEE ON UN-AMERICAN ACTIVITIES HOUSE OF REPRESENTATIVES

EIGHTY-SECOND CONGRESS

SECOND SESSION

MAY 19, 20, AND 21, 1952

Printed for the use of the Committee on Un-American Activities

UNITED STATES
GOVERNMENT PRINTING OFFICE
WASHINGTON : 1952

Above and opposite: The printed, and therefore public, transcript of Lillian Hellman's May 21, 1952, appearance before HUAC (author's collection).

Nine. The Name on the Marquee

COMMUNIST INFILTRATION OF THE HOLLYWOOD MOTION-PICTURE INDUSTRY—PART 8

WEDNESDAY, MAY 21, 1952

UNITED STATES HOUSE OF REPRESENTATIVES,
COMMITTEE ON UN-AMERICAN ACTIVITIES,
Washington, D. C.

PUBLIC HEARING

A subcommittee on the Committee on Un-American Activities met, pursuant to recess, at 11 a. m., in room 226, Old House Office Building, Hon. John S. Wood, chairman, presiding.

Committee members present: Representative John S. Wood and Francis E. Walter.

Staff members present: Frank S. Tavenner, Jr., counsel; Thomas W. Beale, Sr., assistant counsel; John W. Carrington, clerk; Raphael I. Nixon, research director; and A. S. Poore, editor.

Mr. WOOD. The committee will come to order. Let the record show that for the purpose of the hearing I as chairman have set up a subcommittee consisting of Mr. Walter and myself.

Who do you have?

Mr. TAVENNER. Miss Lillian Hellman.

Mr. WOOD. Will you raise your right hand. Do you solemnly swear the evidence you will give to this subcommittee shall be the truth, the whole truth, and nothing but the truth, so help you God?

Miss HELLMAN. I do.

TESTIMONY OF MISS LILLIAN HELLMAN, ACCOMPANIED BY HER COUNSEL, JOSEPH L. RAUH, JR.

Mr. WOOD. Are you represented by counsel?
Miss HELLMAN. Yes, sir.
Mr. WOOD. Counsel will please identify himself for the record.
Mr. RAUH. My name is Joseph L. Rauh, Jr., 1631 K Street.
Mr. WOOD. In Washington?
Mr. RAUH. Washington, D. C.; yes, sir.
Mr. WOOD. Thank you, sir.
Mr. TAVENNER. You are Miss Lillian Hellman?
Miss HELLMAN. Yes, I am.
Mr. TAVENNER. Where were you born?
Miss HELLMAN. I was born in New Orleans, La., in June 1905.
Mr. TAVENNER. Where do you now reside?
Miss HELLMAN. I reside at 63 East Eighty-second Street, New York City.

Hellman's testimony continued and, true to her letter, she found that the only thing left to do was to assert her privilege and use the Fifth Amendment to decline to answer the committee's questions.

The Children's Hour revival opened on December 18, 1952. On December 30, 1952, the conservative columnist Victor Lasky, upon seeing Brooks Atkinson's Sunday piece in the *New York Times*, wrote him a letter. It said in part,

> ... my mind flashed to the more recent testimony given by Miss Hellman before the House Un-American Activities Committee. On the basis of her testimony, would you say I'd be slandering Miss Hellman if I termed her one of Broadway's leading agents for Joe Stalin, who probably did more for Joe Stalin's bloody cause than did her producer, Mr. Herman Shumlin? Well, I'm willing to produce the facts of Miss Hellman; but, of course, there's a new fad on these days. Anyone calling a Red a Red is a witch-hunter.[6]

Atkinson answered the letter the next day using the familiar tone he took when answering such letters:

> Your letter raises a familiar problem. Am I supposed to review what I see on the stage or the outside activities of the author? I have given this question a good deal of

This production photograph is from the premiere production of Lillian Hellman's *The Children's Hour* that ran on Broadway from 1934 to 1936. Left to right: Robert Keith, Anne Revere (the only original cast member in this photograph), Florence McGee, Katherine Emery and Katherine Emmett (Photofest).

thought over the last few years and have concluded that my sole concern is with the material I see on the stage. It seems to me and apparently to most of the other reviewers that "The Children's Hour" is an excellent play. It seems to me my function is to say so.[7]

This revival of *The Children's Hour* closed on May 30, 1953. Hellman's play *The Lark* ran on Broadway in 1955. She wrote the book for the musical *Candide*, which opened in 1956. February of 1960 saw a new Hellman play, *Toys in the Attic*. It received six Tony Award nominations. Of the six, it won two. Best Supporting Actress in a Play went to the blacklisted actress Anne Revere of *National Velvet* fame, who had also been a member of the original company of *The Children's Hour*, while the Tony for Best Scenic Design went to Howard Bay, whose name could be found in the ubiquitous *Red Channels*. But if Broadway belonged to anyone in 1953, it was *Death of a Salesman*'s Arthur Miller and his little skit about witches.

Opening night of Lillian Hellman's *The Lark* that opened on Broadway in November of 1955, three months after the 1955 HUAC "theater" hearings. Left to right: Julie Harris, Boris Karloff, playwright Lillian Hellman and producer Kermit Bloomgarden (Wisconsin Center for Film and Theater Research).

The Crucible opened on Broadway on January 22, 1953, to less-than-stellar notices. But one cannot necessarily trust the critics. Arthur Miller's allegory of the HUAC investigations ran for 197 performances and won the Tony Award as the Best Play of 1953. In addition, Beatrice Straight, the actress playing Elizabeth Proctor, won the award for Best Featured Actress in a Play. In his autobiography *Timebends*, Miller explains why he chose this particular comparison:

> The main point of the hearings, precisely as in seventeenth-century Salem, was that the accused make public confession, damn his confederates as well as his Devil master, and guarantee his sterling new allegiance by breaking disgusting old vows—whereupon he was let loose to rejoin the society of extremely decent people. In other words, the same spiritual nugget lay folded within both procedures—an act of contrition done not in solemn privacy but out in the public air.

HUDSON THEATRE

KERMIT BLOOMGARDEN
presents

JASON   MAUREEN   IRENE
ROBARDS, Jr.   **STAPLETON**   **WORTH**

in

LILLIAN HELLMAN'S
New Play

TOYS IN THE ATTIC
with
Anne Revere

ROCHELLE OLIVER   PERCY RODRIGUEZ

Directed by
ARTHUR PENN

Setting and Lighting by   *Costumes by*
HOWARD BAY   **RUTH MORLEY**

CAST
(In order of appearance)

Carrie Berniers	MAUREEN STAPLETON
Anna Berniers	ANNE REVERE
Gus	CHARLES McRAE
Albertine Prine	IRENE WORTH
Henry Simpson	PERCY RODRIGUEZ
Julian Berniers	JASON ROBARDS, JR.
Lily Berniers	ROCHELLE OLIVER
Taxi Driver	WILLIAM HAWLEY
3 Moving Men	CLIFFORD COTHREN, TOM MANLEY, MAURICE ELLIS

Place: The Berniers house in New Orleans.

ACT I.
Six P.M. on a summer Tuesday.

ACT II.
Eight A.M. the following morning.

ACT III.
Shortly after.

Lillian Hellman's *Toys in the Attic* opened in the 1960 Broadway season. Yet again Hellman's name is as big as the title of her play. She never worked under an alias (author's collection).

Nine. The Name on the Marquee

It was only one year earlier, 1952, that Miller had broken off relations with one of his closest friends and collaborators, Elia Kazan, when Kazan chose to name names before HUAC. Kazan had directed Miller's first two plays, *All My Sons* and *Death of a Salesman*, to great acclaim and a Tony Award for each production. They didn't work together again until 1964, when Kazan directed Miller's semi-autobiographical play *After the Fall*. Miller, after being denied a passport, performed his own interesting song and dance before HUAC in 1956, defending art, relationships, and his production of *The Crucible*.

Blacklisted actress Anne Revere won a Tony Award for her part in *Toys in the Attic*. It is interesting to note that her understudy was Sarah Cunningham, another victim of the blacklist (Wisconsin Center for Film and Theater Research).

MR. MILLER: In relation to censorship, I have always had the same opinion.
MR. SCHERER: This is not censorship.
MR. MILLER: Perhaps I used the word closely, but in relation to the limitation of the artist's right in society, I am opposed to it.
MR. SCHERER: All of us believe in freedom.
MR. KEARNEY: You are putting the artist and literature in a preferred class.
MR. MILLER: I thought we were going to get to this and it places me in a slightly impossible position, and I would be lying to you if I said that I didn't think the artist was, to a certain degree, in a special class. The reason is quite simple and maybe absurd, but if you are asking me what I think, I will tell you.
MR. JACKSON: One brief question.
THE CHAIRMAN: Let him finish that question.
MR. MILLER: I would like to answer Mr. Kearney.
MR. JACKSON: Very well, sir.
MR. MILLER: Most of us are occupied most of the day in earning a living in one way or another. The artist is a peculiar man in one respect. Therefore, he has got a peculiar mandate in the history of civilization from people, and that is he has a mandate not only in his literature but in the way he behaves and the way he lives.
MR. SCHERER: He has special rights?
MR. KEARNEY: Please.
MR. MILLER: I am not speaking of rights.
MR. KEARNEY: I would like to have the question I asked answered.

THE CHAIRMAN: He is trying to answer.
MR. KEARNEY: There are interruptions.
MR. MILLER: The artist is inclined to use certain rights more than other people because of the nature of his work.
Most of us have an opinion. We sit once or twice a week or we may have a view of life which on a rare occasion we have time to speak of. That is the artist's line of work. That is what he does all day long and, consequently, he is particularly sensitive to its limitations.
MR. KEARNEY: In other words, your thoughts as I get it is that the artist lives in a different world from anyone else.
MR. MILLER: No, he doesn't, but there is a conflict I admit. I think there is an old conflict that goes back to Socrates between the man who is involved with ideal things and the man who has the terrible responsibility of keeping things going as they are and protecting the state and keeping an army and getting people fed.[8]

As the hearing continued, the committee asked about comments Miller had purportedly made about his former friend, Elia Kazan. Miller stated unequivocally, "I have never made the statement about Elia Kazan's testimony in my life."[9] The committee continued asking about Miller's donations and involvement with various organizations leading up to this exchange:

MR. ARENS: Now, I believe you alluded a few moments ago to your play the Crucible, is that correct?
MR. MILLER: Crucible.
MR. ARENS: Yes, sir.
MR. MILLER: Yes.
MR. ARENS: Are you cognizant of the fact that your play the Crucible with respect to witch hunts in 1692 was the case history of a series of articles in the Communist press drawing parallels to the investigations of Communists and other subversives by congressional committees?
MR. MILLER: I think that was true in more than the Communist press. I think it was true in the non–Communist press, too. The comparison is inevitable, sir.

Three years after *The Crucible* played on Broadway, Arthur Miller appeared before HUAC on June 22, 1956. Smoking was much more prevalent in those days (Photofest).

Nine. The Name on the Marquee

MR. ARENS: What have been your activities or associations with Howard Fast?
MR. MILLER: In what respect?
MR. ARENS: Do you know him?
MR. MILLER: I have met him.
MR. ARENS: How long do you know him?
MR. MILLER: I don't know how to describe that.
MR. ARENS: Well, have you collaborated with him?
MR. MILLER: Collaborated with him?
MR. ARENS: Yes, sir.
MR. MILLER: No, sir.
MR. ARENS: Are you cognizant of the promotion of yourself by Howard Fast?
MR. MILLER: No
MR. ARENS: I lay before you a copy of the Communist Daily Worker of November 8, 1955, "I Propose Arthur Miller as the American Dramatist of the Day, by Howard Fast." Were you cognizant of his promotion of yourself as the dramatist of the day?
MR. MILLER: Let me say one thing about that sort of thing. The appreciation of dramatic values by people who have behind them an attachment, a remorseless attachment to the political line, is of no import to me. I don't believe it when they are against me and I don't believe it when they are for me. In this case I take no compliment out of this for one simple reason. That is, it happens that the Crucible, which, by the way, I began thinking about in 1938 and which they now say was written about the Rosenbergs about whom I had not heard when I started to write this play, it happened that the line in that play coincided at that moment. I have another example of that which I will go into. This is not literary or dramatic criticism. This is a political article. You are taxing me with what he says. Now, the next play, as with Death of a Salesman which they called "A decadent piece of trash," in the Daily Worker, they were against it. I am not going to guide myself by what they think or don't think. From time to time I am sure Howard Fast or similar critics of plays have praised or blamed one or another of a hundred writers, all of whom you can't tax with that criticism. It isn't fair.[10]

It helps to note that Miller was at this hearing because he wanted to renew his passport, which he let lapse when he had an earlier problem. He also stated that he wasn't very interested in traveling at that time. Now he wanted to go to England for work and to marry his then girlfriend, Marilyn Monroe.

As the hearing proceeded, he was eventually asked about a meeting he attended and, of course, once he admitted going to the meeting, the committee wanted names. His answer was an echo of Lillian Hellman's letter.

MR. ARENS: Can you tell us who was there when you walked into the room?
MR. MILLER:. Mr. Chairman, I understand the philosophy behind this question and I want you to understand mine.
When I say this I want you to understand that I was not protecting the Communists or the Communist Party. I am trying to and I will protect my sense of myself. I could not use the name of another person and bring trouble on him.

These were writers, poets, as far as I could see, and the life of a writer, despite what it sometimes seems, is pretty tough. I wouldn't make it any tougher for anybody. I ask you not to ask me that question.
(The witness confers with his counsel.)
I will tell you anything about myself, as I have.[11]

For anyone who has been following this extended story, it should now be understood that one cannot answer only what one wants in a hearing such as this. Not long after this appearance, Miller was cited for contempt of Congress. As to his passport, when Congress was discussing the matter, they received a visit from Miss Monroe, who agreed to be photographed with various congressmen. In due time, his contempt citation was thrown out, and he got the passport that brought him to England and a marriage to Marilyn Monroe. As for *The Crucible*, like *Death of a Salesman*, it continues to be produced on a regular basis all over the world and has been revived on Broadway four times. In the introduction to the 1959 Bantam paperback of the play, the critic Richard Watts, Jr., wrote,

> It represents quite a victory for Mr. Miller that his play should grow in stature with the passing of time. For it is now clear that "The Crucible" was another victim of a sinister epoch in our history. It isn't that the play has improved, but that the atmosphere surrounding it has. It was judged as a kind of political pamphlet for the stage, when it was actually a work of dramatic art all the time.[12]

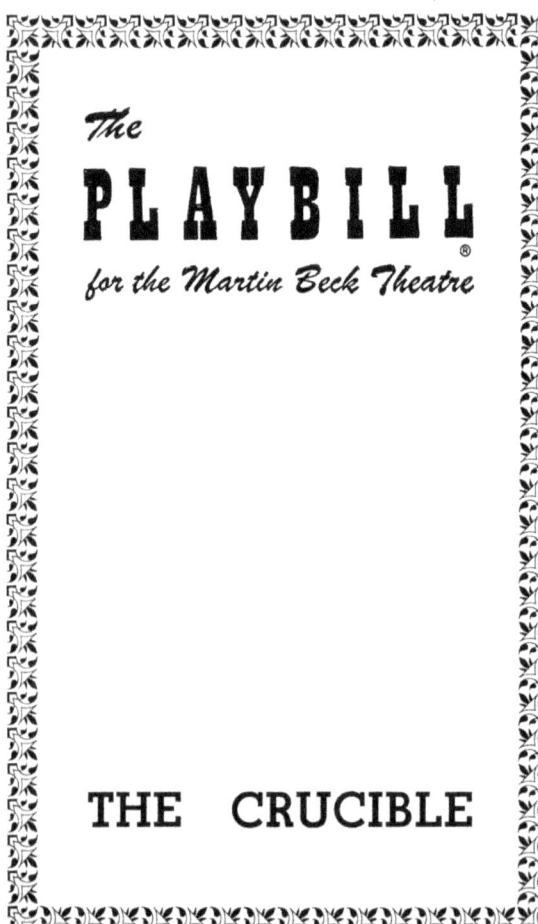

Above and opposite: Although Miller's name in 1953 was not as prominent as Hellman's, it was his name and no one else's. Once again Kermit Bloomgarden is at the helm (author's collection).

Nine. The Name on the Marquee   133

Martin Beck Theatre

Operated by Martin Beck Theatre Corp. — 302 West Forty-fifth Street — Louis A. Lotito, Managing Director

FIRE NOTICE: The exit indicated by a red light and sign nearest to the seat you occupy is the shortest route to the street. In the event of fire please do not run—WALK TO THAT EXIT.
JACOB GRUMET
FIRE COMMISSIONER

Thoughtless persons annoy patrons and distract actors and endanger the safety of others by lighting matches during the performance and intermissions. This violates a city ordinance and renders the offender liable to ARREST. It is urged that all patrons refrain from lighting matches in the auditorium of this theatre.

THE · PLAYBILL · A · WEEKLY · PUBLICATION · OF · PLAYBILL · INCORPORATED

Week beginning Monday, February 2, 1953 • Matinees Thursday and Saturday

IN THE EVENT OF AN AIR RAID ALARM REMAIN IN YOUR SEATS AND OBEY THE INSTRUCTIONS OF THE MANAGEMENT.—HERBERT R. O'BRIEN, DIRECTOR OF CIVIL DEFENSE.

KERMIT BLOOMGARDEN
presents

The JED HARRIS Production of

ARTHUR MILLER'S

THE CRUCIBLE

Starring

ARTHUR KENNEDY   WALTER HAMPDEN
with
BEATRICE STRAIGHT   E. G. MARSHALL

Staged by JED HARRIS

Scenery designed by BORIS ARONSON

Costumes designed by Edith Lutyens

CAST
(In Order of Appearance)

BETTY PARRIS	JANET ALEXANDER
TITUBA	JACQUELINE ANDRE
REVEREND SAMUEL PARRIS	FRED STEWART

GILBEY'S PRESENTS
Spey-Royal Scotch

with "the flavor that Nature made famous"

Gilbey's Spey-Royal Blended Scotch Whisky. 86.8 Proof...100% Scotch Whiskies. Distributed by National Distillers Products Corp., New York, N. Y.

Finally, and most importantly, there was no blacklist on Broadway. Yes, Actors' Equity got anti-blacklisting into their contract, but credit is also very much due to any number of producers who saw in this and other work something worth presenting, and in the interest of full disclosure, some producers did hire certain "blacklisted" theatre artists at a reduced fee which found some paid only what the unions required, even if prior to this period they might have been paid well above minimum. The producers also sometimes suffered the consequences of their hiring decisions. Kermit Bloomgarden, who brought us the plays of Lillian Hellman and Arthur Miller as well as *The Diary of Anne Frank*, received a subpoena to appear before the committee in 1957. Subsequently, and with no reason given, the subpoena was dismissed. In the same boat was Bloomgarden's good friend and often collaborator Herman Shumlin, who produced and directed Hellman's earlier plays including the original production of *The Children's Hour*, *Watch on the Rhine*, and *The Little Foxes*. In 1955 he served both duties again when he presented Jerome Lawrence and Robert E. Lee's *Inherit the Wind*. Shumlin also received a subpoena from HUAC which was later dismissed.

Two producers actually made it as far as executive sessions, but nothing every played out in public hearings. Lee Sabinson had produced *Finian's Rainbow* with music by E. Y. (Yip) Harburg, who was among those listed in *Red Channels*. This found Sabinson called on the carpet by Hartnett's *Counterattack*. The committee thought that producer Bernard Schoenfeld could help them out, but it was not to be. He was also never called to a public hearing. With the exception of the 1955 and 1958 hearings, little was done to the theatre community, and the work continued.

In 1956, HUAC spent days questioning John Cogley, the author of the Fund for the Republic's study *Report on Blacklisting*. Hidden deep in the second volume, which looks at radio and television, is a small but telling section on theatre. Cogley sums up his study as follows:

An early rehearsal shot for *The Crucible*. Left to right: the actor Walter Hampden who played Deputy-Governor Danforth, Miller, and the director Jed Harris (Photofest).

Nine. The Name on the Marquee

Starring as John and Elizabeth Proctor in *The Crucible* were Arthur Kennedy and Beatrice Straight. Straight won the Tony Award for her performance (Photofest).

It is impossible to estimate the role of the intangibles in the theatre and equally impossible to omit them from a discussion of blacklisting. In Hollywood and in radio-television, artistic life has yet to create its own traditions. "There's no business like show business," the dedication to the individualistic, personal milieu of the stage, has been appropriated by the mass entertainment world. Yet on Madison Avenue it has no real roots.... But in the legitimate theatre, tradition still remains intact and functional. The agreement between Equity and the League of New York Theatres, even though it has had little practical value, expresses an attitude, and the attitude is probably more important than any complicated machinery of arbitration...

In and of itself, Equity's experience is noteworthy. It also serves to point up the contrast between Broadway and the mass media. For every element that has worked to keep blacklisting out of the Broadway theatre is absent in the mass media; conversely, it is exactly at those points where the movies and television are unlike the theatre that they are most susceptible to blacklisting pressure...

The movies and radio-tv capitulated to pressure almost as soon as it was applied. The theatre laid down a program to fight the pressure, primarily through the joint action of unions and management....

In a way, it may well have been this element of radian which worked to bring about a sane union situation in Equity. For the ideological mentality of the extreme right militates against the tradition of the theatre, just as the business structure of the movie industry is alien to that tradition...

The result is that the theatre has a better conscience: it is free. The characteristic attitude of industry people in Hollywood or on Madison Avenue is compounded of fear and shame. The theatre people are proud that they have not succumbed. They are proud of their tradition and proud that they have lived by it, even during a period of great stress and assault.[13]

Even as the likes of plays by Miller and Hellman are continually revived and often turned into movies, and even as the careers of formerly blacklisted actors continue to be rewarded, Cogley's words serve to send a chill down the spine of anyone who wonders how the purveyors of today's theatre, the theatre of big conglomerates and mega-stars, might react if faced with a similar situation. In spite of what happened with the hearings in 1955 and testimony like Miller's in 1956, the committee just couldn't quite give up and decided to try one last time to call out the theatre and its related constituents.

Ten

Investigating Broadway ... Again
The 1958 HUAC Hearings

If the witnesses who came before the committee in 1955 "were several steps below star rank"[1] and considered scraping the bottom of the barrel, it begs the question as to why Francis Walter sent the committee back to New York in 1958. If he had a crystal ball, he might have known that 1958 was a mere two years before the film industry blacklist would start to unravel when Dalton Trumbo, one of the Hollywood Ten, saw his own name in the screen credits as writer of both *Exodus* and *Spartacus*. Nonetheless, the hearings occurred even though Walter himself did not deign to make the trip north for the hearings that paid lip service to the notion that the committee was still looking at the theatre community. In his stead, Representatives Morgan M. Moulder (D–Missouri), William H. Tuck (D–Virginia), and Gordon H. Scherer (R–Ohio) alternately filled the chairman duties during the proceedings along with Staff Director Richard Arens. One of the investigators on the committee payroll, Donald T. Appell, was also present during the hearings. Only Scherer and Appell had been present in 1955.

In some ways this hearing was a follow-up to a 1957 hearing also headed by Representative Moulder. That hearing was held

> ... for the purpose of routing out some three dozen musicians associated with the Metropolitan Music School, the Symphony of the Air, and Local 802 of the Musicians Union who had been identified as Communists and duly took the Fifth Amendment.[2]

At the opening of this hearing, Moulder went into more detail as to why they had returned to the Foley Square courthouse yet again:

> This series of hearings by the Committee on Un-American Activities is for the purpose of taking testimony from individuals who, according to investigation, possess knowledge necessary for the consideration of legislation presently pending before the committee. The witnesses called maintain themselves economically by employment

in the entertainment mediums. However, they have been subpenaed [sic] because they possess knowledge of the manner and method by which the Communist Party operates or has operated in the United States by infiltration in the entertainment field. If the witnesses did not possess such knowledge, neither they not their field of employment would be of interest to this committee.

We are interested in learning from these witnesses the extent to which the Communist Party uses talent, similar to the talent of the witnesses under subpoena [sic], for the purpose of facilitating the Communist Party program or assisting the party in formulating or financing its front activities.

Of the 19 witnesses called in 1958, six might be considered leftovers from those 1957 hearings. As to the 13 remaining, five were actors, while the rest were a potpourri of other entertainment workers. Of this group, 18 did not cooperate. The nineteenth was John Lautner, who described himself as a "Government consultant"[3] and provided the committee a respite from the ongoing witness refusals to answer the usual questions. In the committee files there is no information whatsoever on Mr. Lautner. Indeed, these hearings might have been left out of this story completely except for the fact that most of the actors had appeared in groups explored in earlier chapters (the Federal Theatre Project, the Group Theatre and/or the Actors' Lab) and that two of the uncooperative witnesses went on to become two of the most influential leaders in the New York theatre community: Joe Papp, who at the time was a stage manager at CBS and the director of the newly minted New York Shakespeare Festival, which had only recently started free Shakespeare in Central Park, and Bernard Gersten, Papp's friend, colleague and fellow stage manager, who was spending his summer working for the American Shakespeare Festival in Stratford, Connecticut.

The feeling of 1958 as an afterthought is emphasized by much of the archival material. Most of the files are small, with less detailed materials leaving the researcher bereft of the type of memos (save for Joe Papp's) that made the earlier subpoena service so fascinating. Strikingly, in 1958, the landscape for these hearings themselves differed in several significant ways from those of 1955 and earlier. The Supreme Court, whose decision in 1950 sent the Hollywood Ten to jail, handed down two decisions which greatly influenced how witnesses could be made to answer questions: *Watkins vs. the United States* in 1957 and *Sweezy vs. New Hampshire* in the same year. Early on in her testimony, actress Adelaide Klein Annenberg referenced these two cases in her prepared statement on her refusal to answer. Most striking is that in all prior committee hearings, including those in 1955, statements by witnesses the committee expected to be uncooperative were not allowed to be read under any circumstances.

    Mr. Arens: Are you a member of the Communist Party?
    Mrs. Annenberg: I respectfully decline to answer the question.

Ten. Investigating Broadway ... Again

Photographs of Adelaide Klein are hard to come by. This particular one is from a pre *Red Channels* 1948 television episode of *The Naked City*. Left to right are Don Taylor, Barry Fitzgerald, Adelaide Klein and Grover Burgess. Early television depended on the skills of theater actors. Another interesting note: this episode was directed by Jules Dassin, Oakleaf from the Federal Theatre Project's *Revolt of the Beavers* (Photofest).

MR. ARENS: You are reading from a prepared statement now?
MRS. ANNENBERG: Yes, I am.
MR. ARENS: Did you prepare the statement?
MR. ROSS: [Annenberg's attorney]. I object to the witness being asked if she prepared it.
MR. ARENS: I request that counsel be advised that his sole and exclusive purpose is to advise his client.
MRS. ANNENBERG: I prepared the statement with the help of my attorney.
MR. MOULDER: You have a right to use the statement.
MR. ARENS: Kindly proceed.
MRS. ANNENBERG: I respectfully decline to answer the question Mr. Arens has just asked as I have been informed by my counsel that under the decisions of the United States Supreme Court in the Watkins and Sweezy cases, the powers of this committee are strictly limited [in] the areas of my beliefs, expressions, or associations on the grounds that such questioning constitutes an interference with my rights under the first amendment; that the enabling resolution of this

> committee is in itself an unlawful delegation of power and such questioning is in any event beyond the jurisdiction of this committee; that this question or any like question cannot be pertinent to any legitimate subject of inquiry to which this committee can address itself under its enabling resolution; that the purpose of the question addressed to me and any like questions as well as the requirements of my appearance before your committee today, is for the sake of exposure and for the purpose of doing me personal injury and not for the purpose of pursuing any legitimate subject of inquiry which this committee is lawfully authorized to pursue.
> MR. ARENS: Is that all of the statement?
> MRS. ANNENBERG: That is all.

At this point, as if Annenberg had made no statement at all, the questioning and the refusing to answer proceeded.[4]

The six gentlemen identified as members of the music community included Carroll Hollister, who gave his work address as his home where "I teach singing and coach singers—music in general."[5] The committee probed his involvement with the aforementioned Metropolitan Music School, which prompted the following exchange:

> MR. HOLLISTER: I would find it difficult to understand why it is necessary for this committee to ask this question in order to further the aims of legislation which is required. I have no shame about any employment which I have ever had in my life or have at the present time and, as a music teacher, I would consider that I had rights to seek employment in music at any institution of recognized musical standing.
> MR. ARENS: If you are not ashamed of it, then kindly tell us whether or not you have been employed as an instructor at the Metropolitan Music School.
> MR. HOLLISTER: Yes, sir.
> MR. ARENS: Are you a member of the Communist Party?[6]

The questioning continued with Hollister taking the First and Fifth Amendments regarding his activities both in and out of teaching until he was ultimately excused.[7]

Arthur Lief, "a musician by profession," was also made to identify himself by his birth name, Abraham Lipshutz, which he had changed by court order 25 years earlier.[8] Lief was of interest as his current employment was as a guest conductor for the Moiseyev Dance Company, which would be referred to by Mr. Arens as the "Moiseyev Russian Ballet" and then as just the "Russian Ballet" as the questioning continued.[9]

At the time that violinist and assistant conductor Ben Steinberg came before the committee, he was employed in the orchestra for the Broadway musical *The Music Man*, produced by Kermit Bloomgarden. When asked whether or not a particular musician was a member of the Communist Party, Steinberg replied,

> I would like to read a short statement in answer to this question, please:

> The committee's investigation is not in fact being carried on for the purposes set forth in the resolution creating it. It has harmed one of the finest symphony orchestras in the country—an orchestra whose Far Eastern tour for the State Department was so fantastically successful that official citations were received from Far Eastern governments and foreign musical organizations were formed in its honor.
> It is now 11 years sine the first investigations of cultural artists, and this is the fourth consecutive year in New York City. I consider this an illegal harassment of members of the entertainment industry.
> This is beyond the jurisdiction of the committee as it is defined in the House enabling resolution. It is not pertinent to any subject within the committee's jurisdiction.
> The resolution creating this committee is unconstitutionally vague and, hence, invalid as the Supreme Court held in the Watkins case, and the question put by the chairman invades these privileges which I consider to be my birthright, the freedom of association, and the freedom of religion.
> Since I will not testify as to my own associations and beliefs, I would certainly not testify as to others.[10]

The committee members continued to push the witness to answer. In the case of Steinberg, they also pressed him, and then pressed even further, on taking the Fifth Amendment, which he refused to avail himself of as he did not feel it applied to his situation. There is no record of his ever being brought up on contempt charges such as those that dogged the three witnesses in 1955.

Steinberg was followed in quick order by Paul Villard, a singer and musician who did claim the privilege of the Fifth Amendment and was dispensed with in a matter of moments.[11] The same would be true of music teacher Leon Portnoy.[12] Horace Grenell, the last of the music group, followed Portnoy and refused to even answer what his profession was.[13] According to committee questions, it appears that he was, among other things, "one of the principal operators of Abbey Record Manufacturing Company," the "president of Young People's Records" and the "director of the Jefferson Chorus."[14]

Writer Richard Sasuly, when asked, "For purposes of identification, have you been known under any other name?"[15] began his long string of refusals to answer. Publicist James D. Proctor, after detailing some of his theatre credits including three plays for producer Kermit Bloomgarden, *Look Homeward, Angel*, *The Diary of Anne Frank*, and *A View from the Bridge*, was asked by Mr. Arens, "Are you now, or have you ever been, a member of the Communist Party?"[16] Proctor read his statement and refused to answer the ensuing questions based on the First and Fifth Amendments. The committee's frustration with this witness mounted, leading to the following exchange as to the validity of Proctor taking the Fifth:

> MR. ARENS: Are there persons present in the entertainment industry who, to your certain knowledge are, or in the recent past have been members of the Communist Party?

> MR. PROCTOR: Your questions assumes that I would be in a position to know whether or not there are such people in the entertainment industry, and I decline to answer that question on the grounds previously stated.[17]

This exchange would lead to Mr. Arens announcing,

> I respectfully request the witness be ordered and directed to answer the question in order to test his good faith in the invocation of the fifth amendment. He has no right to invoke that unless he truly apprehends that the information could be used against him in a criminal proceeding.[18]

It is unclear as to why Proctor was singled out for this particular admonishment, but the questioning continued along this line for several pages. Ultimately, Proctor was excused and no charges were brought when the hearings were over.

Called before the committee primarily because he also was a publicist, Irwin Silber identified himself as "a writer, editor, publicist."[19] Over the course of his testimony, unlike Proctor's taking the Fifth leading to Arens' statement, Silber refused to take the Fifth Amendment.

> MR. ARENS: Do you invoke the fifth amendment privileges against self-incrimination in response to the question which is outstanding, namely, are you now a member of the Communist Party?
> MR. SILBER: I have great admiration for the fifth amendment of the Constitution, and I do feel that anyone who invokes the fifth amendment has a shadow cast upon him. However, there is a public recognition, however, that the fifth amendment admits some guilt on the part of the person using the fifth amendment. This is not true in my case, and I do not feel it is necessarily true in the case of people invoking the fifth amendment. However, for that reason, I chose not to invoke the fifth amendment.[20]

There is no indication either in the conclusion of Mr. Silber's testimony, in the committee's report, or in their files, that Silber was brought up on contempt charges.

One director, who primarily did television and not theatre appeared before the committee at these hearings: Charles S. Dubin (Dobronofsky until 1929). In a slightly more witty repartee than some witnesses, Dubin still managed to take the Fifth Amendment for basically all the right reasons by the committee's standards. There was, however, one exchange that in retrospect was quite poignant. When Arens told Dubin, "You can definitely help the Committee on Un-American Activities…," Dubin replied, "Mr. Arens, the best way I can help this committee is to go back to my work of good quality material for the American public."[21]

Dubin's work at this time was as the director of the quiz show *Twenty-One*. Four months after his testimony, the show would be over in what was the beginning of the 1950s quiz show scandals. In a 2003 interview for the Television Academy Archives, Dubin says that he was "unaware of the backstage practices." During the same interview he refers to himself as "one of

Ten. Investigating Broadway ... Again

the lucky ones as I was only out [of work] five years," during which time he made a living directing commercials (which any number of blacklistees would call work). When asked by the interviewer why he, Dubin, was blacklisted, he replied that he "didn't want to name names."[22] At no time during this interview did Dubin discuss his executive session of October 24, 1961, three plus years after his first appearance.

In the room for that session held in Washington, D.C., were, among others, Edwin E. Willis, a Democrat from Louisiana, who interrupted Dubin's opening statement:

> MR. WILLIS: It is pleasing to the committee that you have taken the attitude you have taken. After your refusal and then having a change of heart, for whatever reason, it is heartening and as far as we are concerned we are happy about your experience. We will be glad to hear from you. Our job is not a pleasant one but we are appreciative of your attitude, before you say anything. You may be just as frank as you please.
>
> MR. DUBIN: I want you to know that I am very grateful for the opportunity afforded me to be here because with that change of heart as I indicated change of heart primarily on my part is one of wishing to re-establish myself—that may sound corny as we say in show business, but as a good citizen of these United States of America which I dearly love and primarily that is why I am here.[23]

Unlike the five witnesses in 1955 who filed affidavits that, as stated earlier, did not include names, much to the committee's consternation, Dubin's testimony was extensive and included many names. On January 5, 1963, the committee, at Dubin's request, sent him a copy of his transcript.[24] His five years on the blacklist soon ended as he embarked on what would be an award-winning career as a television director. The actors who appeared at this hearing did not fare quite so well.

Before calling on the first of the actors, the committee called William Lazar (William Lawrence), a "spotter by trade."[25] Lazar was being called because the committee had information that he held or had held a leadership position in the Communist Party as Bill Lawrence. Indeed, the major function of Lautner, the one "cooperative" witness, was to confirm Lazar's involvement in the Party.[26] Lazar did reveal, with his lawyer's consent, that he was born in Russia in 1903, came to the United States in 1921 and was naturalized in 1926. Lazar's testimony, which primarily consisted of taking the First and Fifth Amendments, finally ended with statements from the committee:

> MR. ARENS: Mr. Chairman, I respectfully suggest that we conclude the staff interrogation of this witness. I respectfully suggest now if it meets with the Chairman's approval——
>
> MR. SCHERER: I am going to ask that the committee refer the testimony of this witness to the Department of Justice to determine whether or not denaturalization proceedings can be instituted.

There is no indication that this ever actually occurred.

With the actors now being called, the theatre finally took center stage in these hearings. The first actor to appear was Paul Mann (Yisrol Paul Mann Libman): an "actor, director, and teacher by occupation."[27] Mounting a defense of theater occupied much of the opening statement he was allowed to present.

> I challenge the jurisdiction of the House Committee on Un-American Activities to question me and to conduct his investigation of theater people, basing myself on the Supreme Court decision in the Watkins case.
> The way to build the American theater is to subsidize it—not to investigate it. Our country is in need of a national theater, and not of censorship and blacklist.
> … This committee knows that the Congress is forbidden by the first amendment of the constitution to make any laws infringing on the American theater. Where the Congress cannot legislate, this committee knows well that it is forbidden to investigate—nevertheless, you continue to do so.
> … Your purpose is plain—again blatantly disregarding the law, you wish to publicly punish me, to smear me, and by example to attempt to intimidate other theater people.
> Brooks Atkinson, in the New York Times, says: "Ignorant heresy hunters and bigoted character assassination" are draining "the vitality out of the American theater."
> … The theater needs no certificate of Americanism to make it legitimate—the legitimate theater already exists and will continue to exist without this committee. As a member of the American theatre I need no seal of approval from this committee.
> My Americanism is demonstrated by the fact that for 23 years I have worked as a professional actor, director, and teacher in the theater and my work has been judged and accepted by the American theater community—the audience, the critics, the producers, and my fellow artists. I submit myself and my daily work to their standards of Americanism and not to the McCarthyite standards of this committee.[28]

As Paul Mann, like Lazar before, was a naturalized American having been born in Canada, the questioning took a decidedly different turn:

> MR. ARENS: When did you enter the United States for permanent residence?
> MR. MANN: May I ask the specific legitimate purpose of that question?
> MR. ARENS: Yes, sir. I will be as specific as possible. Among others things, the Committee on Un-American Activities has pending before it legislation which could plug certain loopholes in the immigration and naturalization laws.
> … It is our information that you are a Communist. It is our information that you were probably a Communist at the time your were naturalized as a citizen of the United States….
> MR. SCHERER: I have an additional reason for wanting to know it, particularly in your case. I am going to see that the Department of Justice gets the transcript of this testimony. I am going to make a personal request, even if the committee should decide not to, that the Department of Justice determine whether or not denaturalization proceedings should be commenced in your case because of your activities in the Communist Party.[29]
> MR. MANN: Is that a legislative function of this committee?
> MR. SCHERER: I said that is the additional reason of this committee member—-
> MR. MANN: You are threatening me.
> MR. SCHERER: You can take it as you like.

Mann's testimony played out for a considerable length of time. He was excused and the committee went to lunch. When they resumed they once again called John Lautner, who went on in great detail to answer Mr. Arens' request: "Tell us from the background of your experience, how the Communists in the cultural field serve the cause of the international Communist conspiratorial apparatus."[30] Lautner's testimony, although extensive, never once mentioned the name of Paul Mann. Mann went back to his classes, and there is no record of his naturalization ever being challenged.

Earl Jones (also known as Robert Earl Jones), the next witness, would be most well known today as the father of James Earl Jones. It is purported on IMDB that he "had a deep, mellifluous voice like that of his son." From the very first question Mr. Arens asked about his employment, Earl Jones took the First and Fifth Amendments, so it never came up that he had worked in the Federal Theatre Project. As with many other uncooperative witnesses, Arens challenged him with various clippings from the committee's files:

> I have a clipping from the Sunday Worker (July 17, 1949), to which I want to invite your attention, "Broadway Stars Back Rights Parley." It states: "A group of Broadway stars, musicians, and writers today issued an appeal to their colleagues in cultural fields to join them in supporting the Bill of Rights Conference Saturday and Sunday at the Henry Hudson Hotel." Among the signers are a number of persons—I would estimate a dozen—characterized as Broadway stars who lent their prestige and talent. One is identified here as Earl Jones.
> Please look at the article and see if it refreshes your recollection of lending you name and prestige to that particular enterprise.[31]

As he had previously, Jones refused to answer, and, in just a few more sentences, Arens requested, "I respectfully suggest, Mr. Chairman, that would conclude the interrogation of this witness."[32]

The next witness, Will Lee (né William Lubovsky), spent a bit more time before the committee. Early on Lee willingly gave the committee a list of his theatrical accomplishments, which included numerous credits familiar to readers of the previous chapters. Lee was an actor in Federal Theatre, Jules (John) Garfield's replacement in the Group Theatre's original production of *Golden Boy,* and part of a tour of *The World of Sholom Aleichem.*

Once the list was completed, the question of Communist Party membership and the requisite taking of the First and Fifth Amendments occurred. Lee would be the first of the witnesses to be asked if he had been "one of the promoters of a group known as the Actors' Laboratory, Inc. on the West Coast?" To this question Lee replied,

> The pride and joy of being associated with a theatrical organization that contributes tremendously to the theatrical life of the west coast was an honor that was given to me. I earned it in terms of my theatrical life and not in any other way, and I still hold any relationship to this is still in the freedom of creativity of our country, the right

for theater groups to spring up wherever they have a desire to do so, and work and be judged on the creative efforts of their work and this is my relationship to my life, to my theater, to my films, to my TV and to my teachings.

I will not put myself in the dictatorial position in any way to determine who shall live and who shall not live creatively. If we do that, we are having conformity of a severe nature and I will not be any part of it and hence, in relation to your question, I reserve my rights that are given to me."[33]

Earlier in this chapter, readers met actress Adelaide Klein (Annenberg) who had just closed in the play *Jane Eyre* on Broadway. Her career in radio and television had already come to a virtual standstill and never came back. Clifford Carpenter, who appeared before the committee without counsel, fared a bit better. At the time of the hearing, he was appearing on Broadway in *Sunrise at Campobello*. Six months prior to that he had been in Herman Shumlin's production of *Inherit the Wind*. When asked by Mr. Arens his principal employments for the past few years, he replied, "I have been an actor in the theater, and in the last few years I worked practically not at all in radio and television. I used to do a lot in radio and television."[34] His career in television began again in 1964, but most memorably one could hear Carpenter whenever and wherever Friends of Old Time Radio held their conventions.

In an interview with Bernard Gersten at his Lincoln Center offices, he revealed that he had forgotten all about that Wednesday in June when he went to testify. The summer before this interview, the theatre presented the Jules Feiffer play *A Bad Friend*, about a young girl in the Brooklyn of 1953 whose parents were Communists. According to Gersten, it was his daughter who found his testimony and brought it to him. In preparation for the production, they did a reading of his testimony. Gersten listened attentively and was pleased with what he had said when he appeared.[35]

Like many witnesses in 1955, and the ones who followed him in 1958, Gersten took the committee to task, including challenging "the jurisdiction of counsel to ask these questions"[36] as he continued to depend on the Fifth Amendment when questioned. Prior to his appearance before the committee, Gersten had been a member of the Actors' Lab, and the general manager for *The World of Sholom Aleichem*. His current employment was as a stage manager at the American Shakespeare Festival in Stratford, Connecticut, which found the committee especially interested in the actors employed at the festival. Gersten may not have remembered his testimony, but at the time, he was most prepared:

> MR. ARENS: Is Mr. Will Geer engaged in the American Shakespeare Festival company?
> MR. GERSTEN: I think that committee counsel has this ad in front of him, and he probably has a list of all of the actors. I did not have an alphabetical. We have an equal billing clause that requires, if I mention the name of one member, I must mention the name of all of them, and it is a list of 24 actors, and I do not have them memorized and Mr. Geer is certainly among them.

Ten. Investigating Broadway ... Again   147

> MR. ARENS: To your certain knowledge is Will Geer a member of the Communist Party?
> MR. GERSTEN: I know Mr. Geer as an actor and as a member of the company and I know him no other way, I am afraid.[37]

As his testimony continued, Gersten was asked about other employment, and as a result, provides the reader the rare opportunity of an explanation of how the committee pursues its work:

> MR. SCHERER:....You told us that you stage-managed the Mike Todd show. Are there any other shows you managed?
> MR. GERSTEN: To what does such questions relate?
> MR. ARENS: You are entitled to an explanation. If you tell us the principal employments which you have had, I then intend to interrogate you with reference to each of the principal employments as to any Communist activity in which you may have been engaged as a stage manager—undertaking to do the Communist Party bidding in your activity. This would be in furtherance of the objective of this committee of obtaining factual information respecting Communist activities which might be added to the fund of knowledge this committee has in appraising legislation which is pending before it.
> MR. GERSTEN: I decline to answer any questions in relation to employment on the basis of the fifth amendment.[38]

With growing frustration, the committee turned to another of its favorite targets: union membership and activities within the union. This was a popular area in 1955, but only Gersten is questioned about it in 1958.

> MR. ARENS: Are you presently engaged in any professional organization of people in the entertainment industry?
> MR. GERSTEN: I already told you I am. I work for the American Shakespeare Festival.
> MR. ARENS: I mean a fraternal group of people in the professions.
> MR. GERSTEN: Are you asking me about a trade-union affiliation?
> MR. ARENS: Yes, sir.
> MR. GERSTEN: That has always been a bad question to ask, and congressional committees are not supposed to ask it.
> MR. SCHERER: Senator McClellan's committee has been doing that for weeks.
> MR. GERSTEN: I am a member of the Actors' Equity Association.
> MR. ARENS: Have you held any office or post in Actors' Equity Association?
> MR. GERSTEN: No; I have not.
> MR. ARENS: Have you participated in any of the deliberations of Actors' Equity with reference to the question of issuance of passports to Communists?
> MR. GERSTEN: May I have the question repeated, please?
> MR. ARENS: Do you want to withdraw your last answer?
> Perhaps there was a misunderstanding when I asked you whether or not you participated in any proceedings of Actors' Equity with reference to passports to Communists.
> MR. FAULKNER: [Gersten's attorney]. Mr. Gersten was inquiring whether you had a stool-pigeon in Actors' Equity.
> MR. ARENS: What do you mean?

MR. GERSTEN: I wonder how the views come before a congressional committee.
MR. ARENS: I have a publication before me entitled "Equity," June 1958, which is the official organ of this fine organization, Actors' Equity Association. In this magazine I see quoted Bernard Gersten with reference to the matter of the issuance of a passport to international Communist agent Paul Robeson. Now will you tell us whether or not you participated in the deliberations of Actors' Equity with reference to the issuance or denial of passports to Communists!
MR. GERSTEN: It is funny the way you put the question, Counsel. He was a member of our union. He was asked to play a part in a Shakespearean role in Stratford, England, where there is another place where they did Shakespeare. I am interested that a member of our union would be allowed to play in a Shakespearean role when he is offered, and that is what I did, and not the way counsel put it.
MR. ARENS: Tell us whether or not you were a proponent of the issuance of a passport to Paul Robeson.
MR. GERSTEN: Yes, I am afraid that I anticipated the Supreme Court's Monday decision.
... As a matter of fact, as I remember the issue, there was a resolution before the meeting urging that the counsel of Actors' Equity Association support, not propose, support the right of Mr. Robeson, a member of the union, to travel in order to perform in Stratford, England, and I spoke in favor of that resolution....
MR. ARENS: Were you a member of the Communist Party the very instant that you were speaking before the Actors' Equity membership on behalf of the resolution which advocated a passport for Paul Robeson?
MR. GERSTEN: I decline to answer that question on the basis of the fifth amendment.[39]

The ordeal, for the time being, was over. The following year Gersten was hired once again as the stage manager for the American Shakespeare Festival in Stratford, Connecticut, much to the consternation of "five prominent bankers" who resigned as trustees of the Festival. When asked why they had allowed Gersten to continue after testifying in 1958, one of them stated, "The season had just gotten underway and we didn't want to upset things then. We stayed on in the hope that action would be taken this season. But the management saw fit to rehire the stage manager." The Festival chairman of the board and co-director of the Theater Guild responded "that a committee had been appointed to study the Gersten case and had decided to take no action. John Houseman who was the artistic director said that 'artistic continuity was an important factor in rehiring Gersten who has been with the festival for three seasons.'"[40]

In his 2005 interview Gersten opined that no one decided not to come to a show because the stage manager might have been a communist. The next day of the hearings his friend and colleague Joe Papp came before the committee.

In a memo dated August 10, 1956, the ubiquitous Dolores Scotti reported on a visit to the home of one Joseph Papp (Papirofsky). She concluded that she was "reasonably confident that he will take the fifth amendment." But "He could then be an important aspect in the Blacklisting Study of the Fund for the Republic hearings [in July], to establish that at least there is no blacklist. [Vincent] Hartnett asserts that CBS [Papirovsky's employer] knows of his activity."[41] Papp did not get called at that point. In the next memo, dated March 14, 1958, Scotti writes, "I am reliably informed that subject was a 'big wheel in CP on the west coast' and that he has been positively identified as a CP member to the FBI on the west coast." Another obvious reason that Papp is of greater interest is that "The March 6, 1958, issue of the Herald Tribune reports that a drive has been launched to raise $1,000,000 for the Shakespeare Festival under the subject's direction by the sale of 2,000 chairs at $500 each to the public."[42]

And so it came to pass that in a memo headed "Important & Urgent," dated April 25, 1958, Scotti announced that, "Subject has been served with subpoena to appear May 8th. He is enormously important because he is producing the Shakespeare plays in public parks in NYC and a Committee has been formed to raise $1,00,000 for this under auspices of NYC Dept. of Commerce and Public Events."[43] The text of many of Scotti's memos can be found in Appendix B. Due to scheduling conflicts, Papp finally made that appearance on June 19, 1958. At the time of the hearing, Papp was employed by CBS as a stage manager, as well as running the Festival.

Unlike many of the prior testimonies, the committee doesn't get to the "Are you now or have you ever been, a member of the Communist Party?" question until the bottom of page three of a ten page transcript. The committee expends its earlier energies on the Festival and its expenses/funding leading into a brief exchange of his work with the Actors' Lab, the California Labor School, and at People's Drama.

The dapper Joe Papp, aka Joseph Papirovsky, director of the New York Shakespeare Festival (Photofest).

MR. ARENS: During the course of your period of instructing at the California Labor School, the People's Drama School, or the Actors' Laboratory, did you ever recruit anyone into the Communist Party?

MR. PAPIROFSKY: I must decline to answer the question, sir, on the same grounds [the fifth amendment].

MR. PAPIROFSKY: If the intent of that question was whether I used my position to get members into the Communist Party, I must say "No" to that.

MR. ARENS: Did you use your position as director on behalf of People's Drama?

MR. PAPIROFSKY: I taught acting at the People's Drama.

MR. ARENS: I have a therm-faxed reproduction of an article appearing in the Communist Daily Worker entitled, "Theatre Groups, Noted Actors Wire Support to People's Drama."

The wire of support from famous actors signed by half a dozen persons, including Joe Papirofsky, all of the executive committee of Actors' Laboratory Theatre, reads in part:

Outraged at news of brutal hoodlum attack on Actors. Flagrant display of direct censorship.

Kindly look at that article which Mr. Appell is now displaying to you and tell this committee whether or not it refreshes your recollection, whether or not you used you prestige in the entertainment industry in that protest.

MR. PAPIROFSKY: I must say my answer is still unchanged, sir. I have always been opposed to censorship and I would send another wire if there were censorship again, lending my support to an attack of this kind, because this was a direct attack on these people and I felt at the time it was absolutely wrong and I would do it again.

MR. ARENS: Were you a Communist when you sent that wire?

MR. PAPIROFSKY: I must decline to answer on the same grounds.[44]

At this point the hearing is still far from over. The committee asks Papp about negative comments he made about the actor Larry Parks when Parks cooperated with the committee in 1951. Further on, Papp presented a copy of a magazine published by the State Department as well as Voice of American Tapes he made, while continually being asked about his "membership in the Communist Party." Finally, Papp's work came into question:

MR. MOULDER: At any time during your professional career or in connection with the work that you are doing at the present time, do you have the opportunity to inject into your plays or into the acting or the entertainment supervision which you have, any propaganda in any way which would influence others to be sympathetic with the Communist philosophy or the beliefs of communism?

MR. PAPIROFSKY: Sir, the plays we do are Shakespeare's plays. Shakespeare said, "To thine own self be true," and various other lines from Shakespeare can hardly be said to be subversive or influencing minds. I cannot control the writing of Shakespeare. He wrote plays 500 years ago.

I am in no position in any plays where I work to influence what the final product will be, except artistically and except in terms of my job as a producer.

MR. MOULDER: My point is, do you intentionally control the operation of the

Ten. Investigating Broadway ... Again

entertainment which you produce or supervise for the purpose of influencing sympathy toward communism? That is my point.

MR. PAPIROFSKY: The answer to that is obviously "No." The plays speak for themselves.[45]

Not long after appearing, Papp was dismissed from his job at CBS. He opted for arbitration and became the first person to win reinstatement during the blacklist.[46] Shakespeare in the Park continued the following summer, and after a few battles royal with Parks Commissioner Robert Moses, the Delacorte Theatre saw its first production in 1962. Years later Papp noted of those 1958 hearings,

> I was not aggressive before the committee; the circumstances were very intimidating. You can't understand, unless you were part of it, how grim those times were. You saw no future after testifying; you didn't see any light at the end of the tunnel. You didn't even see the tunnel for that matter. Even if you took what might be seen as a heroic position, it was hardly something that you ran around bragging about. You just knew that your situation was terrible.[47]

The Delacorte Theatre in Central Park, New York City. (It seems to be a stock photograph as there was no information connected to it, not even a date.)

Perhaps Joe Papp believed what he said when he told the committee, "the plays we do are Shakespeare's plays. Shakespeare said, 'To thine own self be true,' and various other lines from Shakespeare can hardly be said to be subversive or influencing minds"; or perhaps he was being disingenuous. In the summer of 2017, the Delacorte Theatre hosted a production of Shakespeare's *Julius Caesar* that rained controversy. The critic for the *New York Times* wrote,

> ... this "Julius Caesar" is a deeply democratic offering, befitting both the Public and the public—and the times. If in achieving that goal it flirts a little with the violent impulses it otherwise hopes to contain, and risks arousing pro-Trump backlash, that's unfortunate but forgivable. Mr. Eustis seems to have taken to heart Cassius's admonition to Brutus when Brutus is still on the fence about taking action. "Think of the world," he begs. It's a line that cuts two ways.[48]

Several days later the *Times* interviewed the director, Oskar Eustis, and asked him, "Is Trump Caesar?" Eustis replied,

> Of course not. Julius Caesar is Julius Caesar. What we are doing is what we try and do in every production, which is make the dramatic stakes as real and powerful for contemporary people as we can, in our time and our place.

As the Theatre Guild did with the plays of Eugene O'Neill, as the Group Theatre did with *Awake and Sing!*, *Golden Boy*, and so many others, what the Federal Theatre Project did with the *Living Newspaper*, the *Voodoo Macbeth*, and even *Revolt of the Beavers*, theatre can entertain, it can educate, and it can encourage thought and discussion. Every performance has the chance that something might happen that has never happened before, every audience makes a difference, and even a blacklist was unable to stop it or the family that makes theatre happen.

Epilogue

Inscribed on one of the walls of the River Terrace, just outside the Grand Foyer at the Kennedy Center for the Performing Arts in Washington, D.C., are the words spoken by then President John Fitzgerald Kennedy at Amherst College on October 26, 1963, less than a month before his assassination.

> I look forward to an America which will reward achievement in the arts as we reward achievement in business or statecraft. I look forward to an America which will steadily raise the standards of artistic accomplishment and which will steadily enlarge cultural opportunities for all of our citizens. And I look forward to an America which commands respect throughout the world not only for its strength but for its civilization as well.

These words were spoken just a little more than three years after the blacklist began its slow but inexorable death in the motion picture and television industries.

My father had been invited to be a member of the Academy of Motion Picture Arts and Sciences sometime in late 1959 or early 1960 due to his work in special effects. One of the major perks of membership, especially for his then 14-year-old daughter, was the screenings of movies just prior to their public openings. In early October of 1960, we found ourselves at a screening at the Directors Guild of America West. The movie was *Spartacus*. My father's company had made any number of foam rubber bodies that were strewn across the "fields of battle." My brother, almost six years my senior, had been an extra. But nothing could have prepared us for that day in early October. As the lights dimmed in the theatre, the crowd was extremely quiet. There was great anticipation all around us. And then it happened: a single card on the screen crediting the screenplay to Dalton Trumbo, one of the Hollywood Ten. The audience cheered. A similar event occurred two months later when Trumbo once again got credit for writing the screenplay for *Exodus*.

Two years later, December of 1962, we went to a screening of a little film entitled *David and Lisa*. By this time, screenings were our favorite father-daughter activity, and so we went even though we knew nothing about the movie we were about to see. There we were at the Directors' Guild once again, with comfortable seats and no previews. The lights dimmed, the movie started, and then it happened. I think we heard the voice first—I can't be

Phoebe Brand with Will Lee in the original 1953 production of *The World of Sholem Aleichem* (Wisconsin Center for Film and Theater Research).

sure—but then the "doctor" came around the corner. It was Howard da Silva, and he was back making movies. If others gasped or teared up like my father did, I don't remember. It wouldn't be long before more and more familiar faces finally graced the screens of movies and television.

One person who had never stopped working was Elia Kazan. In 1999, the Academy decided that he was deserving of an honorary Oscar for his undeniably excellent canon of work. The challenge before the Academy was that Kazan had named names, and although the blacklist was gone, the scars had yet to completely heal, as if that was even possible. In his 2005 biography of Kazan, the film critic Richard Schickel wrote,

Phoebe Brand Carnovsky at her home in New York City, Tuesday, May 7, 2002 (photograph by the author).

> They [the Academy board] may have also reasoned that his apostasy had, after all, occurred a very long time ago: forty-seven years had passed since this testimony and no one he named was still alive.[1]

I went to a signing of Schickel's book at the Lincoln Center Barnes and Noble. When I finally reached him and handed him my copy of his book, I asked if perhaps when he did the paperback version he would be so kind as to give Phoebe Brand Carnovsky the last five years of her life back.

Phoebe Brand was one of the founding members of the Group Theatre along with, among others, her husband Morris Carnovsky, both of whom were named by Kazan in his 1952 testimony. Both most definitely helped "raise the standards of artistic accomplishment": standards by which many actors attend to even now as they reach for excellence in their chosen profession. Both made that great commitment to theatre and would have embraced what Chita Rivera said at the 2018 Tony Awards: "Theatre is life." As the only person living when Kazan was being given his Oscar, Phoebe was interviewed extensively. Somehow I guess Schickel missed that. I met Phoebe in her New York City apartment on May 7, 2002; she was 94 years old. She died three years later, teaching her last acting class from her hospital bed. If you wanted to talk to Phoebe, she was more than willing. I didn't want to squander my time with her, so I got right to it. My first question was, "Why did you become radicalized?" And that sweet face looked over at me and said, quite simply, "We had no choice."[2]

As the curtain falls, the house lights come up and the play is over ... for now.

Appendix A: McCarthyism
Why No Joe?

When I began to work in this area of study, I was always amazed to find the name Joseph R. McCarthy and McCarthyism given credit (and blame) for everything that happened between 1947 and 1958. After all, McCarthy was first elected to the Senate in 1946 and sworn in in 1947. He went almost unnoticed until February of 1950 when he made his famous speech in Wheeling, West Virginia, displaying his famous list of 205 communists in the State Department. He was censured in 1954 and died in 1957.

I brought up this issue to many of the people I knew who wrote about this period. It was generally agreed that they accepted McCarthyism as a definition of this period in the same way that Xerox is used for all copy machines and Kleenex for all tissues. When I began teaching, this still rankled, and I made sure that at least my students used his name judiciously.

Please note: Joseph R. McCarthy makes only the rare appearance in the pages of this book because, although he is the shadow over this period, he wasn't at any of the hearings quoted in these pages. This bears noting not just because I yearn for historical accuracy, but also because misuse of his name continues to be promulgated even as I write this. Allow me to posit three examples.

In 2008, the University of Michigan Press published a book on Hazel Scott, an extraordinary jazz pianist and the second wife of a Congressman from New York City, Adam Clayton Powell, Jr. Scott testified before HUAC in 1950 because her husband arranged it. On page 142 of this book, the author writes, "In 1947, McCarthy's House Un-American Activities Committee ... began full-fledged investigations of individual citizens, union leaders, and members of the entertainment community."[1] Wouldn't J. Parnell Thomas be surprised, as well as any sixth grade civics student who knows that a senator doesn't chair a House committee.

In his play *Finks*, screenwriter and playwright Joe Gilford fashioned a semi-fictional story of his parents, Madeline Lee and Jack Gilford, as they took on the House Committee on Un-American Activities (HUAC) and the resulting blacklist. The first full mounting of the play was at the Powerhouse Theater on the campus of Vassar College in Poughkeepsie, New York, the college where Hallie Flanagan taught before and after her "adventure" with federally subsidized theatre. I was fortunate enough to be there. As the audience exited the performance that opening night in 2008, I overheard a woman loudly declaim how amazing it was that McCarthy had done so much damage in so many areas. Where did he get the time? I couldn't help myself—I had to join her group and set them straight.

But sadder yet is that this idea carries on even to 2018. In their delicious documentary *RBG*, producer/directors Betsey West and Julie Cohen bring HUAC into their film. In a scene where John Howard Lawson is testifying before the committee in 1947, a well-known and often used shot of McCarthy and Roy Cohn is seemingly spliced in, as they just weren't there. It was so obvious that it caused my brother to call me frantically after seeing this to ask me why hadn't I told him that those two were there?

At a time in our history where the House and Senate are at loggerheads, isn't it time we put the players on their correct stages? Well, it is for me, and so, at least for this story, Joe McCarthy plays a very small part.

Appendix B:
Serving Subpoenas
The Memos of Dolores Faconti Scotti

The files of the various individual witnesses who came before the House Committee on Un-American Activities are available to the public 50 years after an appearance. One need only request them at the National Archives and Records Administration (NARA) in Washington, D.C. If you are first to request a file, it will be vetted by a member of the archival staff before you see it. For the 1955 and 1958 hearings, all of those files were vetted for me.

One of the more intriguing aspects of many of the files was information on the service of the pink (and they really were pink) subpoenas. Sometimes there was only the time and place, sometimes an extensive memo. The most fascinating and informative of these memos were written by a committee investigator, Dolores Faconti Scotti. Born May 4, 1902, Scotti graduated from Fordham Law School and was an Assistant U.S. Attorney for the Southern District while serving as the only female investigator and process server aligned with the committee. Scotti died on December 5, 1979.[1] Her memos are often revealing, often extremely detailed, and rarely dull. The job Scotti had was much more than just serving the subpoena. As a window into the thought process of the committee, these memos are invaluable and deserving of a place in this story. They are in chronological order.

Over the years following all her adventures in blacklisting, Madeline Lee Gilford regaled anyone who came to interview with the tale of how she was served her subpoena by—and she always used all three names—Dolores Faconti Scotti. As Madeline was such a gifted raconteur, many could not believe it really happened the way she described. In 2005, fifty years after her appearance, her file was vetted for me, and the following memo was found. With the exception of how it all ended (Madeline said she called the police), the story was as she had been telling it. It was my pleasure to hand her a copy of the "truth" of what happened on July 13, 1955. In her memo "Service of subpoena on Madeline Lee (Mrs. Jack Gilford)," Scotti wrote:

> On July 12th, I went to the subject's home at 75 Bank Street, N.Y.C., and ascertained that she had sublet her apartment and was summering at Arcadia, Bungalow Walk, Ocean Beach, Fire Island, New York.
> On July 13th I arrived at the above summer address at approximately 11 a.m. The cottage door was wide open. I knocked and called out if there was any one home and there was no answer. The grounds and porch were strewn with toys and playthings so I concluded that the subject was probably at the beach with her children.
> At 12;40 p.m. I saw subject pushing a baby carriage and accompanied by two other children come up the walk (streets, lanes and alleys are called walks at Fire Island). The children first entered onto the path to the cottage. She then turned into it wheeling the carriage. I quickly followed her and called "Mrs. Jack Gilford." She turned, and on seeing me, hastened her step to a quasi-run up the path. I quickly got in front of her and said "Mrs. Gilford I am serving you with a subpoena to appear before the un-American Activities Committee." With this she struck me on the face, neck and shoulder with a sheaf of letters and magazines she was carrying and screamed, "You did not serve me. I did not say I was Mrs. Gilford. I did not identify myself." She raised her arm to strike me again but I extended by arm at full length and warded her off saying "Don't be foolish, I know you and I have served you with a subpoena," and I touched her body with it but she would not take it and it dropped to the ground. I then walked away but was suddenly confronted by her on the road and she hurled torn scraps of paper in my face shouting "This is what I think of your subpoena and I will not accept it." I answered, "I do not care what you do but if you don't answer the subpoena you will be in contempt of Congress" and I walked away.
> At the end of the walk there was a restaurant and bar and I entered to inquire where I might find the police. I was directed down a road midway to the pier. As I turned this corner for the directed road, I was again confronted by subject and she held out the subpoena to me (in her frenzy she must have torn one of her letters because the subpoena was intact). She said "You take this back. You did not effect legal service. I did not say I was Mrs. Gilford." She continued walking alongside of me reiterating this, commenting on my inability to effect a legal service and at intervals asking who was to take care of her children when she went to the city and would the Congress pay travel expenses for all her children. I told her to leave me alone and that I was going to the police to make a report of the incident. She answered that she would report that I had trespassed on her property.
> When we reached the policemen who was standing outside his booth I handed him credentials and stated that I wanted to report the fact that subject had assaulted me while I was serving her with a subpoena. She, in turn, holding the subpoena in hand said to the officer "She served this on me but it is improper service because I did not say I was Mrs. Gilford." The officer asked, "Well, are you Mrs. Gilford?" "I do not care to say–I want to make a complaint against this woman for trespassing on my property." The officer asked "How can you make a complaint if you won't give your name?" "I had the right to make a complaint in privacy without this woman being present and I will then give my name." The officer said, "Well, if you want privacy, just wait outside until I am finished." (We had entered the booth in the course of the foregoing conversation)

I then made a report of the incident and it, together with any report she may have made after I left, in which she would be compelled to give her name, will be part of the police records of the Town of Islip, Long Island.

The officer's name is Harry Alsing, shield number 77.

Subject could be recognized for her picture in 1955 Players' Guide.

In view of the subject's behavior, which was at the very least contemptuous of the Congress, as well as constituting an assault on my person, it is my respectful opinion that she should not be accorded any extensions as among her many remarks, too numerous to be stated here, was her annoyance in having to come into the city during the summer.[2]

The day before serving Gilford, and then again the day after serving Gilford, Scotti went to a single residence to serve subpoenas on the actor John Randolph and his wife, the actress Sarah Cunningham. For her service, Cunningham dropped any pretext of the Southern belle she would be at the hearings. As for Randolph, Scotti found him incredibly charming as one can see from reading the memo. Most memorable for this writer was to find out that he met Scotti while holding his three year-old daughter Martha in his arms. When I shared this information with her she remarked, "Well, I always knew I was a good prop."

On July 12, 1955 I went to the home of John Randolph, Apartment 1B, 561 West 163rd Street, N.Y.C. with a subpoena for him and one for his wife, also known as Sarah Cunningham. I arrived at 9:00 a.m. and rang the doorbell. Mrs. Randolph in curlers and a wrapper opened the door an inch. I gave her my name and stated I was from Washington. She answered that they were show people and still asleep but I asked if she could not see me then as I had come a long way, whereupon she ushered me in the living room and excused herself.

After a brief interval, she returned with a dress on. I showed her my credentials. Incredulously, and as if a cobra had unwittingly got into her living room, she said "You are from that organization. I have nothing to say to anyone who represents it. You should have told me in the first place and I would not have let you in." I explained that I had stated I was from Washington but she answered they had many friends there and she supposed I had come from one of them. She then said "Mrs. Scotti, you will leave my home immediately." I then served the subpoena on her, explaining what it called for, advised her I had one for her husband and asked if she would not be kind enough to talk to him and see if he would accept it. She answered that he was still asleep and she would not wake him.

During the late afternoon of the same day, I telephoned John Randolph requesting whether he would submit himself to service voluntarily or constrain us to issue it to the U.S. Marshall. He answered the he had no desire to evade service and to telephone him on July 14th at 11 a.m.

At the appointed time, I did telephone John Randolph explaining that I would like to proceed to his home immediately for service of the subpoena and would he receive me. He agreed. The subpoena was served at 11:45 a.m.

During our telephone conversation on July 12th, Randolph had explained that while he had no desire to evade a subpoena, the fact was that he was to be continuously engaged in rehearsals and performances throughout August and being under contract for such, could not appear and could the hearing be put over for him. I advised him that I had no authority whatsoever to make any commitments but that if he cooperated in accepting service that would be considered by the Committee in considering any request he might make.

On the morning of service, he again brought up the fact of his continuous engagements and I stated that I would report that he had voluntarily accepted service but that I could do no more.

Randolph was pleasant and friendly. He stated that he was not a Communist nor did he have any attachment to Communist principles. I then asked him why he did not make a statement and cooperate with the Committee and his answer was that he had been raised in the Bronx where the qualities of fair play and good faith were inculcated in a person and he could not see himself squealing on others. I pointed out that he had larger a duty to his country and also one to his little daughter, whom he held in his arms, not to go on record under the shadow of the 5th Amendment. He said he realized this and he also realized that the moment he took the stand he would jeopardize his livelihood but he felt he could not do otherwise. We chatted along in this vein for a while in an amiable manner until the telephone rang, and he terminated the interview.

I received the impression that Randolph does not give a hoot about the Communists or Communism—having probably embraced them in pursuit of his career. I could be completely wrong however. He was at all times, charming and amiable and slickness and sincerity sometimes wear the same face.[3]

The tenacity of Scotti continues to be demonstrated. It took more than two days in 1955 to serve both Lee and Randolph. For time spans, however, Susan D'Usseau seems to have taken the most advantage. One of the more fascinating things about this memo is that at no time does Scotti include the information as to the identity of the husband she is talking to. It is quite possible that D'Usseau was still married to blacklisted screenwriter Arnaud D'Usseau, who himself had been most uncooperative in May of 1953.

July 12. Went to 409 East 58th St. where subject lives. Husband answered doorbell and stated she was not in. Inquired as to my identity but I stated it was not a matter I could discuss with him. Time. 10:05 a.m.

July 14. Went to subject's home again about 9:20 a.m. Husband again answered and again stated that subject was not at home. I identified myself and stated that I had a subpoena I wished to serve; that the last time subject has [sic] been served, the hearing had been put over to suit the convenience of Royal France, the attorney who represented her and in view of this, subject should make herself available for service. Husband answered that he would have to telephone Mr. France and he went inside to do so. He returned stating that Mr. France could not be reached but that he would consult with him and telephone me as to the result. I left my telephone number.

In view of he foregoing incidents, I realized that it would be difficult, if not impossible to serve Mrs. D'Usseau.

I therefor [sic] telephoned Royal France, who had represented her before our Committee, and who had received the courtesy of an adjournment on a previous subpoena with the end result that Mrs. D'Usseau was never heard, the subpoena having been subsequently cancelled, to enlist his cooperation. He was on vacation and not scheduled to return until the end of August.

Serving Subpoenas 163

On Mr. France's return, I telephoned him and explained the situation to him. After several telephone conversations, he advised that Mrs. D'Usseau would make herself available, which she did, service being effected on August 8th.[4]

The committee had been trying to find Sam "Zero" Mostel for some time when he was finally found to be working at the Capri Theatre in Atlantic Beach, Long Island, New York. On July 19, 1955, the omnipresent, and at this point quite well-traveled, Dolores Faconti Scotti set out to serve her subpoena. This would be one of her rare appearances at a theatre, and it proves to be an excellent example of how a theatre family watches out for one of its own:

At 7:30 p.m. on the evening of July 19th, I went to the Capri Theatre Atlantic Beach, Long Island, N.Y., where subject was appearing in the play "My Three Angels" and asked a young lady at the box office if Mr. Mostel had arrived yet. She said he had. I then stated that I wished to see him and could I go back stage. She asked who I was and I told her that I was Mrs. Scotti from Washington. She answered that she did not know just where subject might be but that she would inquire. The entrance to the theatre is also the entrance to a huge cabana colony, a restaurant, a cocktail lounge, each merging into the other.

After a few moments, an elderly man came out and described himself as the stage manager. He wanted to know what I wished to see subject about. I answered that it was confidential. He said that subject had not yet arrived. I answered that I was definitely informed that he was within. He didn't answer directly to this but stated that I could not see subject until after the performance. I then identified myself as on the staff of the Committee and showed my credentials and requested that since I had traveled a distance to see subject, I would appreciate the courtesy of a few moments now, since it was fully one hour before curtain time. He answered that he could tell subject I was waiting to see him.

After ten minutes, a youth came out and advised me that subject had not yet arrived. I again repeated that I knew subject was inside. I was told in any event I could not see him until after the show and that I would have to wait for him to come out at a gate several hundred feet away from the entrance to the theatre. I advised him that I wanted to see subject now and to send out someone in authority.

While he went in, I walked down to the gate I had been directed to. It was locked tight and was merely an entry to one of the cabana groups. It also led to the kitchen, which was empty as the restaurant was closed at that hour. The only performer who could conceivably use it would be a fugitive from justice.

I returned to the entrance to the theatre. It was now past eight o'clock—a full half hour having been consumed in a "royal run-around."

About 8:10 a woman came out and introducing herself as the theatre manager, again inquired what I wanted to see subject about. I again stated that it was confidential and added that I did not appreciate having been directed to the gate below to wait for subject—that if she did not wish to accord respect to me as a person, she and her associates should do so as a representative of a Congressional Committee. She too asked to see my credentials and I obliged. She too went through the routine that she didn't know if subject had arrived, and that I would have to wait until after the performance. I told her that I was tired of the half-truths and untruths, of the run-around, of the lack of consideration and respect not only for me but for the Congress of the United States and requested that she please go to subject, tell him of the fact that I was outside waiting to see him and bring me his personal message as to whether or not he would see me and exactly when, my preference being before the performance so that I could return to the city. She answered that she would see if she could find him.

In about ten minutes, a fourth individual came out and stated that he was the production manager and could I tell him what I wanted to see subject about. I again answered that it was confidential. He then wanted to know if I could guarantee that what I had to say to subject would not distress him and possibly result in a bad performance. Of course, I gave no such guarantee, asserting however that I did not see why it should disturb him.. The production manager, who later gave his name as Stanley Warren, again refused permission to see subject before the performance but did not attempt all of the evasions and lies previously used, basing his refusal on the fact that he did not want to jeopardize a good performance by subject. At this point, I had no alternative but to agree to wait provided that I was shown the exact way to backstage and this Warren did, leading me through the theatre, back of the wings and up a few steps. I ascertained from him that there was no other way that Mostel could slip away and he assured me that there was not.

The show was over about 11:25. While the performers were taking their bows, I slipped back of the wings and waited for subject to come out. Warren was standing alongside and advised subject I was waiting to see him and would we talk in the kitchen, since people would be milling around waiting to see the various performers.

My conversation with Mostel ran along substantially in this fashion:

> S: As you know we are conducting an investigation in the theatre and it was suggested to the Committee that you might want to cooperate with it and make a voluntary statement as to your associations with the Communist party.
> M: No, I will not cooperate with your Committee.
> S: Why?
> M: Because I do not approve of your Committee, its purposes or activities—why then should I help it.
> S: Perhaps, you would be helping yourself.
> M: How so?
> S: Mr. Mostel, this is the end of the line. The Committee will leave no stone unturned to eradicate Communist influence in the theatre. There will not be a single hearing but possibly a series of hearings, at which many witnesses will be called. The smart performer from the viewpoint of self-interest will be the one who will cooperate and make a statement.
> M: Does making a statement mean stooling?
> S: I wouldn't call it that but you will be asked as to your associations.
> M: Then I refuse to make a statement. And now I suppose you will give me a subpoena.
> S: I'm afraid I will have to.

Mostel took the subpoena and the blue book and walked away so quickly that the kitchen door had shut to before I had reached it. As I was about to open it to exit, Mostel re-entered and said:

If I were you I would resign from a Committee that makes you go serving subpoenas like this.

At this point, the production manager came in to say that there were many people waiting to see Mostel and the matter ended there.

I have written this in detail because I am of the firm opinion that Mostel knew from the very beginning, that is at 7:30 p.m., that I was at the theatre and that I was deliberately affronted, lied to, and given the run-around in contempt of the Committee and its process.[5]

Although she didn't appear before the committee in executive session until May 8, 1958, Ethel Everett was the subject of a February 9, 1956, Scotti memo. Everett, a radio actress and orthodox Jew with a reputation for speaking out at union meetings, proved to be a bit of a frustration to her process server.

> Ethel Everett was identified by Ruth Gilbert. I telephoned Everett for an appointment and she advised that she would speak to me only in the presence of her attorney. An appointment was set for January 24th at the office of Herman Gray, 551 Fifth Avenue, N.Y.C.
>
> Ethel Everett categorically denied being a member of the party, asserting that her only activity had been with some front organization for some veteran relief. She was informed that she had been positively identified as being a member of the party and that in fact, one or more meetings had been held in her home. Of course, she expressed surprise and incredulity. Her attorney talked at length of mistaken identifications. When I expressly asked if I was going to be permitted to question Miss Everett, Mr. Gray stated that he wanted an opportunity first to consult with his client, since there had as yet been no opportunity to do so.
>
> The next day I telephoned Mr. Gray and he stated that Miss Everett had asked for a week in which to seek for confirmation of her position among her records.
>
> The week passed and there was no word. I telephoned Mr. Gray again and he stated that Miss Everett had advised that she had never joined the CP but that she had joined the Communist Political Association in 1945 (he did not have the month) in which she had remained until 1946 or 1947 (again he did not have the month of resignation) and that this had been her only association with the party.
>
> I then specifically asked if I was going to be permitted to interrogate Miss Everett, the information I had received from him being inadequate and unsatisfactory for our purposes, especially in view of the fact that she had been positively identified as a member of the party.
>
> Mr. Gray then asked me to defer this because on February 12th Miss Everett is to be operated for a fibroid tumor on the uturus [sic] and she was worried because until the operation there is never definite knowledge as to whether it is benign or malignant. I did not see any alternative but to agree to such deferment and I have diaried this for further inquiry the last week of February.[6]

Everett was eventually served a subpoena on May 8, 1958, to appear before the committee. This time Scotti did not serve the subpoena, but she was present for the hearing.

The actress and teacher Maureen Holbert was the subject of one of Scotti's memos of March 12, 1956, a month after Scotti served Ethel Everett.

> Our files indicate one item only, namely that subject was a director of the Harlem Unity Theatre–DW, Sept. 2, 1949.
>
> In addition to the above, Vincent Hartnett advises that she taught at the Jefferson School during the 1946–1947 season, and that the FBI has information that she attended party meetings; that G-2 [informants were given identifiers like this] has pictures of subject leaving CP meetings with John Randolph and that indeed she is a CP member.
>
> Another informant advises that subject manned the telephones at the offices of Rachel Productions [producers of *The World of Sholom Aleichem*] during early summer of 1955, incidental to setting up the ECLU protest rally held while our hearings where [sic] in progress in July and that she openly identified herself to all callers; also that subject has been active with the left group at AFTRA, especially before elections.
>
> I recently approached subject for an interview relative to her teaching at the Jefferson School and "allied activities." In a frigid and hostile manner, and making no denial, she answered: "I have nothing I wish to say to you. I am not interested in discussing anything at all with you or with any member of your Committee. I have done noting to be ashamed of."
>
> Is there any way of checking the G-2 information as existing and correct?
>
> In view of the foregoing, it would seem that subject is one of most active and vocal to-day and should be subpoenaed for executive session, in all likelihood she will take the 5th Amendment.[7]

Holbert appeared in an executive session on February 7, 1957, where she did take advantage of the Fifth Amendment as Scotti had predicted. She was one of nine at this hearing, at which time only one person's testimony was marked to be released to the public: not Miss Holbert's, but that of Fred Hellerman, another member of the original Weavers singing group.

Prior to his June 19, 1958, appearance before HUAC, Joe Papp was investigated and ultimately served by Scotti. The result was that Papp was the subject of three of her omnipresent memos. The first one was dated August 10, 1956.

> CBS-TV this day advises that subject is employed as stage manager in network operations. He uses the name Papirofsky.
>
> In addition, according to Vincent Hartnett he is associated with the Parks Department of the City of New York in the production of a series of outdoor Shakespearean plays. Here he uses the name Papp.
>
> Subject's front record evidences attachment to the Communist Line.
>
> On a number of occasions this past week I attempted to communicate with subject but he was not available. Each time I left my name and identity with a message to call but he did not do so.
>
> Early this morning I found subject at home, 410 Central Park West, NYC. After identifying myself, I asked him if he would make a statement relevant to his knowledge of Communism. His answer was that he would make no statement at any time. I then advised him that he had been identified as a Communist and he answered that it was not strange that he was constantly being identified as such. I pressed him further as to whether such identification would not prompt him to affirm or deny, or take any position that he might chose and he again refused.

It is my. respectful opinion that he should be called in executive session preliminarily to public session, being reasonably confident that he will take the 5th amendment.

He could then be an important aspect in the Blacklisting Study of the Fund for the Republic hearings, to establish that at least in this instance there is no blacklist. Hartnett asserts that CBS knows of his activities.[8]

The Fund for the Republic hearings had already been held in July of 1956, so it is curious that she should mention it. Perhaps the committee was looking to hold a hearing in rebuttal. It wouldn't be the first time. Scotti's next memo regarding Papp was written on March 14, 1958.

I am reliably informed that subject was a "big wheel in CP on the west coast" and that he has been positively identified as a CP member to the FBI on the west coast.

In my report of interview with the subject, dated August 10, 1956, I advised that he would either affirm or deny CP membership but quipped hat he was being constantly identified and it was of no importance.

The March 6, 1958 issue of the Herald Tribune reports that a drive has been launched to raise $1,000,000 for the Shakespeare Festival under subject's direction by the sale of 2,000 chairs at $400 each to the public.

The article continues that the committee will work in cooperation with the New York City Department of Commerce and Public Events to solicit support of the venture.

Could not the information stated in the first paragraph of this memo be corroborated.

If correct, could not we call Papp in executive session. This seems to be another municipal activity, at least in part, by support of the City Commerce Department, in which Communists play a leading role.[9]

The lack of question marks at the end of a number of these statements is a curiosity and not this typist's error. I wonder if the key was broken. Scotti's next memo, with "Important & Urgent" handwritten across the top, was dated April 25, 1958.

Subject has been served with subpoena to appear May 8th. He is enormously important because he is producing the Shakespeare plays in public parks in NYC and a Committee has been formed to raise $1,000,000 for this under the auspices of NYC Dept. of Commerce and Public Events.

His attorney Ephraim London has just telephones that his subpoena be extended because subject must go to Houston, Texas and furthermore he is busy producing, building stages, etc.

Mr. London asked that subject's examination be put over to sometime in the middle of June, excepting June 17th. If it is necessary to come to Washington, he is willing to waive per diem fee and mileage.

After ascertaining that subject will take the 5th as of January, 1955, I suggested to Mr. London that he address the above request to you [Richard Arens, Staff Director] directly by letter and he said he would.

Since we know what position subject will take with certainty, I do not see any reason why the subpoena should not be extended indefinitely until further notice.[10]

Appendix B

The final memo I found in the files was written by Scotti on July 7, 1957, and was in regards to the possibility that Lee Sabinson might be a worthwhile witness at a public hearing. I will never cease to be startled by just how deep the involvement of the investigators was at this time.

> Immediately after testifying in executive session, subject went to the west coast so that I never did get a chance to interview him.
>
> Since then, the general impression is that Sabinson could prove a fruitful witness for New York hearings. One of the items that has since come up is that when he was the producer of Finian's Rainbow, he must have known CP members in the cast. Communist propaganda regularly appeared not he stage bulletin board.
>
> In his report, Cosstigan says that he should be questioned about James Proctor and E.Y. Harburg.
>
> If you would consider calling Sabinson for open session in NYC, I would suggest the following:
>
> Please let me have a copy of his testimony in executive session. I will study this and attempt to phrase questions on such matters and individuals as it is reasonable, he might have knowledge of. These can be sent either to Mr. Wheeler, or given to Roy Brewer, who has promised his full cooperation if Sabinson has knowledge of anytime he has not yet testified to.
>
> In view of our need for friendly witnesses, the foregoing seems worth he time and trouble. But again I repeat, only, if you would call him for open hearings.

At some point, and it not clear exactly when, whether the same day or a day after, Scotti hand wrote a note at the bottom of the memo: "Since writing foregoing info, [learned] that Walter Winchell once wrote one had to get CP clearance to play in the orchestra for Finian's Rainbow."[11]

Appendix C:
Who's Who in the Cast
of Witnesses in 1955 and 1958

It is traditional that theatre programs have biographical information introducing the actors appearing in a given production, as well as the writers, producers, directors, designers, and stage mangers. The theatre in Chapters One and Two were only required to do cast lists. Over time, Equity and the other professional unions involved negotiated to end up with today's (2018) highly detailed theatre program. Often biographies are done in order of importance: star first, supporting cast, and then, the chorus. A program like the one Bernard Gersten spoke of is usually called "favored nations" and is done alphabetically. This is the order that has been chosen by this "producer." It has also been negotiated that this program information is submitted by or approved by the artist and often the producer. For obvious reasons, that couldn't happen here. What follows is taken from the witness testimony when applicable, newspaper obituaries, personal files at the National Archives, and personal knowledge.

Principal Players

Adelaide Klein Annenberg: Professionally known as Adelaide Klein (she was married to Norman Annenberg), she had closed in the Broadway production of *Jane Eyre* when appearing before HUAC. Klein was born in New York City on July 4, 1901. She joined Actors' Equity in 1938 when she appeared in *Double Dummy* at the John Golden Theatre. Well known on radio for her ability with dialects, Klein also appeared in television on *The Goldbergs, Kraft Theater*, and *Studio One*. Her movies included *Naked City* and *Splendor in the Grass*. Other Broadway credits included *The Immoralist* and *Marathon 33*. Klein died at Lenox Hill Hospital on March 18, 1983, at the age of 82.

Ivan Black: Born Israel Black in Philadelphia, Pennsylvania, on May 14, 1903, he had been living in New York City full time since 1931. He graduated from Harvard with a fine arts degree in 1924 and practiced architecture in Florida for three years before his eyes went bad. He then became a newspaperman writing for the *Boston Transcript*, the *Boston Post* and the *Philadelphia Record* that led to his writing about theater. He has been a public relations counsel and publicity consultant since 1936. He was director of information for the Federal Theater Radio Division. He "was chosen the number one starmaker in the United States ... by 600 editors throughout the United States and Canada" sometime in the mid 1940s. His clients included Lena Horne, Imogene Coca, Patti Page, and Josh White.

Clifford Carpenter: The Poughkeepsie Journal of January 13, 2014, described Cliff Carpenter as "a prolific actor, concerned citizen and activist" when they announced his passing on January 9 at the age of 98. He was born in San Francisco on March 2, 1915. At the time of his appearance before HUAC, Carpenter was appearing in the Theatre Guild production of *Sunrise at Campobello*. Other Broadway credits included *Inherit the Wind*, produced and directed by Herman Shumlin; George Bernard Shaw's *Caesar and Cleopatra*; and *The Andersonville Trial*. But he was best known as a radio actor where he had been the voice of Terry in *Terry and the Pirates*. With his companion, Jean Rouverol, he attended and performed at the Friends of Old Time Radio conventions.

Sarah Cunningham: Born September 8, 1918, in Greenville, South Carolina, her first professional job was in summer stock in Maine and New York. She made her Broadway debut in 1951 in *The House of Bernarda Alba*. In 1953 she appeared in *The World of Sholom Aleichem* as part of a company that included Morris Carnovsky, his wife Phoebe Brand, Jack Gilford and Howard da Silva. On television she played an Amazon on *Buck Rogers* and was also on *Rocky King* and *Treasury Man*. She is a member of AEA and AFTRA.

She was named in *Counterattack, Facts to Combat Communism* (Vol. 7, No. 39) on September 25, 1953, because of her appearance in *The World of Sholom Aleichem*. They said of Cunningham the she "has played in productions of the Committee for Negro in the Arts, the party's Negro cultural front. She is the wife of **John Randolph**, who has an extensive record of front activity."

Charles Dubin (Dobronofsky): Born in Brooklyn on February 1, 1919, Dubin graduated from Brooklyn College and studied at the Neighborhood Playhouse under Sanford Meisner. As a performer he appeared in small parts on Broadway in 1945 and 1947 before finding his true calling as a television director. In his obituary in the *New York Times* of September 9, 2011, they credit him as helping to "shape early television by directing shows like 'Tales of Tomorrow,' a science fiction anthology series, and 'Two Girls Named

Smith,' a comedy series starring Peggy Ann Garner." At the time of his appearance before HUAC, he was working at NBC on the quiz show *21* and had done an episode of *Omnibus*. After testifying, he was fired by NBC. For the next four years, he made a living directing commercials. In 1961, he appeared again, this time cooperating, before HUAC in an executive session. Dubin's career took off once he started working again in 1963 with an episode of *The Defenders,* and from then on he directed many of the most popular shows on television. He died at his home in Los Angeles at the age of 92.

Susan d'Usseau: Born in New York City in 1902, she is an artist and a painter. She is the wife of writer Arnaud d'Usseau who invoked the Fifth Amendment when he testified in 1953.

Her HUAC file lists some of her activities: "Sponsored May Day Parade that included the Communist Party in 1947; was an instructor at the George Washington Carver School that same year; endorsed the National Council of American-Soviet Friendship and the World Peace Appeal; signed the 'Resolution Against Atomic Weapons' of the National Council of the Arts, Sciences and Professions"

Bernard Gersten: Born January 30, 1923, in Newark, New Jersey, Gersten began his professional theatre life when he joined the Actors' Laboratory Theatre upon being discharged at the end of World War II. Being associated with the Lab would be one of the marks against him when he was called before HUAC. Gersten was an Equity stage manager by trade until 1960, when he joined fellow Actors' Lab member Joe Papp at the Public Theatre with the title of Associate Producer. Gersten stayed at the Public until 1978 when he had a falling out with Papp. Film and theatre jobs followed until 1985 when he became the executive producer of the Lincoln Center Theatre, a position he held until his retirement in 2013. In 1989 Gersten received a Special Award from the Drama Desk, and in 2013 he received the Tony Award for Lifetime Achievement.

Horace Grenell: Born January 19, 1909, Grenell refused to answer every question put to him. What is known comes from what the committee asked: Grenell was associated with Young People's Records, Abbey Record Manufacturing Company, the Jefferson Chorus, People's Radio Foundation and People's Songs, of which he was on the founding committee with, among others, Woody Guthrie, Pete Seeger, Lee Hays, Agnes "Sis" Cunningham, Alan Lomax, and Josh White. He died in early January 1981 at the age of 71.

George Hall: Born November 19, 1916, in Toronto, Ontario, Canada, Hall came to the U.S. in 1938 and studied at the Neighborhood Playhouse. He became a naturalized citizen in February of 1943 in Waco, Texas, where he was serving in the army (from 1942 to 1946). A member of the Communist Party from July or August 1946 through 1947, on March 5, 1954, he went to the FBI and told them about his membership. As an actor he began working professionally in 1946. His first Broadway show was *Call Me Mister*; he also appeared in *Lend an Ear* and *Touch and Go*. On television he appeared on the *Ed Sullivan Show, Celebrity Time* and *Man Behind the Badge* as well as radio soap operas. He was a member of AEA and AFTRA.

Lee Hays: Born March 14, 1914, in Little Rock, Arkansas, he has lived in New York since 1940. A folk singer by profession, he never had an opportunity to go to college because of the Depression. He made a living as a folklorist collecting and researching folk music and also worked in factories as a laborer and in a public library as a page. He worked on numerous farms as a farmhand and in the undesirable part of a good many greasy-spoon restaurants. A member of the folk singing groups The Almanac Singers in the 1930s and the Weavers from 1949 to 1952, he wrote a number of songs including "Kisses Sweeter than Wine" and "Wasn't That a Time." He is a member of Local 802 of the American Federation of Musicians and the American Guild of Variety Artists (AGVA).

Carroll Hollister: Born in Danbury, Connecticut, in 1901, Hollister identified himself as a musician and singing coach when he appeared before HUAC. According to the committee files, he was on the faculty of the Metropolitan Music School and was a founding member of the Musician's Committee to Aid Spanish Democracy during the Spanish Civil War. His work as a pianist is featured on numerous albums with musicians such as Yehudi Menuhin, and singers including Robert Merrill and John Charles Thomas. Hollister died at his home in Manhattan on October 1, 1983. He was 82.

[Robert] Earl Jones: Jones was born in Senatobia, Mississippi, on February 3, 1904. As Earl Jones, he came before HUAC in 1958, and he gave no information whatsoever to the committee. For its part, the committee had little on him in their files. Jones was a boxer in his early years, which found him as a sparring partner for Joe Louis, the world heavyweight champion, in 1937. His first Broadway appearance was in *The Hasty Heart* in 1945, and his last was *Mule Bone* in 1991. In between, Jones appeared in such notable productions as Eugene O'Neill's *More Stately Mansions* and the revivals of Arthur Miller's *Death of a Salesman* and O'Neill's *All God's Chillun Got Wings*. His film credits included *One Potato, Two Potato, The Sting*, and appearances on *The Defenders* and *Lou Grant*. The father of actor James Earl Jones, Robert Earl Jones died at the Lillian Booth Actors Home in Englewood, New Jersey, on September 7, 2006. He was 96.

Irma Jurist: She calls herself a "composer and housewife." She attended Hunter College through her junior year in the mid 1930s. She graduated summa cum laude from the Viller (Diller) Quail (Music) School and then taught there. From 1938–1948 she worked with a comedian in a variety of supper clubs, then at stage-door canteens during the war. In 1943 or 1944, she became Gertrude Lawrence's accompanist in a radio series of musical plays and also composed music for United Nations' films. Her Broadway credits include a revue entitled *Alive and Kicking*, incidental music for *Caesar and Cleopatra*, and ballet arrangements for *Hold It!* (IBDb, Jurist, 2005).

David Kanter: Kanter was born July 12, 1909, in Philadelphia, Pennsylvania, where his education stopped after a year in high school. He has worked as a production stage manager for about the last 18 years. His Broadway credits include the current production of *The Boy Friend*. He also did *Call Me Mister* and *Lend an Ear* (IBDb, Kanter, 2005). He is a member of AEA.

George Keane: Born in 1917 in Springfield, Massachusetts, he graduated from CCNY in 1937. He says he is an actor who occasionally worked as a writer and director. He entered the army in December of 1942 and got out in April 1946. His professional credits include several plays by Shakespeare as well as the musical *Brigadoon* and the play the *Seven Year Itch*. He is a member of AEA and AFTRA. He was named in *Red Channels* (five listings in all). Reported as: "Guest of Honor at the Women's Division Party, to honor Uta Hagen, of the American Relief for Greek Democracy; Speaker at a meeting of the Progressive Citizens of America."

Tony Kraber: Born June 14, 1905, in Pittsburgh, Pennsylvania, he attended Pennsylvania State University, transferred to Carnegie Tech and got his BA in 1927. His acting career began in Paris with Ben Greth, and he first went to Hollywood with a tour of *Journey's End*, but he never made a film in Hollywood, only in Europe. His first Broadway play was in 1927. He is also well known as a folk singer. He was a good friend of Carl Sandburg, who taught him many songs. He also recorded authentic cowboy songs under the title "The Old Chisholm Trail." When given the opportunity, he became an executive with the Columbia Broadcasting System. He was let go in 1951. During 1954 he was director of the theatre at White Lake Lodge. He is a member of AEA and one of the founding members AFTRA. He was named in *Red Channels* (11 listings in all). Reported as: "An entertainer for the American League for Peace and Democracy and the Friends of the Abraham Lincoln Brigade, American Music Alliance; Participant in the American Writers Congress."

John Lautner: When Lautner appeared before HUAC in 1958, he identified himself as a "government consultant." As his testimony proceeded, it turned out that he was testifying as a former functionary in the New York State organization of the Communist Party from 1929–1950. No file information was available.

Peter Lawrence: Born in New York City on June 9, 1919, he is a former stage manager now working as a theatrical producer. He spent two years at night school at Columbia University in 1938 and 1939. The first production he produced in 1950 was the play *Peter Pan* with Jean Arthur and Boris Karloff. He was a member of AEA.

William Lazar (William Lawrence): Born in Kishinev, Russia, in 1903, he came to the United States in 1921 and was naturalized in late 1926 or early 1927. Lazar identified himself as "a spotter by trade" when he appeared before the committee. The committee continually asked him if he was also William Lawrence. To this question, and many others, he took the Fifth. His obituary in the *Daily World* of December 7, 1971, confirmed that indeed William Lazar, a veteran of the Spanish Civil War, was "known in the progressive movement as Bill Lawrence."

Madeline Lee: Born Madeline Rosalind Letterman in New York City in 1923, she took special courses in radio direction and production at NYU. She began her professional acting career at the age of four as Tiny Tim in a radio production of *A Christmas Carol*. From the time she was eight until she was 14, she was "mistress of ceremonies" of her own children's programs. At 17 she became a director in training at the National Youth Administration Workshop while she continued working on radio. Her specialty was baby voices. During the war she directed, produced, and appeared in shows at the only servicemen's canteen in the Bronx for 72 consecutive weeks. In 1945 she appeared in *Embezzled Heaven* with Ethel Barrymore. Her television credits include the *Our Gang* comedies and *Naked City*. She is a member of AEA and AFTRA

She was named in *Red Channels* (two listings in all). Reported as: "Hostess, Cultural Division Party of the National Negro Congress; Performer at Carnegie Hall for the National Council of the Arts, Sciences and Professions" (American, 1950, p. 99).

Will Lee (William Lubovsky): Born in Brooklyn on August 6, 1908, Lee was teaching acting at the American Theatre Wing School. An army veteran, his theatre credits span most of the stories on these pages and are credited as one of the main reasons Lee was called before HUAC. In 1936 he appeared in the Federal Theatre Project's *Johnny Johnson*. He was in the Group Theatre's original production of *Golden Boy* as well as a later revival. When Lee went to Los Angeles for work, he joined the Actors' Lab, and he toured with *The World of Sholom Aleichem*. His other Broadway credits range from 1939's *The Time of Your Life* to 1972's *Enemies*. Although he had film and television roles before and after the blacklist, he will most be remembered as Mr. Hooper on *Sesame Street*. Will Lee died on December 7, 1982, as the age of 74. According to the Internet Movie Data Base (IMDb), "After his death in late 1982, the producers of *Sesame Street* decided to kill off Mr. Hooper instead of hiring another actor.... In a special *Sesame Street* episode that aired in November 1983...Big Bird learned to cope with and grieve the death of his dear friend."

Phil Leeds: Born in the Bronx on April 6, 1916, he's been a working actor since 1938. His first show was *Of Thee I Sing*. His other Broadway credits include *Let Freedom Sing*, *Make a Wish*, and *Can-Can*. During World War II he spent three years in the army. He has appeared on all the major television comedy shows including Milton Berle's, Jimmy Durante's, and Victor Borge's. He even had his own show called *Front Row Center*. His last television appearance was in May 1955. This followed an extensive career in radio. He is a member of AFRA (American Guild of Radio Artists), AEA, AGVA (American Guild of Variety Artists), and AFTRA.

Arthur Lief: Born Abraham Lipshutz in London on June 4, 1907, he came to the United States at 1-1-½ years old. A member of the Musician's Union Local 802, Lief was a conductor both on Broadway and national tours of several international dance companies. When the Old Vic brought Shakespeare to Broadway in the 1950s, Lief was their conductor of choice. He conducted for a tour of London's Royal Ballet and Israel's Invol Dance Company. But it was his work with impresario Sol Hurok and the Moiseyev Dance Company that interested HUAC the most, as they constantly referred to it as the Russian Ballet. Lief died on January 8, 1998. His wife of 45 years was Hurok's daughter Ruth. In his paid notice in *The New York Times*, it was noted that he was "The kindest man, a true gentleman with the heart of a radical."

Paul Mann (Yisroel Paul Mann Libman): An actor, director and teacher, Mann was born on December 2, 1913, in Toronto, Ontario, Canada. Anxious to be an actor, Mann ran away to New York at age 16. He was brought back by his parents, but not for long. When he was 18, he won a scholarship to the Neighborhood Playhouse. He became an American citizen when he graduated. He appeared in the Federal Theatre's *Johnny Johnson* and was the youngest member of the Group Theatre. He was on his way to a possible movie career when the blacklist intervened. He went back to New York and back to teaching. Mann was an original member of the Repertory Theatre of Lincoln Center and the Director of Training there as well as with the Negro Ensemble Company. He was also nominated for Golden Globe awards for the films *America America* and *Fiddler on the Roof*. Eight actresses charged him with sexual abuse and, in September of 1984, he was ordered to pay them each $12,000. A little more than a year later, on September 25, 1985, he died of a stroke.

Alan Manson: Born February 6, 1919, in Brooklyn, he completed high school. He entered the army on April 10, 1941, and was discharged on or about November 1, 1946. After getting out of the army he went into the play *Call Me Mister*. He appeared on television on the *Philco Playhouse*, the *Armstrong Theater*, *Danger*, etc. He is a member of AEA and AFTRA.

Albert M. Ottenheimer: Born in Tacoma, Washington on September 6, 1904, he graduated from the University of Washington in 1927. As one of the founders of the Seattle Repertoire Playhouse, he acted in exactly 150 plays there. He came to New York in 1951 where he did some radio and television. He appeared before one of the "little HUACs," the Cantwell Committee, in Washington State and did not cooperate.

Joseph Papirofsky (Papp): Born in Williamsburg, Brooklyn, on June 22, 1921, Papp was employed as a stage manager at CBS television and had just recently started receiving a salary for his work as founder and producer of the Shakespearean Theatre Workshop, which was already presenting free Shakespeare in various parks. Papp, then still Papirofsky, had studied under the GI Bill at, and was then employed by, the Actors' Laboratory Theatre in Los Angeles between 1948 and 1950. When he returned to New York, like his friend Bernard Gersten, he worked briefly as an Equity stage manager. The rest of his story is a thing of theatre legend. When Papp died on October 31, 1991, at the age of 70, his obituary in the *New York Times* was headlined, "Joseph Papp, Theater's Champion, Dies." The writer went on to call him "one of the most influential producers in the history of the American theater."

Lou Polan: Born June 15, 1904, in Ukraine, Russia, he came to U.S. in 1906 where he completed one year of high school. He started acting in 1920 and traveled with the USO during World War II. He appeared in 27 Broadway shows, including *Cyrano de Bergerac, Hamlet,* the *Merchant of Venice* and *Desire Under the Elms*. He was in the original production of *Bus Stop* when subpoenaed.

Stanley Prager: Born in New York City on January 8, 1917, he attended Johns Hopkins University in Baltimore, Maryland, for three years. He began acting professionally in 1942 with his first Broadway production, *Skin of Our Teeth*. Prior to that production, he appeared in the touring with productions of *Awake and Sing!* and *The Yanks Are Not Coming*. In 1943 he went to Hollywood to do the movie of a play he had been in, *The Eve of St. Mark*. He stayed there for about six or seven years, returning to Broadway with *Two on the Aisle* in 1951. His television credits include *The Colgate Comedy Hour* and *The Jackie Gleason Show*. He is currently appearing on Broadway in *The Pajama Game*. He is a member of AEA and AFTRA.

James D. Proctor: Proctor was born July 8, 1907, in New York City, and received his BA from Cornell University. He was a publicist when he appeared before HUAC and was potentially most interesting to them because of some of the productions he worked on: Kermit Bloomgarden's productions of *Look Homeward Angel, The Diary of Anne Frank,* and *A View from the Bridge* by Arthur Miller. At the hearing he was also accused of using Elia Kazan's wife's name without her permission as a sponsor of the Waldorf Peace Conference.

John Randolph: Born June 1, 1915, in the Bronx, New York, his education included two and a half years at City College of New York and a summer session at Columbia University. Born Emanuel Hirsch Cohen, his mother changed it to Mortimer Lippmann (which he refers to as his "real name") because she didn't like Manny. He was first employed as an actor in the Federal Theater Project's Children's Theater and worked for the project for two years. In 1940 he did his first Broadway show not with the Federal Theater. It was called *Medicine Show*. He served in the Air Force from April 1942 through 1946. In the Chicago company of *The Front Page* in 1946, he was in the original New York companies of *Come Back Little Sheba* and *Paint Your Wagon*, among others, and worked in summer stock. He is a member of AEA and AFTRA. Currently appearing in *Much Ado About Nothing* in summer stock in Massachusetts, he was named in *Counterattack* in 1952.

Harold J. Salemson: Born in Chicago, Illinois, on September 30, 1910, he is currently employed by the company Italian Films Export, which imports foreign films. He handles general problems, straightening out of contracts, translations of the contracts from Italian into English, French into English, and general administrative and executive work of that kind. Prior to that he worked in film publicity, and he worked on a public relations campaign for the leather industry. He lived in Hollywood from 1930 until July 1, 1948, first as a correspondent for French newspapers covering Hollywood then freelancing. He went into the army in December 1941 until October 1945, after which he returned to freelancing and worked for a short time as director of public relations for the Screen Writers Guild.

Richard Sasuly: Born on December 14, 1918, in Washington, D.C., he received his BA from the University of Arizona and an MA in Economics from Columbia. A writer, he was investigated extensively by the committee in 1952. He wrote a column called "On Stage" for *The Worker* magazine and was credited for writing the book on which the film *Der Rat der Götter* was based. The book, *IG Farben*, received four stars on GoodReads, where one reader posted that it was "One of the best books of WWII history I've read." Much later in life, his books took a decidedly different turn with *The Search for the Winning Horse: With a Realistic Guide to Handicapping* and *Bookies and Bettors*. Sasuly died in Palo Alto, California, on January 18, 2011.

Pete Seeger: Born in New York in 1919, he has worked on many things, but his main profession is as a student of American folklore, and he makes his living as a banjo picker, which is damning in some people's opinion. He served in the army from July 1942 to December 1945. He formed the Almanac Singers and then the Weavers, who were blacklisted off of television. He was named in *Red Channels* (14 listings in all). Reported as: "National Chairman of People's Songs; led singing at rallies of the Wallace for President Campaign; entertained at the 'Stop Rankin' Meeting."

Josh Shelley: Born January 27, 1920, he went to New York University for six months in 1937. His acting career began on radio. His television credits included *Studio One* and the *Ed Sullivan Show*. Blacklisted in 1952 by *Counterattack*, his radio and television work stopped. His Broadway credits include *One Touch of Venus* with Mary Martin, *On the Town* and *On Your Toes*. The show he was in when he was subpoenaed, *Phoenix 55*, closed the weekend before he appeared.

Irwin Silber: When Silber came before HUAC in 1958, he identified himself as a writer, editor and publicist. The committee wanted to know about his work and contributions as director of the American Folksay Group, the executive director of *People's Songs*, the editor of *Sing Out*, and the executive secretary of Peoples Artists, all of which he admitted to being involved with, but that was as far as he would discuss it. Silber was born in New York City on October 17, 1925. It was while a student at Brooklyn College that he formed the Folksay Group. His relationships included Pete Seeger, Lee Hays, and Bob Dylan to name a few. He was living in Oakland, California, when he died on September 10, 2010, at the age of 84. The headline for his extended obituary in the *New York Times* called him the "Champion of the Folk Music Revival." *Folkways Magazine*, now a Smithsonian publication, referred to his life as one "of Advocacy, Activism, and Service."

Ben Steinberg: Born in 1916, a violinist and assistant conductor by trade, Steinberg was interesting to the committee primarily because, according to his file, he was "[a] Conductor. Contractor of Orchestras (this means he hires musicians to play in orchestras)." It seems he had also been a judge at a contest held by the Metropolitan Music School. At the time he was called, he was employed by the production of the *Music Man*. Previous Broadway credits include *Peter Pan, Golden Apple*, and *Sandhog*. He was a member of Local 802. When he died on January 29, 1974, at the young age of 58, his obituary noted that he "founded the Symphony of the New World in 1965." It "was believed to be the first fully integrated orchestra in the United States."

Elliott Sullivan: Born in San Antonio, Texas, on July 4, 1907, he spent a semester in college in 1925 and served in the armed forces from 1943–1945. He made his Broadway debut in 1929 in *Red Dust*, appeared in *Lysistrata, Winged Victory,* and was Archie Beaton in the original production of *Brigadoon*. He went to Hollywood in 1937 and appeared in over 80 movies including *Kid Galahad, Yankee Doodle Dandy* and *Winged Victory*. He appeared on almost every major dramatic program on the air including *Big Story, Philco* and *Robert Montgomery Presents*, as well as about 75 radio shows. He is currently employed as director of the stage shows at the Wingdale Lodge in Wingdale, New York. He is a member of AEA and AFTRA. He was named in *Red Channels* (five listings in all). Reported as: "Entertainer for People's Artists and the American Labor Party; Sent greetings in the *Bulletin of People's Songs*."

George Tyne: Born February 6, 1917, in Philadelphia, Pennsylvania, he is also called Buddy Tyne and Buddy Yaros. His education included two semesters spent in night school at the School of Business Administration, City College of New York. His first professional engagement was in the musical *Of Thee I Sing*. He worked in New York from 1941–1942. In 1942 he went to Hollywood and, except for a play in 1945 in New York, stayed in Hollywood until he was blacklisted in 1951. He went to Europe in 1950 and got a movie role while he was there. In April and May of 1952 he did some television work and then returned to New York and the stage.

Paul Villard: When he appeared before HUAC in 1958, Villard identified himself as a musician and singer. Sadly that is almost all we know about him. There are nice mentions of his performing in a number of *Billboard* reviews in the 1940s, but only a single page of information is in his HUAC file. Among those few entries were a quote from the *Sunday Worker* of December 14, 1941, as the committee's list preparers put it, "Villard was eulogized [he hadn't died] in a complete artile [sic] entitled 'HE'S SUNG AT 1,000 PARTIES FOR DEMOCRACY'S FIGHTERS.'"

Martin Wolfson: Born in New York City on April 4, 1904, he received his BA from City College of New York in 1924. He began working as an actor in 1925 both in theater and on radio. His Broadway credits include *Volpone*, *Counselor-at-Law*, *Counterattack*, the original Broadway production of *South Pacific* and the *Threepenny Opera*. He also appeared in the play *Black Pit* by Albert Maltz and did one show for the Federal Theatre Project. He participated in a cultural exchange with Russia where he staged a production of *The Front Page*. He was appearing in a tour of *South Pacific* when he was subpoenaed.

He was named in *Red Channels* (11 listings in all). Reported as: "Sponsor of a dinner for the American Committee for Protection of the Foreign Born, and the Scientific and Cultural Conference for World Peace; United States Sponsor of the American Continental Congress for Peace held in Mexico."

Understudies

Jerome Chodorov: Chodorov was born in New York City on August 10, 1911. With his partner Joseph Fields, his first Broadway writing credit was *Schoolhouse on the Lot* in 1938. They followed two years later with *My Sister Eileen*, which ran for over three years. They would then adapt it to the musical stage and win a Tony Award for their book of *Wonderful Town*.

He was named in *Red Channels* (16 listings in all). Reported as: "Signer of an advertisement in support of the Hollywood 10 sponsored by the National Council of the Arts, Sciences and Professions; a sponsor of the Scientific and Cultural Conference for World Peace; a sponsor of a dinner for the American Committee to Save Refugees, and a member of Writers for [Henry] Wallace."

Jack Gilford: Born Jacob Gelman on July 25, 1908, in New York City (IMDb, Gilford, 2005), he began his Broadway career in 1944 in *Meet the People* (IBDb, Gilford, 2005). He was working at the Musical Tent in Pine Run, Michigan, when he was scheduled to appear at these hearings (AEA,

Box 29, Folder 19). He made his movie debut in 1944 with *Hey Rookie* and had appeared on television prior to being blacklisted.

He was named in *Red Channels* (11 listings in all). Reported as: "A sponsor of the Scientific and Cultural Conference for World Peace; affiliated with the Artists' Front to Win the War; entertainer for the Spanish Refugee Committee and the Civil Rights Congress."

Sam Jaffe: Born Shalom Jaffe on March 10, 1891, in New York City, he made his Broadway debut with The Washington Square Players in 1918, first in *Youth* followed by *Mrs. Warren's Profession*. In 1937 he was the High Lama in *Lost Horizon* and in 1939, at the age of 46, played Gunga Din in the movie of the same title. He was blacklisted in 1951 after completing the film *The Day the Earth Stood Still*.

He was named in *Red Channels* (14 listings in all). Reported as: "Supporter of the Japan Boycott Conference of the American League for Peace and Democracy; Speaker at Carnegie Hall for the Artist's Front to Win the War; Sponsor of the End Jim Crow in Baseball Committee."

Zero Mostel: Born Samuel Joel Mostel on February 28, 1915, in Brooklyn, he made his Broadway debut in *Café Crown* followed in quick succession by *Keep 'em Laughing* and *Top-Notchers*. A graduate of the City College of New York, he completed the first year of a master's program in art at New York University. In 1937 he taught drawing for the Works Progress Administration's Federal Art Project. Prior to being blacklisted in 1951, his movie credits included *Panic in the Streets* directed by Elia Kazan.

He was named in *Red Channels* (5 listings in all). Reported as: "An entertainer at social functions of the Communist Party; a member of American Youth for Democracy; volunteer performer for a benefit for the Joint Anti-Fascist Refugee Committee."

Theodore Saidenberg: Born in Baltimore, Maryland, on March 8, 1908, he is "a concert artist, a pianist, and [he has] been doing concretizing." In 1939 he was Jascha Heifetz's accompanist for the film *They Shall Have Music*. When being served his subpoena, he impressed the investigator Dolores Scotti "as a courteous, cultured, quiet, retiring and sensitive individual."

Angers Wooley: Wooley "was identified as a member of the Communist Party by Judith Raymond when she testified before the House Committee on Un-American Activities on September 11, 1953." He is "reported to be a radio writer" who lives in New York City.

Appendix D:
An Apology from the Unions

On October 27, 1997, fifty years to the day that the Hollywood Ten began testifying in Washington, D.C., SAG and AFTRA as well as the Writers Guild of America (WGA) and Directors Guild of America (DGA) co-hosted an event at the Samuel Goldwyn Theater of the Academy of Motion Picture Arts and Sciences entitled *Hollywood Remembers the Blacklist*.[1] The event, which attracted a capacity crowd, was in effect a *mea culpa* by the talent guilds for failing to support their blacklisted members and for purging them from the ranks of their union.[2] At the time I was working on the staff of Actors' Equity and got to be one of the stage managers for the event.

In a moving ceremony, the WGA, as part of the effort to make amends to the blacklisted, announced proper screenplay credits for the numerous films where a "'front" received a credit instead of the blacklistee. The audience heard HUAC testimony read aloud by well-known Hollywood personalities such as Kevin Spacey, Billy Crystal, and Alfre Woodard. Among the blacklisted who spoke were actress Marsha Hunt and screenwriters Ring Lardner, Jr., and Paul Jarrico. The evening concluded with statements by the then presidents of the various guilds offering words of comfort and apology. Included below are the speeches delivered by the SAG President and the President of the Los Angeles local of AFTRA. Before we did the final rehearsal, Richard Masur took me aside and said that I would like what he would be saying about Equity.

SAG President Richard Masur referred to the "institutionalization of fear" and remarked on the courageous stand of Equity in his comments:

> When I joined Screen Actors Guild in June of 1973, I signed the loyalty oath that twenty years earlier the SAG Board of Directors had made a requirement for membership. I never stopped to consider what it was I was signing. It was one in a series of papers I needed to fill out, and I was so eager to join the Guild, I probably would have signed anything they put in front of me. And I did. That's one of the most frightening legacies of the Blacklist era: the institutionalization of fear and prejudice.

You see, the Guild Board had not yet removed the loyalty oath from our by-laws. In fact, no action was taken until some new members refused to sign it. Those new members were the rock group The Grateful Dead, and the year was 1967. Only after the Dead refused to sign did the Board of Directors reconsider the necessity of a loyalty oath as a pre-condition for joining a union of artists. Even so, the oath had been so ingrained and institutionalized by that time that initially it could not be entirely eliminated. It was simply made optional. Another seven years would pass before, in July of 1974, a year after I joined, the loyalty oath was finally removed from the Screen Actors Guild by-laws.

Tonight Screen Actors Guild would like to express how deeply we regret that when courage and conviction were needed to oppose the Blacklist, the poison of fear so paralyzed our organization. Only our sister union, Actors' Equity Association, had the courage to stand behind its members and help them to continue their creative lives in the theater. For that we honor Actors' Equity Association tonight.

Unfortunately there are no credits to restore, nor any other belated recognition that we can offer our members who were blacklisted. They could not work under assumed names or employ surrogates to front for them. An actor's work and his or her identity are inseparable. Screen Actors Guild's participation in tonight's event must stand as our testament to all those who suffered that, in the future, we will strongly support our members and work with them to assure their rights as defined and guaranteed by the Bill of Rights.

And the organizations represented by the four Presidents on stage tonight, will not have to stand alone. We will be joined by the Alliance of Motion Picture and Television Producers. I have been asked to read a brief statement sent to each of us by AMPTP President Nicholas J. Counter who was unable to be here with us, and I quote:

"The member companies of the AMPTP join with the Guilds in commemorating the 50th Anniversary of the Blacklist era and hope that these efforts will make amends for those who were scarred by the blacklist hysteria. We likewise believe there is no place in a free society for the blacklisting and censorship which took place 50 years ago. The October 27th event represents an industry statement that should assure that history will not repeat itself."[3]

Susan Boyd, President of the Los Angeles section of AFTRA, while offering apologies for the past, also referred to present-day problems as she made promises for the future:

Usually when so many members of the creative community get together it is to celebrate a happy event. Clearly this gathering is exceptional in so many ways.

Tonight we acknowledge a very bitter episode in the history of television, radio and motion pictures. I did not personally live through the blacklist. I didn't experience the suffering as so many of you did. But I have felt its effect and I still do, and so does my union, AFTRA.

I know people whose careers were destroyed. I know performers who spoke in defense of colleagues who were smeared—and although their numbers were not so great as one might hope—their refusal to 'go along' just to 'get along' was all the more heroic because they stood fast against the national tide of fear; they did not hide from the Red Channels, the Counterattacks, the Madison Avenue slander, even the government itself. These heroes are here in this room and I salute you. And so does my union, AFTRA.

Is the age of blacklisting finally over? Or is each generation doomed to repeat the sad mistakes of its predecessors? We've seen in just the last two decades the damage done to so many in our community from whispers circulated about HIV and AIDS. That makes this evening more than a commemoration of those terrifying days which poisoned our profession fifty years ago. It is a lesson in vigilance for those among us who may believe we are safe from lists and files, dossiers and subpoenas. The words we say here tonight must live on to teach our children that compassion without action is not compassion at all; that words are weapons, and labels are equal opportunity destroyers of lives. And the most important lesson: though the blacklist of the Fifties is over, there are others waiting in the wings.

Just two years ago, the new Chairman of the Senate Commerce Committee demanded to know the ethnicity, religious affiliation, sex, age, salary, employment history, political contributions and other information about employees of the Corporation for Public Broadcasting and National Public Radio. Faced with critical publicity and a vigorous protest from AFTRA, which threatened to sue, and by other organizations, the Senator withdrew his request, and was later defeated in his bid for re-election. But the threat is constant. Not long go, AFTRA discovered a plan by the management of a major television station in Washington, DC to fire and hire reporters on the basis of their political beliefs. AFTRA protested once again and the station manager was forced to resign. Executives of the parent company disavowed the plan.

AFTRA's record has not always been so strong. Our leadership considers the Blacklist of the Fifties to be the saddest chapter in our union's history. During the McCarthy era AFTRA was torn apart by this issue, and paralyzed by that division, it failed to fight.

It will not fail again.

I am proud, AFTRA is proud to be a part of this long overdue and very important gathering.[4]

When the evening was over, the blacklisted writer and director Abe Polonsky, who had been honored during the evening's presentations, remarked that it wasn't so much that the guilds had apologized, but that they admitted there was a blacklist in the first place.[5]

Polonsky and many of the others present at the event that evening might have been surprised to learn that Roy Brewer, once an important leader of the International Alliance of Theatrical Stage Employees (IATSE), the last survivor of the fiercely anti–Communist Motion Picture Alliance for the Preservation of American Ideals, and a familiar face before HUAC, was also in the audience. Brewer would be a primary source for Kenneth Lloyd Billingsley whose *Hollywood Party: How Communism Seduced the American Film Industry in the 1930s and 1940s* looked at the evening's activities in a decidedly different way:

> Instead of a courageous reappraisal with a full cast, the industry impresarios had offered a colorized remake of the myth, in which those who had defended the worst

mass murderer in history were still, as Philip Dunne put it, virtually deified. Perhaps that was to be expected.

Hollywood remains a place of fantasy, of dancing shadows, where all dreams are created equal. But it is also a place of shifting fashion and has shown itself capable of change. Films of historical verisimilitude, such as *Schindler's List*, do occasionally emerge. Maybe some day, perhaps in a new century, someone will take the back story of the Hollywood Party and make a movie of it.[6]

On October 27, 1997, at *Hollywood Remembers the Blacklist,* Richard Mazur as SAG's president promised that the Screen Actors Guild would not stand idly by if there was "a next time." In March 2003, SAG remained true to his words as it defended members threatened by a new blacklist for speaking out against the war with Iraq. An industry trade publication reported SAG's stance:

> Some have recently suggested that well-known individuals who express "unacceptable" views should be punished by losing their right to work. This shocking development suggests that the lessons of history have, for some, fallen on deaf ears. Today, having come to grips with its past, having repudiated the insult of loyalty oaths and examined its own failings, our industry, perhaps more than any other, understands the necessity of guarding and cherishing those rights for which Americans have fought and died.
>
> In that spirit, the Screen Actors Guild board of directors, appreciating the value of full and open debate and devoted to the belief that the free flow of information, opinion and ideas contributes to the health of our nation, supports the right of all citizens, celebrated and unknown, to speak their minds freely, on any side of any issue, as is their constitutional right. In the same vein—and with a painfully clear appreciation of history—we deplore the idea that those in the public eye should suffer professionally for having the courage to give voice to their views. Even a hint of the blacklist must never again be tolerated in this nation.[7]

Chapter Notes

Prologue

1. Tallulah Bankhead in http://www.notable-quotes.com/t/theatre_quotes_v.html
2. https://intimateexcellent.wordpress.com/2017/11/22/new-study-proves-that-our-hearts-beat-together-at-the-theatre/.
3. Diep Tran, "When Writer's Rights Aren't Right: The 'Virginia Woolf' Casting Fight," *American Theatre,* May 22, 2017.
4. https://www.nytimes.com/2017/11/21/theater/rajiv-joseph-alley-theater-describe-the-night.html?emc=edit_th_20171126&nl=todaysheadlines&nlid=53934763&_r=1.

Chapter One

1. Phyllis Hartnoll ed., *The Oxford Companion to the Theatre,* 3rd ed. (London: Oxford University Press, 1967).
2. Therese Helburn, *A Wayward Quest: The Spirited Memoir of a Dynamic Personality in the American Theater* (Boston: Little, Brown, 1960), p. 51.
3. Lawrence Langer, *The Magic Curtain* (New York: E.P. Dutton, 1951), p. 94.
4. *Ibid.,* p. 95.
5. Hartnoll, ed., *The Oxford Companion to the Theatre,* 3rd ed.
6. Langer, *The Magic Curtain,* p. 116.
7. Langer, *The Magic Curtain,* p. 115.
8. *Ibid.,* pp. 123–124.
9. *Ibid.,* p. 124.
10. *Ibid.,* p. 125.
11. Helburn, *A Wayward Quest,* p. 7.
12. Langer, *The Magic Curtain.*
13. *Ibid.*
14. *A Wayward Quest,* p. 218.
15. *Ibid.,* p. 219.
16. Harold Clurman, *The Fervent Years: The Story of the Group Theatre and the Thirties* (New York: Hill and Wang, 1957), p. 25.
17. Langer, *The Magic Curtain,* pp. 250–251.
18. Wendy Smith, *Real Life Drama: The Group Theatre and America, 1931–1940* (New York: Grove Weidenfeld, 1990), p. 3.
19. *Ibid.*
20. Brooks Atkinson, *Broadway* (New York: Macmillan, 1970), p. 223.
21. https://timesmachine.nytimes.com/timesmachine/1935/02/20/93673799.pdf.
22. https://timesmachine.nytimes.com/timesmachine/1939/03/08/94687225.pdf.
23. *Ibid.,* p. ix.

Chapter Two

1. Hallie Flanagan, *Arena: The Story of the Federal Theatre* (New York: Limelight Editions, 1940/1969), p. 28.
2. *Ibid.,* p. 29.
3. A Brief Delivered by Hallie Flanagan, Director, Federal Theatre Project, Works Progress Administration before the Committee on Patents, House of Representatives, Washington, D.C. February 8, 1938. National Archives and Records Administration, Washington, D.C.
4. https://www.britannica.com/art/Living-Newspaper.
5. *Federal Theatre Plays, 1. Triple-A Plowed Under, 2. Power, 3. Spirochete* (New York: Random House, 1938), pp. vii–viii.
6. http://historymatters.gmu.edu/d/5105/.
7. https://timesmachine.nytimes.com/timesmachine/1937/05/21/94377803.pdf.
8. Bonnie Nelson Schwartz and the Educational Film Center, *Voices from the Federal Theatre* (Madison: University of Wisconsin Press, 2003), pp. 44–45.
9. Flanagan, *Arena: The Story of the Federal Theatre,* p. 202.
10. Courtesy of the da Silva family: Howard da Silva interview with Sol Schulman. George Mason University, May 24, 1976.

11. Schwartz, *Voices from the Federal Theatre*, p. 195.
12. August Raymond Ogden, *The Dies Committee: A Study of the Special House Committee for the Investigation of Un-American Activities 1938–1944* (Washington, D.C.: The Catholic University of America Press, 1945), p. 47.
13. *Ibid.*, p. 48.
14. Hearings before a Special Committee on Un-American Activities House of Representatives, Seventy-Fifth Congress, August 19, 1938, p. 775.
15. *Ibid.*, p. 777.
16. *Ibid.*, p. 778.
17. *Ibid.*, August 20, 1938, pp. 858–860.
18. Adam Lapin, *The Chicago Defender (National Edition) (1921–1967)*; Sep 3, 1938; ProQuest Historical Newspapers The Chicago Defender, p. 4.
19. Hearings before a Special Committee on Un-American Activities House of Representatives, Seventy-Fifth Congress, December 6, 1938, p. 2839.
20. *Ibid.*, p. 2844.
21. *Ibid.*, p. 2847–8.
22. *Ibid.*, pp. 2851–2.
23. *Ibid.*, p. 2856.
24. *Ibid.*, p. 2857.
25. *Ibid.*, pp. 2858–60.
26. *Ibid.*, p. 2867.
27. *Ibid.*, p. 2885.
28. Flanagan, *Arena: The Story of the Federal Theatre*, pp. 364–5.
29. *Ibid.*, pp. 334–5.
30. National Republic Records, Collection #60006, Hazel Huffman office records, reel 625, Hoover Institution Library and Archives.
31. Flanagan, *Arena: The Story of the Federal Theatre*, p. v.
32. Martin Dies, *Martin Dies' Story* (New York: Bookmailer, 1963), pp. 91–2.

Chapter Three

1. Committee on Un-American Activities, House of Representatives, Eightieth Congress, First Session, October 20, 1947, pp. 1–2.
2. *Ibid.*, October 22, 1947, pp. 165–166.
3. Larry Ceplair & Steven Englund, *The Inquisition in Hollywood* (Urbana: University of Illinois Press, 2003), p. 455.
4. Communist Infiltration of Hollywood Motion-Picture Industry—Part 1, Hearings before the Committee on Un-American Activities, House of Representatives, Eighty-Second Congress, First Session, March 21, 1951, pp. 115–6.
5. *Ibid.*, p. 120–1.
6. *Ibid.*, April 11, 1951, p. 177.
7. Communist Infiltration of Hollywood Motion-Picture Industry—Part 2, Hearings before the Committee on Un-American Activities, House of Representatives, Eighty-Second Congress, First Session, April 24, 1951, p. 391.
8. United States House of Representatives, Committee on Un-American Activities, Washington, D.C. Executive Session, January 14, 1952, National Archives and Records Administration, pp. 3–4.
9. *Ibid.*, p. 5.
10. *Ibid.*, pp. 10–11.
11. *Ibid.*, p. 23.
12. Communist Infiltration of Hollywood Motion-Picture Industry—Part 7. United States House of Representatives, Committee on Un-American Activities, Washington, D.C. Executive Session, April 10, 1952, National Archives and Records Administration, pp. 2408–9.
13. *Ibid.*, p. 2409.
14. *Ibid.*, p. 2410.
15. *Ibid.*, p. 2414.
16. *Ibid.*, May 19, 1952, pp. 3456–7.
17. *Ibid.*, May 20, 1952, p. 3511.

Chapter Four

1. American Business Consultants, *Red Channels: The Report of Communist Influence in Radio and Television*, New York: Counterattack, p. 161.
2. *Ibid.*, pp. 9–160.
3. *Ibid.*, pp. 161–213.
4. For a detailed look at the blacklist, television, and the Faulk trial see David Everitt's *Shadow of Red: Communism and the Blacklist in Radio and Television*.
5. Martha E. Randolph interviews with the author, June 28–30, 2004.
6. Arnold Perl Papers, Box 3, Folder 7. Wisconsin Historical Society/Wisconsin Center for Film and Theater Research.
7. Brooks Atkinson Papers, *T-MSS 1968-001, Box 3, Folder 14. The New York Library for the Performing Arts, The Billy Rose Collection.
8. *Ibid.*, Box 3, Folder 34.
9. *Ibid.*, Box 5, Folder 32.
10. Brooks Atkinson, *Broadway*, New York: The Macmillan Company, 1970, p. 426.
11. Arnold Perl Papers, Box 2, Folder 4.
12. Committee on Un-American Activities, House of Representatives, Eightieth Congress, First Session, October 30, 1947, p. 482.

Chapter Five

1. Dan Wakefield, "Whole Lotta Shakin' Goin' On," *Nation*, 20 September 1993, p. 287.
2. Howard Zinn, *A People's History of the United States* (New York: Perennial Classics, 2001), p. 425.

3. Thomas Rosteck, *See It Now Confronts McCarthyism: Television Documentary and the Politics of Representation* (Tuscaloosa: University of Alabama Press, 1994), p. 12.
4. Douglas T. Miller and Marion Nowak, *The Fifties: The Way We Really Were* (New York: Doubleday, 1977), pp. 6, 13.
5. Jean Rouverol Butler interview with the author, Thursday, January 10, 2002.
6. Miller & Nowack, *The Fifties: The Way We Really Were*, pp. 6–7.
7. David Thomson, *The Whole Equation: A History of Hollywood* (New York: Alfred A. Knopf, 2004), p. 74.
8. Diana Anhalt, *A Gathering of Fugitives* (Santa Maria, CA: Archer Books, 2001); Norma Barzman, *The Red and the Blacklist* (New York: Nation Books, 2003); Jean Rouverol, *Refugees from Hollywood* (Albuquerque: University of New Mexico Press, 2000); Rouverol, interview, January 10, 2002.
9. David F. Prindle, *The Politics of Glamour: Ideology and Democracy in the Screen Actors Guild* (Madison: The University of Wisconsin Press, 1988), p. 2.
10. Quoted in Eric Bentley, Ed., *Thirty Years of Treason: Excerpts from Hearings before the House Committee on Un-American Activities, 1938–1968* (New York: The Viking Press, 1971), pp. 146–147.
11. Gale Sondergaard in HUAC Files and Reference Section Name Files at the National Archives and Records Administration, Washington, DC.
12. *Ibid.*
13. Gale Sondergaard: http://www.imdb.com/name/nm0814216/.
14. T. F. Brady, "Anne Revere Quits Actors Guild Post," *The New York Times*, May 31, 1951; Revere quoted in "Anne Revere" www.spartacus.schoolnet.co.uk/USArevere.htm.
15. "Screen Actors Ask for Loyalty Oath," *New York Times*, 1 July 1953; Actors Move to Bar Communists, *Los Angles Times*, 1 July 1953.
16. "Screen Guild Acts to Bar Communists," *New York Times*, 28 July 1953; "Screen Actors Guild Closes Door on Reds," *Los Angles Times*, 28 July 1953.
17. Larry Ceplair, "SAG and the Motion Picture Blacklist" in a special issue of the *National Screen Actor,*www.sag.com/blacklist.html; "Actors Guild votes down anti-Communist bylaws," *Daily World*, 28 August 1974.
18. Peter Schweizer, *Reagan's War: The Epic Story of His Forty-Year Struggle and Final Triumph Over Communism* (New York: Doubleday, 2002), p. 12. For more information on the strike of studio technicians please see Gerald Horne's *Class Struggle in Hollywood 1930–1950: Moguls, Mobsters, Stars, Reds, & Trade Unionists.* (Austin: University of Texas Press, 2001).

19. *Ibid.*, p. 13.
20. Patrick McGilligan and Paul Buhle, *Tender Comrades: A Backstory of the Hollywood Blacklist* (New York: St. Martin's Press, 1997), p. 462.
21. Murrow quoted in Rosteck, p. 20.
22. McCarran quoted in Thomas Doherty, *Cold War, Cool Medium: Television, McCarthyism, and American Culture* (New York: Columbia University Press, 2003), pp. 23–24.
23. David Halberstam, *The Fifties.* (New York: Random House, 1993), p. 192.
24. AFTRA/History/Leadership from www.aftra.org/aftra/history.htm.
25. *Ibid.*, Rita Morley Harvey, *Those Wonderful, Terrible Years: George Heller and the American Federation of Television and Radio Artists* (Carbondale, IL: Southern Illinois University Press, 1996), *passim*.
26. "TV-Radio Union to Hit Unfriendly Witnesses," *Los Angeles Times*, 20 March 1953.
27. "Trio Silent in Red Quiz Radio Artists Suspend," *Los Angeles Times*, 24 June 1953.
28. *Ibid.*
29. "Artists' Union Drops 3," *The New York Times*, 27 July 1953.
30. Jack Gould, "TV: More about AWARE," *New York Times*, 11 July 1955.
31. Adams, "A.F.T.R.A. Ratifies Hearings Clause." *New York Times*, 11 August 1955; interview with George Ives, September 30, 2005.
32. Gould, "TV: More about AWARE." 11 July 1955.
33. Ives interview.
34. Adams, "A.F.T.R.A. Ratifies Hearings Clause," 11 August 1955.
35. Gould, "House Group to Hold Hearings on Reds in Show Business Here," *The New York Times*, 20 July 1955.
36. *Ibid.*

Chapter Six

1. Alfred Harding, *The Revolt of the Actors* (New York: William Morrow, 1929), *passim*
2. Actors' Equity Association, General Files (1945–1960). Tamiment Library/Robert F. Wagner Labor Archives, Bobst Library, New York University, Box 10, Folder 21.
3. L. I. Pearlin & H. E. Richards, "Equity: A Study of Union Democracy." *Equity*, September 1951, p. 7.
4. Equity Collection Box 10, Folder 21.
5. *Ibid.*, Box 10, Folders 19 & 20.
6. *Ibid.*, Box 22, Folder 12.
7. Alfred Harding, "Equity to Receive Brotherhood Award," *Equity*, September 1952.
8. Quoted in Harding, "Subpoenas, Blacklisting and Communism," *Equity*, June 1951, p. 3.
9. *Ibid.*
10. *Ibid.*

11. Equity Collection, Box 19, Folder 23.
12. Actors' Equity Association, Minutes of Council, Tamiment Library/Robert F. Wagner Labor Archives, NYU, Labor Documentation Project, Actors' Equity R-7421, 10,670.
13. Equity Collection, Box 18, Folder 22.
14. Equity Minutes of Council, Actors' Equity R-7421, 10,691–10,692.
15. *Ibid.*, 10,692.
16. *Ibid.*, 10,697.
17. *Ibid.*, 10,698.
18. *Ibid.*, 10,751–10,756.
19. Equity Collection, Box 1, Folder 35: "Rules Governing Employment," Rule 9, 1952.

Chapter Seven

1. George Ives interview with the author, September 30, 2005; Prager subpoena in his HUAC Investigation Name Files, at the National Archives and Records Administration, Washington, DC.
2. Madeline Lee Gilford interviews with the author, April 11, 2002, and January 28, 2006.
3. *Ibid.*
4. Pete Seeger interview with the author, May 20, 2005.
5. David King Dunaway, *How Can I Keep from Singing: Pete Seeger* (New York: McGraw-Hill, 1982).
6. Ives interview with the author, September 30, 2005.
7. U.S. Congress, House Committee on Un-American Activities, *Investigation of Communist Activities in the New York Area—Part VI (Entertainment)* Eighty-Fourth Congress, August 15–18, 1955, pp. 2259, 2325, 2373, 2431.
8. *Ibid.* p. 2265.
9. *Ibid.* p. 2268.
10. *Ibid.* pp. 2269–2270.
11. *Ibid.* p. 2274.
12. *Ibid.* p. 2275.
13. *Ibid.* pp. 2284–2285.
14. *Ibid.* pp. 2286–2300.
15. Ives interview with the author, September 30, 2005.
16. U.S. Congress, House Committee on Un-American Activities, *Investigation of Communist Activities in the New York Area—Part VI (Entertainment)* Eighty-Fourth Congress, August 15–18, 1955, p. 2302.
17. *Ibid.* pp. 2311–2312.
18. *Ibid.* p. 2317.
19. *Ibid.* pp. 2321–2322.
20. *Ibid.* p. 2327.
21. Norma Sullivan interview with the author, May 2007.
22. When I met Sullivan's widow, Norma, she commented that when Victor Navasky wrote about these hearings in his book *Naming Names* he only mentioned that George Tyne and Pete Seeger were cited for contempt. I promised her that when I wrote about the 1955 hearings that I would make sure to say that Elliott Sullivan was also cited.
23. Pete Seeger interview with the author, May 20, 2005; U.S. Congress, House Committee on Un-American Activities, *Investigation of Communist Activities in the New York Area—Part VI (Entertainment)* Eighty-Fourth Congress, August 15–18, 1955, p. 2327.
24. Irma Jurist interview with the author, February 12, 2005.
25. U.S. Congress, House Committee on Un-American Activities, *Investigation of Communist Activities in the New York Area—Part VI (Entertainment)* Eighty-Fourth Congress, August 15–18, 1955, p. 2368.
26. *Ibid.* p. 2373.
27. *Ibid.* p. 2375.
28. *Ibid.* p. 2383.
29. *Ibid.* p. 2387.
30. Madeline Lee Gilford interview with the author, April 11, 2002.
31. U.S. Congress, House Committee on Un-American Activities, *Investigation of Communist Activities in the New York Area—Part VI (Entertainment)* Eighty-Fourth Congress, August 15–18, 1955, 2397.
32. *Ibid.* p. 2398
33. *Ibid.* p. 2411.
34. *Ibid.* p. 2414.
35. *Ibid.* p. 2415.
36. *Ibid.* p. 2434.
37. *Ibid.* pp. 2446–2447.
38. Pete Seeger interview with the author, May 20, 2005.
39. U.S. Congress, House Committee on Un-American Activities, *Investigation of Communist Activities in the New York Area—Part VI (Entertainment)* Eighty-Fourth Congress, August 15–18, 1955, p. 2452.
40. *Ibid.* p. 2456.
41. *Ibid.* p. 2464.
42. *Ibid.* p. 2470.
43. *Ibid.* p. 2474.
44. *Ibid.* pp. 2487–2488.
45. Angers Wooley, Jerome Chodorov, Sam Jaffe, HUAC Investigation Name Files, at the National Archives and Records Administration, Washington, DC.
46. *Ibid.* p. 2488.
47. M. Bracker, "6 More Witnesses Balk Red Inquiry; Hearings Ended," *The New York Times,* 19 August 1955, p. 1; "House Committee Ends Quiz on New York Reds," *Los Angeles Times,* 19 August 1955, p. 27.
48. D. Platt, "Walter Folds Tent, Steals Out of Town." *Daily Worker,* 19 August 1955. John Randolph papers, Robert F. Wagner Labor Archives, Bobst Library, New York University.

Chapter Eight

1. Griffin Fariello, *Red Scare: Memories of the American Inquisition, an Oral History* (New York: Avon, 1995), p. 346.
2. "Cambridge Actor Spurns Red Quiz," *Boston Daily Record*, 16 August 1955, p. 2. John Randolph papers, Robert F. Wagner Labor Archives, Bobst Library, New York University.
3. "Sarah Cunningham," *New York Times*, 5 April 1986, p. 32.
4. "Ivan Black, 75, a Publicity Agent," *New York Times*, 27 March 1979, p. B14.
5. "Susan d'Usseau," *New York Times*, 13 June 1973, p. 50.
6. "George Hall, 85, Broadway Character Actor," *New York Times*, 1 December 2002, p. 58.
7. "Lee Hays, a Co-Founder of the Weavers, Dies," *New York Times*, 27 August 1981, p. D19.
8. Irma Jurist interviews with the author, February 12 & March 12, 2005.
9. David Kanter in Records of the U.S. House of Representatives HUAC, Executive Session Transcripts p. 24, RG 233, Box 34, at the National Archives and Records Administration, Washington, DC.
10. W. Edwards, "Probe Defied by 22 out of 23 at Red Hearing," *Chicago Daily Tribune*, 19 August 1955, p. 2.
11. "George Keane, 78, Stage and TV Actor," *New York Times*, 25 October 1995, p. D21.
12. "Tony Kraber Dead at Age 81: An Actor, Singer and Director," *New York Times*, 12 September 1986, p. D20.
13. Albert M. Ottenheimer in HUAC Investigation Name Files, Series 1, Box 35, File 9E 3/3/15/4, at the National Archives and Records Administration, Washington, DC., Appell document, October 1955.
14. "Lou Polan, Broadway Actor in Over 50 Plays, is Dead," *New York Times*, 4 March 1976, p. 32.
15. "Martin Wolfson, Who Portrayed Captain in 'South Pacific,' Dead," *New York Times*, 13 September 1973, p. 52.
16. Madeline Lee Gilford interviews with the author, April 11, 2002, and January 28, 2006.
17. "Madeline Lee Gilford," *New York Times*, 21 April 2008, p. A19.
18. "Phil Leeds, 82, Comic on Stage and Screen," *New York Times*, 21 August 1998, p. D17.
19. "Alan Manson, 83, A Soldier Transplanted to the Stage, Dies," *New York Times*, 11 March 2002, p. B9.
20. "Harold Salemson, 78, Film and Book Critic," *New York Times*, 28 August 1988, p. 36.
21. Joshua Shelley. Retrieved April 17, 2006, from http://www.answers.com/topic/joshua-shelley.
22. John Cogley, *Report on Blacklisting II: Radio-Television [and Theatre]* (New York: Fund for the Republic, 1956), p. 211.
23. "Actor Elliott Sullivan Acquitted of Contempt of Congress," *Washington Post*, 7 June 1974, p. 12; in Sullivan HUAC Files and Reference Section Name Files at the National Archives and Records Administration, Washington, DC.
24. Walter Goodman, *The Committee: The Extraordinary Career of the House Committee on Un-American Activities* (New York: Farrar, Strauss and Giroux, 1968), p. 378.
25. George Tyne, IMDb.com, 2005.
26. "Lasting Music, Social Legacy: Pete Seeger dies at 94," *Los Angeles Times*, 29 January 2014, p. D7.
27. "Elliott Sullivan, 66, Actor and Witchhunt Victim, Dies," *Daily Worker*, 5 June 1974, p. 10 (Sullivan HUAC Name Files).
28. Francis Walter. Retrieved February 3, 2006, from http://www.spartacus.schoolnet.co.uk/USAwalterF.htm.
29. Gordon H. Scherer. Retrieved April 17, 2006, from http://en.wikipedia.org/wike/Gordon_H_Scherer.
30. Edwin E. Willis. Retrieved April 17, 2006, from http://en.wikipedia.org/wike/Edwin_Edward_Willis.
31. HUAC. Retrieved March 5, 2006, from http://www.spartacus.schoolnet.co.uk/USAhuac.htm.
32. John Cogley, *Report on Blacklisting II: Radio and Television* (New York: Fund for the Republic, 1956), pp. 211–212.
33. Bernard Gersten interview with the author, November 9, 2005.
34. Cogley, *Report on Blacklisting II: Radio and Television*, p. 212.
35. George Ives interview with the author, September 30, 2005.
36. Dorothy Thompson, On the Record: "All the World's a Stage." *Daily News*, Newport News, VA. August 1955. John Randolph papers, Robert F. Wagner Labor Archives, Bobst Library, New York University.

Chapter Nine

1. *The Peoria Journal*, October 27, 1950, Kermit Bloomgarden papers, U.S. Mss 8AN, Box 72, Folder 4, Wisconsin Center for Film and Theater Research.
2. Ibid.
3. Ibid., *Daily Variety*, October 23, 1950.
4. U.S. Congress, House Committee on Un-American Activities, *Communist Infiltration of the Hollywood Motion-Picture Industry—Part*, Eighty-Second Congress, Second Session, May 21, 1952, p. 3545.
5. Ibid., pp. 3545–46.

6. Brooks Atkinson Papers, *T-MSS 1968-001, Box 5, Folder 13. The New York Library for the Performing Arts, The Billy Rose Collection,
7. Ibid.
8. U.S. Congress, House Committee on Un-American Activities, Investigation of the Unauthorized Use of United States Passports—Part 4. Eighty-Forth Congress, Second Session, June 21, 1956, pp. 4675–6.
9. Ibid., p. 4677.
10. Ibid., pp. 4683–4.
11. Ibid., p. 4686.
12. Arthur Miller, *The Crucible* (New York: Bantam Classics, 1959), p. x.
13. Cogley, *Report on Blacklisting II: Radio and Television*, pp. 215–217.

Chapter Ten

1. Goodman, *The Committee: The Extraordinary Career of the House Committee on Un-American Activities*, p. 375.
2. Ibid.
3. U.S. Congress, House Committee on Un-American Activities, *Communism in the New York Area (Entertainment)* Eighty-Fifth Congress, Second Session, June 18 and 19, 1958, 2493.
4. U.S. Congress, House Committee on Un-American Activities, *Communism in the New York Area (Entertainment)* Eighty-Fifth Congress, Second Session, June 18 and 19, 1958, 2584–5.
5. U.S. Congress, House Committee on Un-American Activities, *Communism in the New York Area (Entertainment)* Eighty-Fifth Congress, Second Session, June 18 and 19, 1958, p. 2528.
6. Ibid.
7. Ibid., p. 2533.
8. Ibid., p. 2537.
9. Ibid., p. 2538–41.
10. Ibid., p. 2560.
11. Ibid., p. 2565–6.
12. Ibid., p. 2573–5.
13. Ibid., p. 2575.
14. Ibid., p. 2576.
15. Ibid., p. 2566.
16. Ibid., p. 2544.
17. Ibid., p. 2545.
18. Ibid., p. 2545–6.
19. Ibid., p. 2579.
20. Ibid., p. 2581.
21. Ibid., p. 2526.
22. Charles Dubin interview was conducted on September 9, 2003: http://www.emmytvlegends.org/interviews/people/charles-dubin#.
23. Executive Session transcript Testimony of Charles S. Dubin, United States House of Representatives, Subcommittee of the Committee on Un-American Activities. October 24, 1961.
24. Charles S. Dubin in HUAC Files and Reference Section Name Files at the National Archives and Records Administration, Washington, DC.
25. U.S. Congress, House Committee on Un-American Activities, *Communism in the New York Area (Entertainment)* Eighty-Fifth Congress, Second Session, June 18 and 19, 1958, p. 2490.
26. Ibid., p. 2493–5.
27. Ibid., p. 2498.
28. Ibid., p. 2499–2500.
29. Ibid., p. 2503–4.
30. Ibid., p. 2912.
31. Ibid., p. 2516.
32. Ibid., p. 2517.
33. Ibid., p. 2519–20.
34. Ibid., p. 2571.
35. Bernard Gersten, interview with the author, November 9, 2005.
36. U.S. Congress, House Committee on Un-American Activities, *Communism in the New York Area (Entertainment)* Eighty-Fifth Congress, Second Session, June 18 and 19, 1958, p. 2480.
37. Ibid., p. 2483.
38. Ibid., p. 2486–7.
39. Ibid., p. 2488–9.
40. New York Post, May 26, 1959, p. 33 in U.S. Congress, House Committee on Un-American Activities Organizations files, Box 474.
41. Joseph Papirovsky (Papp) in HUAC Files and Reference Section Name Files, Box 14, at the National Archives and Records Administration, Washington, DC.
42. Ibid.
43. Ibid.
44. U.S. Congress, House Committee on Un-American Activities, *Communism in the New York Area (Entertainment)* Eighty-Fifth Congress, Second Session, June 18 and 19, 1958, p. 2553–4.
45. Ibid. p. 2556.
46. Joseph Papirovsky (Papp) in HUAC Files and Reference Section Name Files, Box 14, at the National Archives and Records Administration, Washington, DC.
47. Kenneth Tynan & Joseph Papp, *Free for All: Joe Papp, The Public, and the Greatest Theater Story Ever Told* (New York: Doubleday, 2009), p. 132.
48. https://www.nytimes.com/2017/06/09/theater/review-julius-caesar-delacorte-theater-donald-trump.html.

Epilogue

1. Richard Schickel, *Elia Kazan, A Biography* (New York: HarperCollins, 2005), p. xvi.
2. Phoebe Brand Carnovsky, interview with the author, May 7, 2002.

Appendix A

1. Karen Chilton, *Hazel Scott: The Pioneering Journey of a Jazz Pianist from Cafe Society to Hollywood to HUAC* (Ann Arbor: The University of Michigan Press, 2008), p. 142.

Appendix B

1. https://wlh.law.stanford.edu/biography_search/biopage/?woman_lawyer_id=12235 and https://www.findagrave.com/memorial/171632785/dolores-faconti-scotti.
2. Madeline Lee Gilford, Scotti memo of July 13, 1955, in HUAC Files and Reference Section Name Files at the National Archives and Records Administration, Washington, DC.
3. John Randolph, Scotti memo of July 14, 1955, in HUAC Files and Reference Section Name Files at the National Archives and Records Administration, Washington, DC.
4. Susan D'Usseau, Scotti memo, undated, in HUAC Files and Reference Section Name Files at the National Archives and Records Administration, Washington, DC.
5. Sam (Zero) Mostel, in HUAC Files and Reference Section Name Files, Series 2, Box 74, at the National Archives and Records Administration, Washington, DC.
6. Ethel Everett, Scotti memo dated February 9, 1956, in HUAC Files and Reference Section Name Files at the National Archives and Records Administration, Washington, DC
7. Maureen Holbert, Scotti memo of March 12, 1956, in HUAC Files and Reference Section Name Files at the National Archives and Records Administration, Washington, DC
8. Joseph Papirovsky (Papp) in HUAC Files and Reference Section Name Files, Box 14, letter dated August 10, 1956, at the National Archives and Records Administration, Washington, DC.
9. Ibid., letter dated March 14, 1958.
10. Ibid., letter dated April 25, 1958.
11. Lee Sabinson, Scotti memo of June 7, 1957, in HUAC Files and Reference Section Name Files at the National Archives and Records Administration, Washington, DC

Appendix D

1. Kenneth Lloyd Billingsley, *Hollywood Party: How Communism Seduced the American Film Industry in The1930s and 1940s* (Rockland, CA: FORUM, 1998), 1–10, 283–289.
2. Greg Krizman, "Hollywood Remembers the Blacklist," www.sag.com/blacklist.html, *passim*.
3. Judith Chaikin (Executive Producer/Director), Michael Seel (Producer), J. Angier (Writer), *Hollywood Remembers the Blacklist: AFTRA/DGA/SAG/WGA*.[Unaired television program]. Los Angeles: AMulti-Guild Production.
4. *Ibid*.
5. Abe Polonsky, conversation with the author, October 27, 1997.
6. Billingsley, 288–289.
7. Roger Armbrust, "SAG Sees Blacklist Mentality," *Backstage*, 13 March 2003, pp. 6–7.

Bibliography

American Business Consultants, *Red Channels: The Report of Communist Influence in Radio and Television,* New York: Counterattack, 1950.
Anhalt, Diana. *A Gathering of Fugitives.* Santa Maria, CA: Archer Books, 2001.
Atkinson, Brooks. *Broadway.* New York: Macmillan, 1970.
Barranger, Milly. *Unfriendly Witnesses: Gender, Theater, and Film in the McCarthy Era.* Carbondale: Southern Illinois University Press, 2008.
Barzman, Norma. *The Red and the Blacklist.* New York: Nation Books, 2003.
Bentley, Eric. *Are You Now or Have You Ever Been: The Investigation of Show Business by the Un-American Activities Committee, 1947–1958.* New York: Harper Colophon Books, 1972.
Bentley, Eric, ed. *Thirty Years of Treason: Excerpts from Hearings before the House Committee on Un-American Activities 1938–1968,* New York: Nation Books, 2002.
Bentley, Joanne. *Hallie Flanagan: A Life in the American Theatre.* New York: Alfred A. Knopf, 1988.
Bernstein, Walter. *Inside Out: A Memoir of the Blacklist.* New York: Alfred A. Knopf, 1996.
Bigsby, Christopher. *Arthur Miller.* Cambridge: Harvard University Press, 2009.
Billingsley, Kenneth Lloyd. *Hollywood Party: How Communism Seduced the American Film Industry in the 1930s and 1940s.* Rockland, CA: FORUM, 1998.
Blue, Howard. *Words at War: World War II Era Radio Drama and the Postwar Broadcasting Industry Blacklist.* Lanham, MD: Scarecrow Press, 2002.
Brenman-Gibson, Margaret. *Clifford Odets: American Playwright, the Years from 1906–1940.* New York: Atheneum, 1981.
Brown, Jared. *Zero Mostel: A Biography.* New York: Atheneum, 1989.
Buckley, William F., Jr. *The Committee and Its Critics: A Calm Review of the House Committee on Un-American Activities.* New York: G.P. Putnam's Sons, 1962.
Buhle, Paul, and Dave Wagner. *Hide in Plain Sight: The Hollywood Blacklistees in Film and Television, 1950–2002.* New York: Palgrave Macmillan, 2003.
Burton, Michael C. *The Making of a Liberated Mind: John Henry Faulk, a Biography.* Austin, TX: Eakin Press, 1993.
Buttita, Tony, and Barry Witham. *Uncle Sam Presents: A Memoir of the Federal Theatre, 1935–1939.* Philadelphia: University of Pennsylvania Press, 1982.
Caute, David. *The Great Fear: The Anti-Communist Purge Under Truman and Eisenhower.* New York: Simon & Schuster, 1978.
Ceplair, Larry, and Steven Englund. *The Inquisition in Hollywood.* Urbana and Chicago: University of Illinois Press, 2003.
Charles, Searle F. *Minister of Relief: Harry Hopkins and the Great Depression.* Westport, CT: Greenwood Press, 1963.
Chilton, Karen. *Hazel Scott: The Pioneering Journey of a Jazz Pianist from Café Society to Hollywood to HUAC.* Ann Arbor: University of Michigan Press, 2008.
Clurman, Harold. *The Fervent Years: The Story of the Group Theatre and the Thirties.* New York: Hill and Wang, 1957.

Cogley, John. *Report on Blacklisting, I-Movies; II-Radio-Television*. The Fund for the Republic, 1956.
Collins, Sheila D., and Gertrude Shafner Goldberg, eds. *When Government Helped: Learning from the Successes and Failures of the New Deal*. New York: Oxford University Press, 2014.
Corey, Jeff, with Emily Corey. *Improvising Out Loud: My Life Teaching Hollywood How to Act*. Lexington: University of Kentucky Press, 2017.
Crawford, Cheryl. *One Naked Individual: My Fifty Years in the Theatre*. Indianapolis: Bobbs-Merrill, 1977.
Dies, Martin. *Martin Dies' Story*. New York: The Bookmailer, 1963.
Dmytryk, Edward. *Odd Man Out: A Memoire of the Hollywood Ten*. Carbondale: Southern Illinois University Press, 1996.
Doherty, Thomas. *Cold War, Cool Medium: Television, McCarthyism, and American Culture*. New York: Columbia University Press, 2003.
Dunaway, David King. *How Can I Keep from Singing: Pete Seeger*. New York: McGraw-Hill, 1982.
Epstein, Helen. *Joe Papp: An American Life*. Boston: Little, Brown, 1994.
Everitt, David. *A Shadow of Red: Communism and the Blacklist in Radio and Television*. Chicago: Ivan R. Dee, 2007.
Fagan, Myron C. *Red Treason on Broadway*. Hollywood: Cinema Educational Guild, 1954.
Fariello, Griffin. *Red Scare: Memories of the American Inquisition*. New York: Avon Books, 1995.
Fast, Howard. *Being Red*. Boston: Houghton-Mifflin, 1990.
Federal Theatre Plays, 1. Prologue to Glory, 2. One-Third of a Nation, 3. Haiti. New York: Random House, 1938.
Federal Theatre Plays, 1. Triple-A Plowed Under, 2. Power, 3. Spirochete. New York: Random House, 1938.
Flanagan, Hallie. *Arena: The Story of the Federal Theatre*. New York: Limelight Editions, 1975.
Frommer, Myrna K., and Harvey Frommer. *It Happened on Broadway: An Oral History of the Great White Way*. New York: Harcourt Brace, 1998.
Frost, Jennifer. *Hedda Hopper's Hollywood: Celebrity Gossip and American Conservatism*. New York: New York University Press, 2011.
Goldman, Eric F. *The Crucial Decade—and After: America, 1945–1960*. New York: Vintage, 1969.
Goodman, Walter. *The Committee: The Extraordinary Career of the House Committee on Un-American Activities*. New York: Farrar, Strauss and Giroux, 1968.
Gorney, Sondra K. *Brother Can You Spare a Dime? The Life of Composer Jay Gorney*, Lanham, MD: Scarecrow Press, 2005.
Graff, Ellen. *Stepping Left: Dance and Politics in New York City, 1928–1942*. Durham, NC: Duke University Press, 1997.
Halberstam, David. *The Fifties*. New York: Random House, 1993.
Harding, Alfred. *Revolt of the Actors*. Rahway, NJ: Quinn & Boden Co., 1929.
Hartnoll, Phyllis, ed. *The Oxford Companion to the Theatre*, 3rd ed. London: Oxford University Press, 1967.
Harvey, Rita Morley. *Those Wonderful, Terrible Years: George Heller and the American Federation of Television and Radio Artists*. Carbondale: Southern Illinois University Press, 1997.
Haynes, John E. *Red Scare or Red Menace? American Communism and Anticommunism in the Cold War Era*. Chicago: Ivan R. Dee, 1996.
Helburn, Theresa. *A Wayward Quest: The Spirited Memoir of a Dynamic Personality in the American Theater*. Boston: Little, Brown, 1960.
Hellman, Lillian. *Scoundrel Time*. Boston: Little, Brown, 1976.
Hill, Errol G., and James V. Hatch. *A History of African American Theatre*. Cambridge, UK: Cambridge University Press, 2005.
Hill, Jason. *Red Channels: The Bible of Blacklisting*. Albany, GA: BearManor Media, 2016.
Himmelstein, Morgan Y. *Drama Was a Weapon: The Left-Wing Theatre in New York 1929–1941*. New Brunswick, NJ: Rutgers University Press, 1963.

Holtzman, Will. *Judy Holliday*. New York: G. P. Putnam's Sons, 1982.
Horne, Gerald. *Class Struggle in Hollywood 1930–1950: Moguls, Mobsters, Stars, Reds, & Trade Unionists*. Austin: University of Texas Press, 2001.
Houchin, John H. *Censorship of the American Theatre in the Twentieth Century*, Cambridge, UK: Cambridge University Press, 2003.
Jeezer, Marty. *The Dark Ages: Life in the United States, 1945–1960*. Boston: South End Press, 1982.
Jellison, Charles A. *Tomatoes Were Cheaper: Tales from the Thirties*. Syracuse, NY: Syracuse University Press, 1977.
Josephson, Barney and Terry Trilling-Josephson. *Café Society: The Wrong Place for the Right People*. Urbana: University of Illinois Press, 2009.
Kanfer, Stefan. *A Journal of the Plague Years: A Devastating Chronicle of the Era of the Blacklist*. Cambridge, MA: Atheneum, 1973.
Kazan, Elia. *A Life*. New York: Alfred A. Knopf, 1988.
Kessler-Harris, Alice. *A Difficult Woman: The Challenging Life and Times of Lillian Hellman*. New York: Bloomsbury Press, 2012.
Kisseloff, Jeff. *The Box: An Oral History of Television, 1920–1961*. New York: Penguin Books, 1997.
Langer, Lawrence. *The Magic Curtain*. New York: E.P. Dutton, 1951.
Lardner, Kate. *Shut Up He Explained: The Memoir of a Blacklisted Kid*. New York: Ballantine Books, 2004.
Lardner, Ring, Jr. *I'd Hate Myself in the Morning*. New York: Thunder Mouth Press/Nation Books, 2000.
Mank, Gregory William. *Women in Horror Films, 1940s*. Jefferson, NC: McFarland, 1999.
Martinson, Deborah. *Lillian: A Life with Foxes and Scoundrels*. New York: Counterpoint, 2005.
Matthews, Jane Dehart. *The Federal Theatre 1935–1939: Plays, Relief and Politics*. Princeton, NJ: Princeton University Press, 1967.
McGilligan, Patrick, and Paul Buhle. *Tender Comrades: A Backstory of the Hollywood Blacklist*. New York: St. Martin's Press, 1997.
Miller, Arthur. *Timebends: A Life*. New York: Grove Press, 1987.
Miller, Douglas T., and Marion Nowak. *The Fifties: The Way We Really Were*. New York: Doubleday, 1977.
Mostel, Kate, and Madeline Gilford. *170 Years of Show Business*. New York: Random House, 1978.
Murphy, Brenda. *Congressional Theatre: Dramatizing McCarthyism on Stage, Film and Television*. Cambridge, UK: Cambridge University Press, 1999.
Navasky, Victor S. *Naming Names*. New York: The Viking Press, 1980.
Nott, Robert. *He Ran All the Way: The Life of John Garfield*. New York: Limelight Editions, 2003.
O'Connor, John and Lorraine Brown, eds. *Free, Adult, Uncensored: The Living History of the Federal Theatre Project*. New York: New Republic Books, 1978.
Ogden, August Raymond. *The Dies Committee: A Study of the Special House Committee for the Investigation of Un-American Activities 1938–1944*. Washington, D.C.: Catholic University of America Press, 1945.
Prindle, David F. *The Politics of Glamour: Ideology and Democracy in the Screen Actors Guild*. Madison: University of Wisconsin Press, 1988.
Quinn, Susan. *Furious Improvisation: How the WPA and a Cast of Thousands Made High Art Out of Desperate Times*. New York: Walker, 2008.
Rabkin, Gerald. *Drama and Commitment: Politics in the American Theatre of the Thirties*. Indianapolis: Indiana University Press, 1964.
Radosh, Ron, and Allis Radosh. *Red Star Over Hollywood: The Film Colony's Long Romance with the Left*. New York: Encounter Books, 2005
Ross, Steven J. *Hollywood Left and Right: How Movie Stars Shaped American Politics*. New York: Oxford University Press, 2011.
Rosteck, Thomas. *See It Now Confronts McCarthyism: Television Documentary and the Politics of Representation*. Tuscaloosa: University of Alabama Press, 1994.

Bibliography

Rouverol, Jean. *Refugees from Hollywood.* Albuquerque: University of New Mexico Press, 2000.
Sainer, Arthur. *Zero Dances; A Biography of Zero Mostel.* New York: Limelight Editions, 1998.
Schickel, Richard. *Elia Kazan: A Biography.* New York: HarperCollins, 2005.
Schrecker, Ellen. *Many Are the Crimes: McCarthyism in America.* Boston: Little, Brown, 1998.
Schultz, Bud, and Ruth Schultz. *It Did Happen Here: Recollections of Political Repression in America.* Berkeley: University of California Press, 1989.
Schwartz, Bonnie Nelson, and the Educational Film Center, eds. *Voices from the Federal Theatre.* Madison: University of Wisconsin Press, 2003.
Schweizer, Peter. *Reagan's War: The Epic Story of His Forty-Year Struggle and Final Triumph Over Communism.* New York: Doubleday, 2002.
Simonson, Robert. *The Gentleman Press Agent: Fifty Years in the Trenches with Merle Debuskey.* New York: Applause Theatre & Cinema Books, 2010.
_____, *Performance of the Century: 100 Years of Actors' Equity Association and the Rise of Professional American Theater.* New York: Applause Theatre & Cinema Books, 2012.
Slide, Anthony. *Actors on Red Alert: Career Interviews with Five Actors & Actresses Affected by the Blacklist.* Lanham, MD: Scarecrow Press, 1999.
Smith, Glenn D., Jr. *"Something of My Own": Gertrude Berg and American Broadcasting, 1929–1956.* Syracuse: Syracuse University Press, 2007.
Smith, Wendy. *Real Life Drama: The Group Theatre and America, 1931–1940.* New York: Grove-Weidenfeld, 1990.
Swain, Martha H. *Ellen S. Woodward: New Deal Advocate for Women.* Jackson: University Press of Mississippi, 1995.
Swortzell, Lowell, ed. *Six Plays for Young People from the Federal Theatre Project (1936–1939): An Introductory Analysis and Six Representative Plays.* New York: Greenwood Press, 1986.
Taylor, Nick. *American Made: The Enduring Legacy of the WPA: When FDR Put the Nation to Work.* New York: Bantam Books, 2008.
Thomson, David. *The Whole Equation: A History of Hollywood.* New York: Alfred A. Knopf, 2004.
Tynan, Kenneth, and Joseph Papp. *Free for All: Joe Papp, the Public, and the Greatest Theater Story Ever Told.* New York: Doubleday, 2009.
Vaughn, Robert. *Only Victims: A Study of Show Business Blacklisting.* New York: G.P. Putnam's Sons, 1972.
Wallach, Eli. *The Good, the Bad, and Me: In My Anecdotage.* New York: Harcourt, Inc., 2005.
Webster, Margaret. *Don't Put Your Daughter on the Stage.* New York: Alfred A. Knopf, 1972.
Whitfield, Stephen J. *The Culture of the Cold War.* Baltimore: Johns Hopkins University Press, 1991.
Zinn, Howard. *A People's History of the United States.* New York: Perennial Classics, 2001.

Index

Numbers in ***bold italics*** indicate pages with illustrations

Abbey Record Manufacturing Company 141, 171
Abbott, George 116
Abe Lincoln in Illinois 49
Abraham Lincoln Brigade 59, 173
Abzug, Bella 101, ***101***
Academy of Motion Picture Arts and Sciences 153, 181
Actors' Equity Association ix, 3, 7, 69–70, 80, 82–87, 89–94, ***91***, 98, 101, 103, 106, 134–135, 147–148, 181–182; *see also* Anti-Blacklisting Resolution
Actors' Laboratory Theatre 2, 59, 145, 150, 171, 178
Adelphi Theatre ***27***
Adler, Luther ***11***, 14, 59
Adler, Stella ***11***, 13, 14, 59
AEA *see* Actors' Equity Association
Affidavit of Noncommunist Union Officer ***88–89***
AFRA *see* American Federation of Radio Artists
After the Fall 129
AFTRA *see* American Federation of Television and Radio Artists
Ah, Wilderness! 8
The Aldrich Family 80
Aleichem, Sholom 61, 65; *see also The World of Sholom Aleichem*
Alive and Kicking 173
All God's Chillun Got Wings 172
All My Sons 118, 120, 129
"All the World's a Stage" 119
Alley Theatre, Houston, TX 4, 185
Alliance of Motion Picture and Television Producers 182
Ally McBeal 115
Almanac Singers 172, 177

American Academy of Dramatic Arts, NYC 2
American Business Consultants 58, 67, 186, 192
American Committee to Save Refugees 179
American Federation of Musicians Local 802 137, 172, 175, 178
American Federation of Radio Artists 80, 175
American Federation of Television and Radio Artists x, 69–70, 80, 187; cooperating with HUAC rule 81–82
American Folksay Group 178
American Guild of Variety Artists 172, 175
American League Against War and Fascism 59
American League for Peace and Democracy 173, 180
American Legion 120–121
American Relief for Greek Democracy 173
American Shakespeare Festival, Stratford, Connecticut 138, 146
American Theatre (magazine) 3, 185
American Theatre Wing 174
Amos and Andy 79
Anderson, Maxwell 13
The Andersonville Trial 170
Annenberg, Adelaide Klein *see* Klein, Adelaide
Anthony Adverse 75
Anti-AWARE Resolution 114
anti-blacklisting contract language 93
Anti-Blacklisting Resolution 83, 87, 90–93, ***91***
Anti-Nazi League 41
Appell, Donald T. 97, 137, 150, 189
Are You Now or Have You Ever Been…? see Bentley, Eric
Arena 40–41, 185–186, 193
Arens, Richard 130–31, 137–148, 150, 167

197

Armstrong Theater 175
Ashworth, Christine x
Associated Actors and Artistes of America 83
Atkinson, Brooks 13, 21, 23–24, **27**, 39, 67–68, 118, 126, 144, 185–186, 190, 192
Atlantic Theatre Company 4
atomic bomb 71
audience xi, 2–4, 7–8, 10–11, 17–18, 26–27, 38, 40, 50, 65, 68, 118–119, 144, 152–153
Awake and Sing 13, **14–15**, 152, 178
AWARE 82, 98–99, 106, 114, 187

Baar, Carl xi
Baar, Ella ix, **65**
Baar, Keith xi
Baar, Rowan xi
Baar, Tim ix, **31**
A Bad Friend 146
Bandbox Theatre 5
Bankhead, Tallulah 2, 185
Barbizon-Plaza Theatre **64, 66**
Barker, Margaret 11
Barlin, Anne 2
Barlin, Paul 2
Barrymore, Ethel 174
Barzman, Norma xi
Bateson, Gregory 1
Bay, Howard 127
Beale, Thomas W., Sr. 97
Belasco Theatre **15**
Bellamy, Ralph 92
Ben-Ami, Jacob **65**
Bentley, Eric 3, 187, 192
Benton, Dr. Lori x
Berg, Gertrude 80, 195
Berlin blockade 71
Bernstein, Walter xi, 192
Bessie, Alvah 47, **49**
Beveridge, Glen **25**
Biberman, Herbert **9**, 10, **49, 74**, 75
Bierly, Ken 58
Big Night 13
Billingsley, Kenneth Lloyd 183, 191–192
Black, Ivan 108, 111, 170, 189
Black Pit 179
Blackmer, Sidney 90
Blitzstein, Marc 25–27, **30**, 59
Bloomgarden, Kermit **11**, 120–121, 122, **127–128, 134**, 140–141, 178, 189
Bloor, Mother 50–51
Bogart, Humphrey 42
Bohnen, Roman **11**
"Bonche Schweig" *see The World of Sholom Aleichem*
bonding provisions 83
The Bonds of Interest 7
Bonner, Herbert C. 43
Bonora, Frank 95, 97, 109
Book Find Club 59
Borland, James x

Boudin, Leonard 105
Boy Friend 112–113, 173
Boyd, Susan 182
Brand, Phoebe **11**, 13, 14, 51, 54, 56, **60**, 61, 84, **154–155**, 170, 190
Brattle Summer Theatre, Cambridge, Massachusetts 111
Brecht, Bertolt 19, 46, 104
Brewer, Roy 168, 183
Brigadoon 173, 178
Briggs, Matt 92
British Actors Equity 116
Broadway Bound 111, **112**
Broadway Dissents **117**
Bromberg, J. Edward **11**, 54–56, 59, 84
Brookfield Center, Connecticut 11
Brooklyn College 61, 178
Brother Can You Spare a Dime xi, 193
Burke, Libby 80
Bus Stop 176
Butler, Hugo 72
Butler, Jean Rouverol *see* Rouverol, Jean
Byrd, Caren x

Caesar and Cleopatra 170, 173
Café Crown 180
Cagney, James 42
Cagney & Lacey 115
California Labor School 149–150
California Un-American Activities Committee ix, 53
Call Me Mister 172–173, 175
Camp David 17
"Campaign for Americanism" 59
Candide 127
Cantwell Committee 114, 175
Capek, Karel **31**
Capri Theatre, Atlantic Beach, Long Island, New York 163
Carnegie Hall 113, 174, 180
Carnegie Tech, Pittsburgh, Pennsylvania 2, 173
Carnovsky, Morris **11**, 14, 54, 56, 59, 61, **68**, 84, 155; testimony **51**, 52
Carnovsky, Phoebe Brand *see* Brand, Phoebe
Carousel 8
Carpenter, Clifford 84, 146, 170
Celebrity Time 172
Center for the Study of Cold War America x
Central High School, Little Rock, Arkansas 79
Challee, William 11
Chekov, Anton 7
The Children's Hour 122, **126**, 127, 134
Chodorov, Jerome 110, 179, 188
A Christmas Carol 174
Churchill, Winston 43, 71
Civilian Conservation Corps 19
Clurman, Harold **8**, 9, 10, **11–12**, 13, 53–54, 185, 192
Cobb, Lee J. **11**, 84, 97

Cogley, John 118, 134, 136, 189, 193
Cohen, Emanuel Hirsh *see* Randolph, John
Cohen, Julie 158
Cold War 71, 103, 187, 193, 195
Cole, Lester 47, **49**
The Colgate Comedy Hour 178
Come Back Little Sheba 177
Committee for Negro in the Arts 170
Communism 30, 32, 35, 39, 61, 72, 105, 121, 151, 162, 166
Communist front 56, 68, 72, 121, 138, 166
Comstock, Ned x
contempt citation 75, 100, 102, 107–108, 116, 120, 122, 141
Contempt of Congress 47, 119, 132, 160–161
Cooper, Gary 74
cooperative witness 42, 45, 80, **102**, 103, 111, 143, 168
Corey, Jeff 84, 193
Cornell, Katherine 8
Corporation for Public Broadcasting 183
Costello, Frank 79
Council *see* Actors' Equity Association
Counselor-at-Law 179
Counter, Nicholas J. 182
Counterattack 67, 81, 90, 98, 120, 134, 170, 177, 179, 186, 192
Coy, Walter 11
The Cradle Will Rock 25–27, **29–30**, 41, 49–50
Crawford, Cheryl **8**, 9–11, 53–54, 193
The Crucible 127, 129, **130**, 131, 132 **134–135**, 190
Crystal, Billy 181
Cunningham, Agnes "Sis" 171
Cunningham, Sarah x, **60**, 61, **62–64**, 65, **68**, 69, 96, 103, 111, **129**, 161, 170, 189; testimony **99**, 101
Cyrano de Bergerac 51, 176
Czechoslovakia 71

Daily Press, Newport News, Virginia 110, 189
Daily Variety 75, 77, 115, 121, 189
Daily Worker 37, 50, 56, 110, 114, 131, 150, 188–189
da Silva, Daniel xi
da Silva, Howard v, xi, 1, 26, 46, 49, **29**, 56, 59, 61, 65–**67**, 69, 155, 170; testimony 49, **50**–51
da Silva, Marjorie **63**
Dassin, Jules 21, **28**, **139**
David and Lisa 154
Davis, Ossie 61, **67**
The Day the Earth Stood Still 180
Death of a Salesman 118, 120–**121**, 122, 127, 129, 131–132, 172
Dee, Ruby **60**–61, **67**
Dekker, Albert 120–**121**
Delacorte Theatre **151**–152, 190
Dempsey, john J. 28, **32**
Derwent, Clarence 90, 92

de-segregation of theatres 84
Desire Under the Elms 176
d'Eustachio, Ellie x
DGA *see* Directors Guild of America
The Diary of Anne Frank 134, 141, 176
Dies, Martin 27, **32–33**, 35, 38, 40–43, 73, 186, 193–194
Dies Committee *see* Special House Committee for the Investigation of Un-American Activities
A Different Woman xi
Directors Guild of America 73, 154, 181
Directors' Guild of America West 153
Disney, Walt 45
Dmytryk, Edward 47, **49**, 193
Donath, Ludwig **60**
Dougherty, Marion 81
Doyle, Clyde 48
Dreyfus, Mike 81
Dubin, Charles S. 170–171, 190; testimony 142–143
Dunne, Philip 184
d'Usseau, Arnaud 102, 162, 171
d'Usseau, Susan 162–163, 171, 189, 191; testimony 102
Dylan, Bob 178

ecology and ethics 1
Ed Sullivan Show 172, 177
Eldridge, Florence 42
Embezzled Heaven 174
End Jim Crow in Baseball Committee 180
Enemies 174
An Enemy of the People 124
Equity (magazine) **85–86**
Equity *see* Actors' Equity Association
Erickson, Lief **11**
Ervine, St. John 7; *see also John Ferguson*
"Ethics and Social Responsibility" ix
Ethiopia 21
Eustis, Oskar 152
Evans, Maurice 90
The Eve of St. Mark 176
Everett, Ethel 165, 191
Ewen, Frederic **60**, 61, **62**
Exodus 137

Farmer, Frances **11**
Farmer, (Mary) Virginia 11
Fascism 23, 27, 27, 59, 82
Fast, Howard 131, 193
Faulk, John Henry 59, 81, 186, 192
Faulkner, Stanley 147
favored nations 169
Federal Art Project 180
Federal Theatre Project xii, 2, 9, 17, **18–19**, 21, 23, 15, **27**, 28–30, **31**, 32–34, 36–37, 40–43, 49, 138–**139**, 145, 152, 174, 176, 179, 185, 194–195; *see also Ethiopia; Injunction Granted; It Can't Happen Here; "Living Newspaper"; One-Third of a Nation;*

Power; Revolt of the Beavers; R-U-R; Triple-A Plowed Under; Voodoo Macbeth
Federal Writers' Project 28
Feiffer, Jules 146
Feningston, Sylvia 11
Fiddler on the Roof 175
Fields, Joseph 179
Finian's Rainbow 134, 168
Finks xi, 158
Flanagan, Hallie **18-19**, 21, 28, 32-33, 158, 185, 192-193; testimony 35-40, 41
Foley Square Courthouse 4, 96, **100**, 137
Fontanne, Lynn 8
Ford, Friendly 11
Four A's *see* Associated Actors and Artistes of America
France, Royal 162
franchising of agents 83
Frank, Allen **28**
Frank, Yasha 40
Frazier, James B. 148
Fried, Walter **11**, 120
Friedman, Peter ix
Friendly, Fred W. 79
friendly witness *see* cooperative witness
Friends of Old Time Radio 146, 170
Front 53, 56, 68, 72, 121, 138, 165-166, 180-182
The Front Page 177, 179
Front Row Center 175
Fund for the Republic 118, 134, 149, 167, 189, 193

Gardenia, Vincent **63**
Garfield, Jules (John) 14, 59, 84, 145, 194
Geer, Will 51, 56, 59, 146-147; testimony 51
Gelman, Jacob *see* Gilford, Jack
Gentleman's Agreement 52
George Washington Carver School 171
Gersten, Bernard xi, 65, 118, 138, 171, 176, 189; testimony 146-148; Tony Award 171
Gilbert, Ronnie xi; *see also* The Weavers
Gilbert, Ruth 165
Gilford, Jack xi, 59, 65, 158, 160, 170, 179
Gilford, Joe xi, 158
Gilford, Madeline Lee ix-xi, 59, 95, 115, 158-159, 188-189, 191, 194; Scotti memo 160-161; testimony **104-105**
Gillmore, Margalo 90
The Goldbergs 80, 169
Golden Boy 13, 145, 152, 174
Goodman, Edward 5
Goodrich, Trudy 35
Gorney, Jay xi
Gorney, Sondra xi, 193
Gough, Lloyd 84
Gould, Jack 81, 187
The Grateful Dead 78, 182
Gray, Herman 165
Great Depression 10, 17-18, 172, 192
Greek Theatre **20**

Green, Paul 10, 12
Greene, Alexis ix
Grenell, Horace 171; testimony 141
Greth, Ben 173
Group Theatre 2, **8**, 10-14, **11**, **12**, **14**, **15**, 16, 36, 50-56, 114, 121, 152, 154, 174-175, 185, 192, 195
Guggenheim Foundation 36
Gunga Din 180
Guthrie, Woody 171

Hall, George 105-107, 111, 171-172, 189; testimony **102**-103; Walter closing statement 103-104
Hamlet 176
Hammerstein, Oscar 8
Hampden, Walter **134**
Harburg, E. Y. (Yip) 134, 168
Harris, Jed **134**
Harris, Julie **127**
Hartnett, Vincent 81, 120-121, 134, 149, 166
The Hasty Heart 172
Hays, Lee 107, 109, 113, 171-172, 178, 189; testimony 102; *see also* The Weavers
HCUA *see* House Committee on Un-American Activities
Healey, Arthur D. 28
Heartbreak House 8
The Heavenly Twins 114
Heifetz, Jascha 180
Helbrun, Theresa 7, 10; *A Wayward Quest* 5, 9, 185, 193
Heller, George 80, 187, 193
Hellerman, Fred 166; *see also* The Weavers
Hellman, Lillian xi, 3, 59, 78, 96, 118, **126-128**, 131-**132**, 134, 136, 193-194; testimony **124-125**, 122-123
Herald Tribune 149, 167
"The High School" (Gymnasium) *see The World of Sholom Aleichem*
Hiss, Alger 71, 104
Holbert, Maureen 165-166, 191
Hold It 173
Hollister, Carroll 172; testimony 140-141
Hollywood, California 2, 9, 12-13, 41-43, 45, 48, 50-51, 53, 58, 68, 73, 87, 96-97, 135-136, 173, 177-179, 18, 184, 186-187, 189, 192-195
Hollywood Party: How Communism Seduced the American Film Industry in the 1930s and 1940s 183, 192
Hollywood Remembers the Blacklist 181, 184
Hollywood Ten **9**, **47**, **49**, 68, **74**-75, **85**, 104, 120, 137, 153, 181
Hopkins, Harry 17-**18**, 21, 26, 192
House Committee on Un-American Activities 43-44, 47, 97-102, 124-125
The House of Bernarda Alba 170
The House of Connelly 10, 12-13
Houseman, John 25, 41, 148
HUAC *see* House Committee on Un-American Activities

Hudson Theatre **128**
Huelsbeck, Mary x
Huffman, Hazel 28, 36, 40–41, 43, 186; testimony 30, 32, **33–34**
Human Science ix
Hunt, Marsha 181
Hurok, Sol 175
Hurricane Harvey 4

Ibsen, Henrik 7, 124
The Iceman Cometh 8
Inherit the Wind 134, 146, 170
Injunction Granted 21, 37–38
Internal Security Act 72, 117
International Alliance of Theatrical Stage Employees (IATSE) 183
Invol Dance Company 175
Iraq War 184
Iron Curtain 43, 71
It Can't Happen Here **23–25**
Ives, George xi, 81, 95–96, 99, 118, 187–189

The Jackie Gleason Show 176
Jackson, Donald L. 48, 129
Jaffe, Dr. Dennis ix
Jaffe, Sam 110, 180, 188
Jaffe, Shalom *see* Jaffe, Sam
Jane Eyre 146, 169
Jarrico, Paul 181
Jarrico, Sylvia xi
Jefferson Chorus 141, 171
Jefferson School 166
Jewish Center Lecture Bureau 61
John Ferguson 7
Johnny Johnson 174–175
Johnson, Laurence 59, 98
Johnston, Eric 47
Jones, James Earl 145
Jones, (Robert) Earl 172; testimony 145
Joseph, Rajiv 4, 185
Journey's End 173
Julius Caesar 152, 180
Jurist, Irma xi, 103, **113**, 172–173, 188–189; testimony 102

Kanter, David 103, 108, 113–114, 173, 189; testimony 109–110
Karam, Elena 28
Karloff, Boris **127**, 173
Kazan, Elia **11**–12, **52**, 56, 116, 129–130, 155, 180, 190, 194–195; testimony 52–54
Keane, George 59, 103, 106, 114, 173, 189
Kearney, Bernard W. 48, 53, 55, 129–130
Keenan, Jack 58
Keep 'Em Laughing 180
Kefauver, Estes 79
Kennedy, Arthur **135**
Kennedy, John Fitzgerald 153
Kennedy Center for the Performing Arts 153
Kenney, Robert W. **49**
Kessler-Harris, Alice xi

Kid Galahad 178
Kingsley, Sidney 13
Kirkpatrick, Theodore 58
Klein, Adelaide 59, **139**, 146, 169; testimony 138–139
Korea 71
Kraber, Gerrit (Tony) 11, 54, 56, 59, 106, 114, 173, 189; testimony 107
Krahulik, Dr. Karen x
Kuluva, Will **63**

Labor Council of the National Conference of Christians and Jews National Brotherhood Award 84, 187
LaCour, Joan xi
Langer, Lawrence 5, 7, 10, 185, 194
Lardner, Ring, Jr. **49**, **68**, 104, 181, 194; testimony **47**, 69
The Lark **127**
Lasky, Victor 126
Lautner, John 138; testimony 143, 145, 173
Law and Order 96
Lawrence, Gertrude 172
Lawrence, Jerome 134
Lawrence, Mark 84
Lawrence, Peter 114, 173; testimony **105**–106
Lawson, John Howard 13, 47, **49**, 158
Lazar, William (William Lawrence?) 144, 174; testimony 143
League of American Theatres 84
League of New York Theatres 90, 93, 135
Lee, Madeline *see* Gilford, Madeline Lee
Lee, Robert E. 134
Lee, Will 65, **154**, 174; testimony 145–146
Leeds, Phil 99, 115, 174, 189; testimony **100**–101
Lend an Ear 172–173
Let Freedom Sing 174
Let the Record Speak 119
Letterman, Madeline Rosalind *see* Gilford, Madeline Lee
Leverett, Lewis 11, 54, 56
Levittowns 71
Lewis, Robert (Bobby) **11**, 13
Libman, Yisrol Paul Mann *see* Mann, Paul
Library of Congress x, **19**, **21**, **23**–24, **27**–28, **33**, **43**
Lief, Arthur 175; testimony 140
Lincoln Center Theatre 118, 146, 171
Lippman, Mortimer *see* Randolph, John
Lipshutz, Abraham *see* Lief, Arthur
The Little Foxes 134
"Living Newspaper" 19, **20**–**22**, 23, **26**, 152, 185
Local 1199 of the United Healthcare Workers 61–**62**
Loeb, Philip 80, 84
Lomax, Alan 171
London, Ephraim 167
Look Homeward Angel 141, 176
Los Angeles Times 110, 187–189

Louis, Joe 172
loyalty oath 181–182, 184, 187
Lubovsky, William *see* Lee, Will
Lunatics and Lovers 116
Lunt, Alfred 8
Lynn, Eleanor *11*
Lysistrata 178

Make a Wish 174
Malmgreen, Gail ix
Maltz, Albert 47, *49*, 179
Man Behind the Badge 172
Mann, Paul 175; testimony 144–145
Manoff, Arnie 95
Manson, Alan 115, 175, 189; testimony 106
Many Are the Crimes xi
March, Fredric 42
Margolis, Ben 49
Marlowe, Christopher 38
Martin Beck Theatre 10, *132–133*
Mason, Noah H. 28, *32*
Master Institute of United Arts *60*–61
Masur, Richard 181–182
The Matchmaker 115
Mayer, Louis B. 45
Maynard, Mab 11
McAllister, Dr. JoAnn ix
McCarran, Pat 79–80, 187
McCarthy, Joseph R. 68, 79–80, 144, 157–158, 183, 187, 192
McCarthyism 157, 187, 193–195
McDowell, John 43–*44*
McFarland & Company xi, 194
Medicine Show 177
Meet the People 181
Meisner, Sanford *11*, 13, 170
Men in White 13
Menjou, Adolph 74
Menuhin, Yehudi 172
Merchant of Venice 176
Mercury Theatre *30*
Merin, Eda Reiss 84
Merrill, Robert 172
Metropolitan Music School 137, 140, 178
Miller, Arthur 59, 118, 120–*121*, 122, 127, *133–134*, *136*, 172, 176, 190, 192, 194; Pulitzer Prize 120; testimony 129–*130*, 131–132; Tony Award 120, 127
Miller, Paula 11, 54
Miltner, Barbara xi
minimum wage guarantee 83, 134
Moeller, Philip 5
Moiseyev Dance Company 140, 175
Mollan, Katherine x
Monroe, Marilyn 131–132
Montoya, Dr. Maria x
More Stately Mansions 172
Morley, Karen 46, 84
Morris, Mary 11
Mosier, Harold G. 28
Mostel, Samuel Joel *see* Mostel, Zero

Mostel, Zero 59, 111, 163–165, 180, 191–192, 195
"Mother Goose Marx" 23, *27*
Motion Picture Alliance for the Preservation of American Ideals 183
Motion Picture Artists' Committee 50
Motion Picture Association of America 47
Moulder, Morgan M. 48, 137, 139, 150
Mourning Becomes Electra *6*, 8
Mrs. Warren's Profession 180
Much Ado About Nothing 111, 119, 177
Muir, Jean 80, 87
Mule Bone 172
Mundt, Karl E. 43
Murphy, George 45
Murphy Brown 115
Murrow, Edward R. 79, 187
Musicians' Congress Committee 59
My Sister Eileen 110, 179

The Naked City *139*, 169, 174
Naming Names 188, 194
NARA *see* National Archives and Records Administration
Nash, Michael x
National Archives and Records Administration x, 159, 169, 185–191
National Council of American-Soviet Friendship 171
National Council of the Arts, Sciences and Professions 171, 174, 179
National Endowment for the Arts 4
National Labor Relations Board *88–89*
National Lawyers Guild
National Negro Conference 174
National Public Radio 183
National Republic 28
National Theatre Conference, Iowa 18
National Theatre, Washington, D.C. 84
National Velvet 127
National Youth Administration Workshop 174
Navasky, Victor xi, 188, 194
Negro xii
Negro Cultural Committee 59
Negro Ensemble Company 175
Neighborhood Playhouse 170–171, 175
Nelson, Ruth *11*
New Theatre League 59
New Theater Magazine 56
New York Labor History Association ix
New York Library for the Performing Arts x, 190
New York Shakespeare Festival *149*
New York University ix; College of Arts and Sciences x; Department of History x; Tisch School of the Arts x
Newspaper Guild 109
Night Music 13
Night Over Taos 13
1931 13

Nixon, Richard M. **43-44**, 48, 52-53, 79, 104, 117
Nizer, Louis 59
NYU *see* New York University

Ober, Philip 90, 92
O'Brien, Christopher 84
O'Casey, Sean 61
Odets, Clifford 10, 11, 13-**14**, **15**, 54, 192; testimony 55-56
Of Thee I Sing 174, 178
Oklahoma 8
O'Neill, Eugene **6**, 7-8, 152, 172
"On the Record" 119
On the Town 177
On Your Toes 177
One-Third of a Nation 21-**22**, 193
One Touch of Venus 177
Ornitz, Samuel 47, **49**
Ottenheimer, Albert M. **63**, 106, 114, 175, 189
Our Gang 174

Paint Your Wagon 177
The Pajama Game 95, 115, 119, 176
Panic in the Streets 52, 180
Papirofsky, Joseph *see* Papp, Joe
Papp, Joe 138, 148-**149**, 152, 166-167, 171, 176, 190-191, 193, 195; testimony 150-151
Paradise Lost 13
Parks, Larry 150
Patten, Dorothy 11
People's Artists 178
People's Drama 140, 150
People's Songs 59, 171, 177-178
People's Theatre of Cleveland v, 1
Peoria, Illinois 120-121
Peoria Journal 189
Peretz, I.L. 65
Perl, Arnold 61, 66-67, 186
Peter Pan 173, 178
Peterson, J. Hardin 43
Philco Playhouse 175, 178
Phoenix 55 115, 177
Pinocchio 40
Piscator, Erwin 19
Platt, David 110, 188
Polan, Lou 99, 114, 176, 189; testimony 100
Polonsky, Abe 95-96, 105, 183, 191
Popper, Martin **49**, 99
Portnoy, Leon 141
Potter, Charles E. 48
Powell, Adam Clayton, Jr. 157
Powell, Dawn 13
Power 21, **26**, 185, 193
Prager, Stanley 95, 115-116, 176, 188; testimony 99
Pritzker, Dr. Steven ix
Prizzi's Honor 111
Proctor, James D. 168, 176; testimony 141-142
Producing Managers Association 83
Provincetown Players 7

Quartette Productions **63**

Rachel Productions 166
A Raisin in the Sun 114
Randolph, John x, 24, **28**, **60**, 61, **62-63**, 84, 92, 101, 103, 111, 115, 161-162, 166, 170, 176, 188-189, 191; testimony **98**-99; Tony Award **112**
Randolph, Martha x, 161, 186
Rankin, John E. 43, 177
Ratner, Herbert 11
Rauh, Joseph 124
Raymond, Judith 180
RBG 158
Reagan, Ronald 45, 78, 81, 187, 195; testimony **73**-75
Red Channels 58-**59**, 61, 67, 80-81, **85**, 90, 118, 120-121, 127, 134, **139**, 173-174, 179-180, 182, 186, 192-193
Red Rust **8-9**, 10, 47, 76
Red Scare 82, 84, 189, 193
Repertory Theatre of Lincoln Center 118, 146, 171, 175
Report on Blacklisting 149, 167, 189, 190, 193
Resolution Re Blacklisting 87, 90-**91**, 92-93
restriction of foreign actors 83
Retreat to Pleasure 13
Revere, Anne 59, 78, **126**, **128**, 187; letter to SAG 77; testimony **78**; Tony Award 127, **129**
Revolt of the Beavers 23-25, **27-28**, 38-39, 61, 98, **139**, 152
Rhapsody in Blue 51
Rice, Elmer 7, 19
Rice, Vernon 65
Richie Brockelman, Private Eye 111
Ritt, Martin 78
Ritz Theatre 40
Rivera, Chita 155
Robbins, Barbara 90
Robert Montgomery Presents 178
Robinson, Philip 11-12
Roche, Eugene **60**
Rocket to the Moon 13
Rodgers, Richard 8
Romancing the Soul 119
Romano, Amelia **63**
Roosevelt, Franklin Delano 2, 17, 21, **22**, 23, **24**-25
Rosenberg, Ethel 71, 131
Rosenberg, Julius 71, 131
Ross, Bill 90
Ross, Paul M. 109, 139
"Round Table Review" **60**-61
Rouverol, Jean x, 72, 170, 187, 195
Royal Ballet 175
Royale Theatre 113
R-U-R **31**
Ruskin, Shimen 80
Sabinson, Lee 134, 168, 191
SAG *see* Screen Actors Guild

Index

Salemson, Harold 115, 177, 189; testimony 108–109
Sandburg, Carl 173
Sasuly, Richard 177; testimony 141
Saunders, Sallie 33, 35
Saybrook University ix
Scherer, Gordon H. **97**, 99, 102, 104, 107–110, 116–117, 129, 137, 143–144, 147, 189
Schickel, Richard 155, 190, 195
Schoenfeld, Bernard 34
Schoolhouse on the Lot 179
Schrecker, Ellen xi, 195
Schwimmer, Harry 109
Scientific and Cultural Conference for World Peace 179–180
Scott, Adrian 47, **49**
Scott, Hazel 157, 191–192
Scotti, Dolores Faconti 95, 113, 148–149, 160–168, 180
Screen Actors Guild 45, 70, **73**–74, 76–78, 181–182, 184, 187, 194
Screen Writers Guild 69, 177
Seattle Repertoire Playhouse 175
See It Now 78, 187
Seeger, Pete xi, 2, 59, 96, 102, 104, 113, 116, 171, 177–178, 188–189, 193; testimony 107–**108**; *see also* The Weavers
Seeger, Toshi 96, 116
segregation 84
SEIU1199 61–**62**
Senate Commerce Committee 183
Sesame Street 174
The Seven Year Itch 114, 119, 173
Shakespeare in Central Park 138, 149, 151, 167
Shaw, George Bernard 7–8, 170
Shaw, Irwin 10–**11**, 13
Shelley, Josh 103, 115, 177, 189; testimony 106
Shrog, Will **63**
Shuberts 13
Siegel, Andrea x
Sifton, Claire 10, 13
Sifton, Paul 10, 13
Silber, Irwin 178; testimony 142
Simon, Louis 87
Sing for Your Supper 33, 35
Skin of Our Teeth 176
Skouras, Spyros P. 54
Smith, Art **11**–12, 54, 56
Smith, Kent 90
Smith, Wendy 16, 185, 195
Sondergaard, Gale **9**–10, 187; letter to SAG 75–77; testimony **74**, 75
South Pacific 179, 189
Southern California Library for Social Science and Research x
Soviet Union 10, 32, 78
Spacey, Kevin 181
Sparer, Paul **60**
Spartacus 137, 163
Special House Committee for the Investigation of Un-American Activities 27, **32-33**, 42–43, 186, 194
Spirochete 21, 185, 193
Spolin, Viola 2
Stage for Action 59
Stalin, Joseph "Joe" 126
Stanislavski, Constantine 36
Stanton, Olive **29**
Starnes, Joe 28–30, 35–39
Starr, Dr. G. Gabrielle x
State Fair 8
Steele, Walter S. 28
Steinberg, Ben 178; testimony 140–141
Stevenson, Janet x-xi
Stoddard, Eunice 12
Straight, Beatrice 127, **135**
Strange Interlude 8
Strasberg, Lee **8**, 9–10, **11**–13, 53–54
A Streetcar Named Desire 52
Stripling, Robert E. **32**, **43-44**, 45–46, 69
Studio One 169, 177
Success Story 13
Sullivan, Elliot xi, 101, 65, 116, 178, 189; testimony **101**–102
Sullivan, Norma xi, 188
Sullivan Show 172, 177
Sunrise at Campobello 146, 170
Sweezy vs. New Hampshire 138–139
SWG *see* Screen Writers Guild
Symphony of the New World 178

"A Tale of Chelm" *see* The World of Sholom Aleichem
Tamiment Library and Robert F. Wagner Labor Archives x, 3, 187–188
Tavenner, Frank 48–52, 55–56, 97–99, 101–110, 124
Taylor, Robert 74; testimony 45–**46**
Television Authority 80
Terry and the Pirates 170
Thalberg, Irving 73
Theatre Arts Committee 59
Theatre 1199 **62**
The Theatre Guild 5–**6**, 7–10; *see also* Goodman, Edward; Helbrun, Teresa; Langer, Lawrence; Moeller, Philip
Theatre Section of the Communist Party **34**
They Shall Have Music 180
This Is the Army 115
Thomas, J. Parnell 28–30, **32**–33, 36–38, **43-44**, 45–**46**, 48, 157
Thomas, John Charles 172
Thompson, Dorothy 119, 189
Thomson, David 72, 187, 195
Threepenny Opera 179
Till the Day I Die 13
The Time of Your Life 174, 194
Timebends 127
Tone, Franchot 12–13
Top-Notchers 180
Touch and Go 172

Index

Toys in the Attic 78, 127, **128–129**
Tracy, Lee 90
Tran, Diep 3, 185
"Trial by Jurist" **113**
Triple-A Plowed Under **20–21**, 185, 193
Truman, Harry 71, 192
Trumbo, Dalton **47**, **49**, 137, 153
Tuck, William H. 137
TVA *see* Television Authority
Twentieth Century Fox 54
Twenty-One 142
Two on the Aisle 176
Tyne, George 116, 178, 188–189; testimony 97–98

Un-American Activities in California 53, 120
uncooperative witness 42, 45–46, 57, 104, 118, 145, 162, 187, 192
un-friendly witness *see* uncooperative witness
unemployed 3, 17–18, 36, 55, 94
United American Artists 59
U.S. Congress Committee on Patents 18, 185
University of California, Los Angeles x
University of Southern California x

Vail, Richard B. 43–**44**.
Van Duzer, Michael x
Vassar College 18, 158
Velde, Harold H. 48, 56
Venice Theatre 26
A View from the Bridge 141, 176
Villard, Paul 179; testimony 141
Viva Zapata! 54
Voice of America 150
Volpone 179
Voodoo Macbeth 152

Wagner, Murry 80
Waiting for Lefty 13
Wakefield, Dan 71, 186
Waldorf Astoria Hotel 47
Waldorf Peace Conference 176
The Waldorf Statement 47–48
Walker, Alixe 12
Wallach, Eli **85**, 195
Walter, Francis E. 48, 96, **97–98**, 110, 116–117, 124, 137, 189
Wanamaker, Sam 84
Ward, Janet **63**
Ware, Herta 51
Warner, Jack 45

Washington Square Players 5, 7–8
Wasn't That a Time? 113, 172
Watch on the Rhine 134
Watkins vs. the United States 138–139, 141, 144
Watts, Richard 132
A Wayward Quest see Helbrun, Theresa
The Weavers 113, 116, 166, 177, 189
"Week of the Angry Arts Against the War in Vietnam" **117**
Welles, Orson 25, 59
West, Betsy 158
West Coast Advisory Board 84; letter to Council 84, 87
West Side Story 114
White, Josh 170–171
"WHY THROW THE BABY OUT THE WINDOW" 40
Wilenchick, Clement 12
Willis, Edwin E. **97**, 117, 143, 189
Winchell, Walter 168
Windsor Theatre **30**
Wingdale Lodge 178
Winged Victory 178
Winkler, Betty 103
Wisconsin Historical Society x
witch hunt 76, 110, 126, 130, 189
Wolfson, Martin 59, 114, 179, 189; testimony 99
Wonderful Town 110, 179
Wood, John S. 43, 48, 50–51, 124–125
Woodard, Alfre 181
Wooley, Angers 110, 180, 188
Works Progress Administration 17–**18**, 39, 180, 185
The World of Sholom Aleichem 61, **63–64 66–67**, 68–69, 101, 118, 145–146, 166, 170, 174; "Bonche Schweig" **65**; "The High School" **68**; "A Tale of Chelm" **154**
World Peace Appeal 171
WPA *see* Works Progress Administration
Writers for (Henry) Wallace 179

Yankee Doodle Dandy 178
Yanks Are Not Coming 176
Yaros, Buddy *see* Tyne, George
Young, Dr. Marilyn x
Young Actors Company ix, 2
Young People's Records 59, 141, 171

Zinn, Howard 71, 188, 195
Ziter, Dr. Edward x

www.ingramcontent.com/pod-product-compliance
Lightning Source LLC
Chambersburg PA
CBHW061348300426
44116CB00011B/2034